Collaborative Research in Language Education

Trends in Applied Linguistics

Edited by
Ulrike Jessner

Volume 20

Collaborative Research in Language Education

Reciprocal Benefits and Challenges

Edited by
Gudrun Erickson, Camilla Bardel and David Little

ISBN 978-3-11-221417-6
e-ISBN (PDF) 978-3-11-078771-9 e-
ISBN (EPUB) 978-3-11-078786-3
ISSN 1868-6362

Library of Congress Control Number: 2023936595

Bibliographic information published by the Deutsche Nationalbibliothek
The Deutsche Nationalbibliothek lists this publication in the Deutsche Nationalbibliografie;
detailed bibliographic data are available on the internet at http://dnb.dnb.de.

Chapter Reciprocity and challenge in researcher–student collaborative labour in a multilingual secondary school @ Marie Källkvist, Henrik Gyllstad, Erica Sandlund and Pia Sundqvist;
Chapter National graduate schools in language education: Dimensions of collaboration and reciprocity © Camilla Bardel and Gudrun Erickson

© 2025 Walter de Gruyter GmbH, Berlin/Boston
This volume is text- and page-identical with the hardback published in 2023.
Cover image: Martin Zech, Bremen, using a photo by Roswitha Schacht/morguefile.com
Typesetting: Integra Software Services Pvt. Ltd.
Printing and binding: CPI books GmbH, Leck

www.degruyter.com

Preface

This book had its origin in the AILA 2021 symposium 'Collaborative research in language education: Reciprocal benefits and challenges', which was held online in August 2021. The success of the symposium and the level of interest it generated prompted the organizers, Camilla Bardel and Gudrun Erickson, to consider publishing a collection of papers. Eight of the book's twelve chapters (1, 2, 3, 4, 6, 7, 8, 10) started life as contributions to the symposium; four further chapters were solicited (5, 9, 11, 12) to increase the book's range and thematic balance. After the symposium, the organizers invited David Little to join the editorial team. This book is the result of their joint labours.

We are grateful to the authors of the twelve chapters for their contributions and for meeting our various deadlines; to Ema Ushioda for so readily agreeing to write the afterword; to Natalie Fecher and Kirstin Börgen of De Gruyter for accepting our book proposal; and to Ulrike Jessner for welcoming the book into the applied linguistics series of which she is editor.

Gudrun Erickson
Camilla Bardel
David Little

Contents

Preface —— V

Gudrun Erickson, Camilla Bardel and David Little
Introduction —— 1

Part 1: Addressing challenges in the classroom

Jessica Berggren, Silvia Kunitz, Malin Haglind, Amanda Hoskins, Anna Löfquist and Hanna Robertson
1 Combining theory and practice: Findings from a collaborative project on oral task design —— 11

Katherine Mueller, Roswita Dressler, Anja Dressler Araujo, Frank Moeller and Tanya Ronellenfitsch
2 Improving second language education through Intensive German Weeks: An action research collaboration between teachers and researchers —— 29

Anna Elgemark, Alastair Henry and Petra Jansson
3 An affordance-focused approach for working with authentic materials: A practice–research initiative —— 41

Part 2: Learners as collaborative agents

Marie Källkvist, Henrik Gyllstad, Erica Sandlund and Pia Sundqvist
4 Reciprocity and challenge in researcher–student collaborative labour in a multilingual secondary school —— 59

Annamaria Pinter
5 The organic processes of learning in an exploratory collaborative action research (CAR) project —— 71

David Little and Déirdre Kirwan
6 Managing linguistic diversity in an Irish primary school: Reciprocal collaboration in practice and research —— 85

Part 3: Collaborative research in professional development

Tanya M. McCarthy
7   Collaboration, reciprocity, and challenges: Professional development-in-practice —— 101

Gabriele Pallotti, Claudia Borghetti, Stefania Ferrari and Greta Zanoni
8   Teachers and researchers collaborating to develop effective language education: The project *Observing Interlanguage* —— 119

Ofra Inbar-Lourie and Orly Haim
9   Learning to become an English teacher: Collaboration, context and the self —— 133

Part 4: Collaborative research and national policy

Batia Laufer
10   From research to a national curriculum: The case of a lexical syllabus —— 151

Karita Mård-Miettinen and Anne Pitkänen-Huhta
11   Tensions in collaborative research with teachers in the context of language education policy change in Finland —— 165

Camilla Bardel and Gudrun Erickson
12   National graduate schools in language education: Dimensions of collaboration and reciprocity —— 179

Afterword

Ema Ushioda
13   An ethical perspective on collaborative research —— 197

Contributors —— 207

Index —— 211

Gudrun Erickson, Camilla Bardel and David Little
Introduction

This book is concerned with the reciprocal benefits that accrue from effective collaboration between the various actors in language education – teachers and researchers but also learners and policy makers: the fruitful interdependence of policy aims and pedagogical goals and approaches on the one hand and research purposes and methodologies on the other. At the same time, challenges are addressed, not least the gulf that so often separates applied linguistic and other educational research from classroom practice (most recently, Sato and Loewen 2022) and policy-related frame factors like curricula and assessment (van den Akker 2003). There is a growing tendency to argue that we need more teaching-informed research (e.g., Rose 2019). This implies modes of collaboration between policy makers, schools, teachers and learners on the one hand and researchers on the other that are mutually beneficial, mutually respectful, mutually relevant, non-exploitative and ethically aware. Quality and validity in educational research should promote quality and validity in educational practice and vice versa, with reciprocity and ethics assumed to be intrinsic aspects of these concepts (Hammersley 2017). These considerations determined our recruitment of contributions to the book. Arranged in four sections – *Addressing challenges in the classroom*, *Learners as collaborative agents*, *Collaborative research in professional development*, and *Collaborative research and national policy* – the twelve chapters report on research in a wide variety of educational contexts in eight countries on three continents: Canada, Finland, India, Ireland, Israel, Italy, Japan and Sweden. They have in common a core commitment to reciprocity and relevance and an awareness of the many ethical challenges posed by classroom research. In her afterword, Ema Ushioda reviews the twelve chapters from an ethical perspective.

The first part of the book reports on collaborative research that seeks solutions to specific pedagogical problems. Chapter 1, by Jessica Berggren, Silvia Kunitz, Malin Haglind, Amanda Hoskins, Anna Löfquist and Hanna Robertson, describes a Swedish project funded by the local school authorities and designed to stimulate spontaneous oral interaction in the language classroom. The researchers hypothesized that pupils' reluctance to engage in reciprocal communication was due to the kind of tasks they were asked to perform. Working closely with teachers, the researchers proposed a cyclical approach – task design, implementation, analysis – that was intended to reduce the gap between theory and practice and strengthen the ecological validity of the project. Perhaps unsurprisingly, task design was found to affect pupil interaction. More importantly, too detailed instructions and too many instructional materials were obstacles to pupil interaction. The project used the techniques of conversation analysis (Sidnell 2010) to explore the nature of effective task-oriented interaction, concluding that the co-construction of reciprocal oral communication depends on pupils attending to one another's turns-at-talk and making contributions that move the activity in question forward.

Canada's Bilingual (partial immersion) Programs are often confronted with a problem similar to the one addressed in Chapter 1: although they develop strong listening skills in their target language, students are reluctant to speak. In Chapter 2, Katherine Mueller, Roswita Dressler, Anja Dressler Araujo, Frank Moeller and Tanya Ronellenfitsch report on the solution adopted by one German Bilingual Program in the province of Alberta: the introduction of intensive German weeks at the beginning, middle and end of the school year for Kindergarten–Grade 6 students (5–12 years old). The project adopted strategies from the Neurolinguistic Approach (Germain 2018), which emphasizes oral before written production, the modelling of full sentences, and language use for purposes of meaningful, authentic communication. For participating teachers, classroom practice was enhanced by the creation of year, unit and single lesson plans and the use of games, songs and other activities. For the researchers, language education theory was informed by the establishment of clear, grade-specific goals, consistent implementation of the Neurolinguistic Approach, and analysis of teachers' perception of students' success in attaining these goals.

Chapter 3, by Anna Elgemark, Alastair Henry and Petra Jansson, brings us back to Sweden, where it is officially recognized that classroom teaching is not always informed by relevant research findings. To address this problem, and to develop and test sustainable models of researcher–practitioner collaboration, the Swedish government has introduced a national system of partnerships between schools and universities. Research projects are initiated not just by academics but also by teachers, and the purpose of each school–university partnership is to develop and test a model that can support sustainable, research-based practice. The project described in Chapter 3 addresses one of the major challenges currently facing teachers of English in Sweden, namely the need to create activities that go beyond the textbook: activities which students can experience as relevant and meaningful, and which promote the development of linguistic competence. Working with primary, secondary and upper secondary teachers of English in a rural municipality, the authors – two language teacher educators and an upper secondary teacher of English – set out to enable the teachers to develop design skills that include language awareness. The chapter examines the conditions under which the collaboration took place, the challenges faced, the beneficial influences on teachers' practice, the potential for sustainability, and opportunities to replicate the model in other contexts.

While Part I is concerned with collaboration between teachers and researchers, the three chapters in Part II explore the role of learners as collaborative agents in classroom research. Chapter 4, by Marie Källkvist, Henrik Gyllstad, Erica Sandlund and Pia Sundqvist, focuses on reciprocity and challenge in researcher–student collaborative labour in a large multilingual secondary school in Sweden. In particular, the authors explore the challenge of recruiting a sufficient number of students to provide written, informed consent and thus contribute research data. They define reciprocity in terms of the benefits that both parties need or desire from the collaboration, towards which they adopt an ethical stance (Trainor and Bouchard 2013). Their data collection followed ethnographic principles, according to which researchers build rapport with participants over time. Besides securing the research data they needed, the researchers acquired new knowledge about students' heritage languages and the multilingual territories they had left. Students were given the opportunity to communicate with the researchers in either English or Swedish, and the data suggest that students felt empowered when positioned as experts on their multilingual repertoires and on the language ecology in their prior home territories.

In Chapter 5, Annamaria Pinter reflects on a collaborative action research project, 'Children and teachers as co-researchers in Indian primary classrooms', that involved two universities, one in the UK and one in India, 25 Indian teachers of English, and some 800 children from different types of school in various regions of the country. The aim of the project was to explore the concept of the agentic child, borrowed from the Childhood Studies literature, by giving children active roles in classroom action research. In particular, the project set out to discover how teachers implemented changes in their classrooms as a result of (re-)conceptualizing their learners as partners in classroom research. During the two years of the project, in addition to focussing on the children's experiences, Pinter and her colleagues documented how the research team benefited from multiple learning opportunities that emerged organically in the process of working collaboratively. The chapter shows that by involving learners as co-researchers, the project had a transformative impact on classroom practice: teachers frequently adopted pedagogical approaches calculated to harness and further develop the agency of their learners.

Chapter 6, by David Little and Déirdre Kirwan, describes the approach that one Irish primary school has adopted to the management of extreme linguistic diversity – more than 50 home languages among 320 pupils. In keeping with the ethos of the Primary School Curriculum, the school aims to harness and extend the agency of each individual pupil by including home languages in classroom discourse. Each pupil's home language, after all, is central to her identity and the default medium of her consciousness and discursive thinking. The chapter describes what the school's approach looked like in 2014–2015, after an evolution of some twenty years. This description is itself the result of reciprocal collaboration between the former principal of the school (Déirdre Kirwan) and a researcher (David Little). Behind this description, the chapter explores the multiple collaborations on which the development and implementation of the school's approach depended: collaborations involving principal, teachers, pupils, parents and the wider school community. The reciprocities that characterize these collaborations have generated an especially close relation between pedagogical principles, classroom practice and ongoing research.

Part III focuses on collaborative research in professional development. In Chapter 7, Tanya McCarthy describes an initiative carried out at two national universities in Japan to prepare young researchers in master's and doctoral programmes to meet the challenges of communicating in English in their life beyond the laboratory. Supported by a government grant, the initiative took the form of a research exchange programme that identified five core principles of collaborative research: dynamic relationships, autonomous learning, knowledge transfer, sharing resources, and professionalism. Three distinct types of partnership emerged during the programme: student/student, researcher/student and researcher/researcher. Partnerships functioned effectively when they were reciprocal; that is, when individuals identified shared problems, devised shared solutions, made personal breakthroughs, and committed to common as well as individual needs. The principal challenges the initiative encountered had to do with scheduling, trust and technological issues.

One of the greatest challenges in the field of language education is to identify effective strategies for developing students' language competences, whether they are using their first, second or an additional language. In Chapter 8, Gabriele Pallotti, Claudia Borghetti, Stefania Ferrari and Greta Zanoni report on Osservare l'Interlingua/Observing Interlanguage, a teacher training and action research initiative designed to meet this challenge. Carried out since 2007 by the Reggio Emilia municipality and the University of Modena and Reggio Emilia, the initiative is founded on the principle that effective teaching should be grounded in the observation and analysis of students' needs, existing competences and learning strategies. The initiative involves 12 primary and three middle schools, 28 teachers and 35 classes, with about 650 pupils. Teachers and researchers meet every two or three months to analyse pupils' written and/or oral texts, plan pedagogical actions, and monitor the impact of those actions, sometimes revising them along the way. The chapter describes the overall pedagogical approach and the reciprocal dynamics of teacher–researcher collaboration, explaining how teachers learn from one another's experience and from the researchers' inputs, while the researchers expose their academic insights to the test of everyday classroom reality.

The process of learning to teach has been described as 'socially negotiated and contingent on knowledge of self, students, subject matter, curricula, and setting' (Johnson 2009: 20). This is the perspective adopted by Ofra Inbar-Lourie and Orly Haim in Chapter 9, which reports on a collaborative project involving a teacher education college and mentoring schools situated in the centre of Israel. Each school accommodates a group of EFL student teachers working collaboratively with mentor teachers and school staff on various school-based activities and projects. Mentor teachers, school principals and pedagogical advisors from the college collaborate in a professional development programme aimed at enhancing the learning-to-teach process and attaining shared educational goals. Building on Opfer and Pedder (2011), the chapter examines pre-service EFL teachers' learning through an ecological lens comprised of three overlapping systems: the pre-service teacher (prior experience, beliefs and assumptions about teaching and learning), the school (context, policy and culture, and interactions with the students, mentor teacher and staff), and the professional development activities teachers perform as part of their learning process.

It is widely accepted that the success of large-scale educational reform depends on effective collaboration between all relevant stakeholders, including the policy level. This is the concern of Part IV. In Chapter 10, Batia Laufer describes the collaborative research processes that informed the construction of the lexical syllabus in the new English curriculum in Israel. Researchers, teachers, textbook writers, curriculum planners, assessment specialists, and education administrators all contributed to the construction of the syllabus, whose design was based on the following research findings and (in brackets) collaborations:

- gaps between learners' lexical knowledge and the amount of lexis necessary for performing language tasks (researchers, teachers, assessment specialists);
- vocabulary treatment in textbooks: amount of exposure and type of activities (researchers and textbook writers);
- challenges in reaching the productive level of word knowledge (researchers, textbook writers, curriculum planners);
- establishing a new word-counting unit – the Nuclear Word Family (researchers and curriculum planners);
- importance and difficulty of multi-word units (researchers, textbook writers, curriculum planners);
- presentation of words with multiple meanings (researchers and curriculum planners);
- representation of orthographic patterns (researchers and curriculum planners).

The impact of major change in national education policy is felt most immediately by teachers and learners in classrooms. One such change happened in Finland in 2020, when primary pupils began to learn the first foreign or second domestic language in first rather than third grade. In Chapter 11, Karita Mård-Miettinen and Anne Pitkänen-Huhta present a collaborative case study that they carried out with one primary school. Their original goal was to engage in close collaboration with the school for the first three years of teaching English as a foreign language to first graders. They planned their study as a series of cycles: classroom observation, stakeholder interviews and questionnaires, and collaboratively developed classroom activities. With the arrival of Covid-19, however, responsibility for data collection passed from the researchers to the school. At the same time, the researchers' perspective on emerging classroom practices was broadened by including the language teachers' collegial network in online interviews, which foregrounded both challenges and opportunities in researcher–practitioner collaboration. Teachers' sense that they were falling short of expectations as early language teachers sometimes led to defensiveness; on the other hand, they were empowered by becoming researchers of their own work.

According to the Swedish Education Act, all education should be based on scientific knowledge and evidence (Skollag 2010:800 §5). Since 2008, the Swedish government has followed this principle by funding national graduate schools to enable teachers and teacher educators to undertake educational research. In Chapter 12, Camilla Bardel and Gudrun Erickson describe and discuss two such schools in language education. One brought ten lower and upper secondary teachers to a Licentiate degree; the other will bring nine language teacher educators to a PhD. The design of both programmes entailed collaboration between Swedish universities – four in the first programme, three in the second – and followed the same basic structure: an overarching theme, three common courses, and regular joint seminars with presentations of work in progress and discussion of draft texts. In some seminars, especially in the PhD programme, members of the international advisory boards attached to the programmes acted as readers and discussants, thereby adding another dimension of collaboration. The chapter pays particular attention to the collaborative and reciprocal elements embedded in the pedagogical model used, highlighting benefits as well as challenges for the parties involved: graduate students, researchers, schools and pupils, universities and policy makers.

In her concluding commentary, Ema Ushioda reviews the twelve chapters from the perspective of reciprocity as an ethical principle. She argues that truly reciprocal collaborative research meets the needs of all partners in the collaboration; insists on the interdependence of pedagogical theory, classroom practice and empirical exploration; addresses the relational complexities among the individuals, communities and institutions involved; and seeks to reduce asymmetries of power. This captures the essence of our rationale for putting the book together in the first place. For all their diversity of purpose, theme and focus, our authors share a commitment to reciprocity as an ethical principle, and their chapters contribute to a debate that is of increasing importance to researchers, teachers, teacher educators, policy makers and funding agencies.

References

Akker, Jan van den. 2003. Curriculum perspectives: An introduction. In Jan van den Akker, Wilmad Kuiper & Uwe Hameyer (eds.), *Curriculum landscapes and trends*, 1–10. Amsterdam: Kluwer Academic Publishers.
Germain, Claude. 2018. *The neurolinguistic approach (NLA) for learning and teaching foreign languages*. Newcastle upon Tyne: Cambridge Scholars Publishing.
Hammersley, Laura. 2017. Language matters: Reciprocity and its multiple meanings. In Judyth Sachs & Lindie Clark (eds.), *Learning through community engagement: Vision and practice in higher education*. Singapore: Springer. https://doi.org/10.1007/978-981-10-0999-0_8 (accessed 24 October 2022).
Johnson, Karen E. 2009. *Second language teacher education: A sociocultural perspective*. New York: Routledge.
Opfer, V. Darleen & David Pedder. 2011. Conceptualizing teacher professional learning. *Review of Educational Research* 81(3). 376–407. DOI: https://doi.org/10.3102/0034654311413609 (accessed 24 October 2022).
Rose, Heath. 2019. Dismantling the ivory tower in TESOL: A renewed call for teaching-informed research. *TESOL Quarterly* 53(3). 895–905.
Sato, Masatoshi & Shawn Loewen (eds.). 2022. *Connecting second language research and practice: Observations and interventions*. Special issue, *Modern Language Journal* 106(3).
Sidnell, Jack. 2010. *Conversation analysis: An introduction*. Chichester: Wiley-Blackwell.
Skollag 2010:800 [Education Act] (accessed 24 October 2022).
Trainor, Audrey & Kate A. Bouchard. 2013. Exploring and developing reciprocity in research design. *International Journal of Qualitative Studies in Education* 26(8). 986–1003.

Part 1: **Addressing challenges in the classroom**

Jessica Berggren, Silvia Kunitz, Malin Haglind, Amanda Hoskins, Anna Löfquist and Hanna Robertson

1 Combining theory and practice: Findings from a collaborative project on oral task design

Abstract: This chapter presents the collaborative research project 'From monologues to dialogues'. The project included several small-scale classroom studies conducted by a research team of teachers and researchers. The collaboration encompassed all stages of the project (design, implementation and analysis), which combined theory and practice to produce findings relevant for the teaching profession. The project was grounded in a practice-based problem: How do we get the pupils to talk to each other in the target language in the classroom? The research team hypothesized that the issue might lie with oral classroom activities and that the problem could be solved by designing meaningful tasks aimed at promoting co-constructed interaction. Our findings related to task design indicate that problem-based tasks with brief instructions and artefacts can elicit 'good interaction', which – with the analytical affordances of conversation analysis – we empirically defined as co-constructed interaction where pupils attend to each other's turns-at-talk and formulate fitting turns that foster the progressivity of the activity. Challenges in our collaboration included negotiating different expectations and perspectives; we argue, however, that the benefits outweigh the challenges. Most importantly, by working side by side in the research process our research team has produced findings that are both actionable and sustainable for the teaching profession.

1 Introduction

This chapter presents a collaborative classroom study in which a research team of teachers and researchers worked side by side to produce knowledge by solving a practice-based problem. Our work was grounded on the belief that combining practice and theory is necessary to build a knowledge base for teaching and that an authentic collaboration needs a shared research object. As such, collaboration in our study entailed working together throughout the research process towards a common goal, which in our case implied the production of knowledge relevant for the teaching and learning of English as a foreign language (EFL). More specifically, the research team explored task design for oral interaction in English in primary and secondary school in Sweden.

https://doi.org/10.1515/9783110787719-002

Bulterman-Bos argues that '[t]he way in which researchers view education differs fundamentally from the way in which teachers view education' (2008: 412). This idea can be related to the traditional dualism of skill (practice) and knowledge (theory), which is in turn associated with the distinction between people who act (teachers/practitioners) and people who think (university-based researchers; see Bulterman-Bos 2008; Sensevy et al. 2013). Even if this duality is far from clear-cut, there is a perceived gap between practice and theory in educational research, a gap which can be explained by different views on what constitutes relevant knowledge, and accordingly, by the disparity between what university-based researchers study and what teachers need to know to improve teaching (Cochran-Smith and Lytle 1990; Hiebert, Gallimore, and Stigler 2002). One way of overcoming this divide is to form collaborative research teams of teachers and researchers who explore teaching problems and formulate research questions together. In other words, this kind of collaboration entails working on a shared research object (Eriksson 2018), which is exactly what we have done in our project.

Having a shared research object and aiming to produce public and shareable knowledge are two important factors that distinguish collaborative classroom research from action research, for example Andrée and Eriksson (2019), Kunitz et al. (2022). Action research is commonly perceived as professional development resulting in individual or local knowledge (Burns 2010; Carlgren 2012; Eriksson 2018); sometimes, in this kind of research, the teachers themselves constitute the research object rather than teaching and learning (Carlgren 2012).

Indeed, some examples of teacher–researcher partnerships, rooted in the assumption that researchers know more than teachers (or, put another way, that researchers are knowledge-producers while teachers are knowledge-consumers), seem to accentuate the gap between theory and practice by emphasizing that, in the research process, teachers learn from the researchers/experts. 'Closing the gap' is also frequently interpreted as a one-directional need for practice to move towards research (Hamza et al. 2018). On the contrary, we conceptualize collaboration in line with Sensevy et al.'s (2013: 1032) idea of 'cooperative engineering', which denotes a joint process involving a 'collective of teachers and researchers'. This collective rests on a notion of symmetry and reciprocity. That is, as the differences between the two professions are vital in that 'every agent plays "her game"' (Sensevy et al. 2013: 1033), each agent also benefits from the different perspectives that different 'games' bring to the collaboration. These types of collaborative endeavours pave the way for a knowledge base for teaching by formulating relevant research questions that combine practice and theory (cf. Cochran-Smith and Lytle 1990) and by forming a research team in which teachers are 'included in the research as interpretative professionals making professional sense of particular educational events' (Carlgren 2012: 126).

2 The setting

The present project, 'From monologues to dialogues', was carried out within Stockholm Teaching & Learning Studies (STLS). STLS is a research environment for teacher-driven classroom studies, organized as a partnership between school organizers[1] and Stockholm University. It started in 2009 as an attempt to bring theory and practice closer by developing the idea that schools need an in-built apparatus for research and development in which teachers are primarily knowledge producers rather than consumers (Berggren and Carlgren 2015). Today, STLS employs three senior university professors, researchers with a teaching background, and teachers who are working towards a research degree in different disciplinary areas. Their job is to promote, initiate and participate in collaborative classroom studies with schoolteachers whose participation is funded by their school organizer. New classroom studies are conducted on a yearly basis and are part of larger projects; every year new schoolteachers join new sub-projects and become members of subject-specific research teams. Collaboration in STLS is also fostered by a set of guidelines that establish shared ownership of the data and require acknowledgement of all people involved for dissemination purposes.

'From monologues to dialogues' is a small-scale, long-term project conducted by the STLS network for English and foreign languages. It consists of various sub-projects that have been implemented over the years through the participation of more than 30 language teachers. All the participants have contributed to the cumulative research process, in which findings from the sub-projects were pooled and further developed in subsequent sub-projects. In this chapter, we zoom in on two of the sub-projects in English.

3 Our research process

3.1 Background

The starting point for our project was the observed practice-based problem that pupil–pupil interactions in the language classroom often resemble parallel monologues, with each pupil giving the floor to the co-participant (e.g., through fixed phrases such as *what do you think?* or *what about you?*) but then not showing any sign of active listenership and engagement with the co-participant's talk. That is, it

---

[1] In Sweden, a school organizer can be a municipality or the board of an independent school (Swedish *friskola*). School organizers are responsible for following national guidelines in their schools.

seems difficult to involve pupils in co-constructed oral interaction in the second language classroom (see Kunitz et al. 2022 for a thorough description of the problem). At the beginning of the project, we formulated this pedagogical problem as: *How do we get our pupils to talk to each other in the target language in the classroom?*

In the planning process of the present research project, a meeting was held with a teacher group at a local school. These teachers, relying on steering documents, their own experience, and video recordings of pupil–pupil interactions, had compiled a list of features perceived as important for successful oral interaction, such as eye contact, vocabulary, discourse strategies, etc. We then set out to collaboratively identify the cause of the problem and watched a video-recorded conversation between two pupils who were engaged in the task of planning a party. The task instructions included a list of points to discuss, such as date and food. The conversation was implemented as a series of suggestions followed by confirmations, which resulted in task completion (i.e., the pupils did plan a party), but without any collaborative co-construction of the interaction. We hypothesized that the problem might lie in the task itself. On these grounds we formulated a joint research objective; that is, an exploration of task design to promote classroom oral interaction. More specifically, the planning process involved a transformation of the pedagogical problem identified at the beginning into a research question; this transformation entailed narrowing the scope of the problem to turn it into a 'researchable' – i.e., answerable – question. In our case *How do we get the pupils to talk to each other in the target language in the classroom?* became *How can we design classroom tasks that elicit oral interaction in the target language?*

Over time our understanding of the pedagogical problem has developed. On the basis of the participating teachers' experience and of our interpretation of the steering documents, it has become clear that the assessment culture in Swedish schools, where pupils expect to be assessed at any time (cf. Sivenbring 2016), has contributed to the emergence of the problem. More specifically, the oral national standardized test influences classroom teaching and activities (see Kunitz et al. 2022) to the point that oral activities are often perceived as opportunities to display language rather than to use it for meaningful communicative purposes (Ellis 2003). This perception can be reinforced by the fact that many teacher-initiated activities also include language support, such as glossaries with fixed phrases that the students are encouraged to use when they speak in the target language; that is, students' attention is drawn to form/accuracy rather than meaning/purposeful communication. Indeed, the focus on assessment rather than teaching in the language classroom attracted some of the schoolteachers to our project; that is, some of the participating schoolteachers joined our research team on this particular project because of their willingness to shift from a focus on assessing speaking to a focus on teaching speaking in the classroom. The opportunity to create oral tasks that would engage students in meaningful communication (versus mere language display), which was the goal of our project, seemed to aid in the implementation of such a shift.

In terms of collaboration, the process of pinpointing the problem was a joint endeavour where every participant played their game (Sensevy et al. 2013) towards a common goal; the teachers brought their knowledge and experience of classroom practice to the table, while the researchers posed questions and provided input intended to deepen the research team's understanding of the issue. The following sections describe the research design and process.

3.2 Phase 1: How can we design tasks that elicit oral interaction in the target language?

As mentioned previously, our project was organized as a series of sub-projects, each lasting an academic year. The first two years of the project focused on task design to promote 'good interaction' in the EFL classroom and each sub-project worked with a separate task. Our research design relied on collaboration, intervention and iteration. The intervention (i.e., the task implementation) was conducted and video-recorded in classrooms in three cycles. Each cycle comprised task design, testing with a new group of pupils, analysis, and revision (see Figure 1.1).

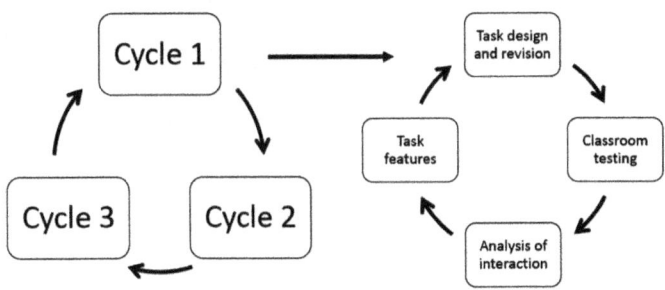

Figure 1.1: Project structure.

The intervention involved pupils in the six primary and secondary schools represented by the twelve teachers participating in this phase of the project. To ensure ecological validity, all pupils present in the classroom engaged with the task, but we only video-recorded those who had consented to take part in the study, following the guidelines issued by the Swedish Research Council (Vetenskapsrådet 2017). The collaboration in this phase of our project entailed regular seminars including all sub-projects; all participants were considered members of the same research team.

Task design in our project was based on Ellis's design features (2003: 21; see Table 1.1 below). These features proved useful in task revision as the research team could manipulate specific parts of the task to improve the predicted outcomes (Berggren et al. 2019). This manipulation was grounded on an analysis of the pupil–pupil interaction, that is, the intended process outcome of the task. Task revision could entail introducing a feature that had functioned well in another task or testing something new. For instance, we decided not to use split information since this condition did not elicit co-constructed talk in our tasks. One of the tasks designed during the first phase (i.e., *What happened to Kim?*) is presented in the next section.

Table 1.1: Design features (Ellis 2003: 21).

Design feature	Description
1 Goal	The general purpose of the task (e.g. to practise the ability to describe objects concisely; to provide an opportunity for the use of relative clauses)
2 Input	The verbal or non-verbal information supplied by the task (e.g., pictures, a map, written text)
3 Conditions	The way in which the information is presented (e.g., split vs. shared information) or the way in which it is to be used (e.g., converging vs. diverging)
4 Procedures	The methodological procedures to be followed in performing the task (e.g., group vs. pair work, planning time vs. no planning time)
5 Predicted outcomes:	
Product	The product that results from completing the task (e.g., a completed table, a route drawn in on a map, a list of differences between two pictures). The predicted product can be open (i.e., allow for several possibilities) or closed (i.e., allow for only one correct solution).
Process	The linguistic and cognitive processes the task is hypothesized to generate

As mentioned above, the manipulation of task design features was grounded in data analysis. Our analytical process consisted of preparing words-only transcripts of the video-recorded task-based interactions and analysing the data with a colour-coding scheme that was empirically developed by the research team. Table 1.2 presents the latest version of the colour-coding scheme (for an example of how it was used see the next section).

Table 1.2: Colour-coding scheme elaborated in Phase 1.

Colour	Function
Red	Introducing a new idea
Yellow	Developing ideas (perspectives, angles)
Green	Agreeing, 'oiling element'
Blue	Disagreeing
Purple	Talking about instructions
Pink	Searching for words

In this phase, we were inspired by genre theory (Burns 2013), and the colour coding exemplified different functions of the interaction in relation to the task. The categories were developed through several data sessions which involved all sub-projects. During data sessions, various excerpts of task-based interactions that had been video-recorded in the sub-projects were shown and discussed, with the help of words-only transcripts; all participants in the data sessions contributed with analytical observations.

Once the first phase had been completed, the research team came to the conclusion that the open-ended, problem-solving tasks that had been designed in the latest sub-projects (such as *What happened to Kim?*; see below) did elicit the kind of 'good' (i.e., co-constructed) interaction that the research team had been aiming for all along. In other words, an answer to the original research question had been found, and with it a solution to the pedagogical problem identified at the beginning of the project.

3.3 Phase 2: What are the interactional features of 'good interaction'?

In a subsequent phase, a new research question emerged, concerning more specifically the interactional features that characterize the task-based interactions in which the pupils engaged. That is, we aimed to unpack, in a more detailed fashion, what the 'good interaction' we had observed meant. To answer this new research question, the data were (re-)analysed through the lens of Conversation Analysis (CA; see Sidnell and Stivers 2013).

CA is an observational discipline that works with primary data (i.e., audio and video recordings of naturally occurring interactions) and focuses on how the participants in interaction make sense of each other's actions turn by turn, by relying on interactional mechanisms such as turn-taking, sequence organization, and repair. In recent years, the branch of CA that works within the field of second language acquisition (called CA-SLA) has particularly focused on exploring and describing the features of interactional competence (IC) in a second language (see Skogmyr Marian and Balaman 2018 for an overview; see Salaberry and Kunitz 2019 for a collection of studies on L2 IC).

It therefore made sense to apply CA's set of analytical tools to the data, in order to describe in more detail the interactional features that characterize the pupils' IC. To this end, the words-only transcripts that had been used in the previous phase were refined in order to include at least some of the conventions adopted by CA and, most importantly, some notations regarding embodiment (e.g., gaze, gestures, etc.). The transcripts were produced in preparation for data sessions, during which all members of the research team participated in multiple viewings of the video-recordings and in subsequent rounds of observations. Overall, the findings resulting from this analytical phase confirmed the findings from the first phase with the addition of some relevant details.

In what follows we have selected one excerpt from the *What happened to Kim?* task (produced in phase 1) to illustrate how the analysis was conducted, first with colour-coding (Excerpt 1a) and later with CA (Excerpt 1b). The input (i.e., one of the design features; see Tables 1.1 and 1.3) for *What happened to Kim?* included instructions delivered as a 'Background' for the task (see Figure 1.2) and a set of artefacts in a paper bag.

```
Background
12-year old Kim left home at 7:30 yesterday morning, but did
not arrive at school.
Kim was found at a petrol station at 11 in the night, but
doesn't remember anything from the day.
The 8 things you have in your paper bags were found next to
Kim.
What happened to Kim?
Choose the five things you think can help Kim remember and
put them in the paper bag. Close the bag when you are
finished.
```

Figure 1.2: Instructions for the task *What happened to Kim?*

The pupils were asked to determine what had happened to Kim, a 12-year-old who did not attend school on the day in question and was later found at a petrol station together with a bag containing eight objects (i.e., a cell phone, some coins, a receipt for a bag of apples, a roller coaster ticket, a note saying 'I miss you', a photo of a girl, a cuddly toy, and a key). The pupils were then instructed to choose the five objects that would help Kim remember the day's events.

Excerpt 1 is extracted from the task-based interaction of three grade 8 students (lower secondary school). The excerpt starts with Ed's proposal that Kim, referred to as a she, must have been at a Tivoli; his co-participants (Isa and Anna), however, disagree with the idea that Kim is a girl and suggest instead that 'Kim is a guy'. They then provide an account for their disagreement, arguing that the assumption that Kim is a boy would help clarify the role of two artefacts, namely, the note saying 'I miss you' and the photo of a girl. Specifically, if Kim were a boy, then one could assume that the photo is of his girlfriend and that the two went to the amusement park together.

Excerpt 1a reproduces the words-only transcript used in phase 1. The excerpt was colour-coded with yellow and green, where yellow was used to mark the proposal of ideas that led to the development of the story, while green was used to mark parts of the interaction that simply functioned as an 'oiling element' (see Table 1.2 above), providing confirmation. The research team considered this to be an example of good interaction in that the students engaged with each other's ideas as they collaboratively constructed the story of what had happened to Kim.

Excerpt 1a (Lower secondary) – Yeah but I start to think that Kim is a guy
Ed: my guess is that she has been at a öh öh öh a tivoli or something similar
Isa: **yeah but i** still think that kim is a guy because it would really explain] **[Anna: yeah it has]** this note and this photo **[Anna: the photo maybe]** a girlfriend or something
Anna: maybe they were there together
Isa: yeah
Ed: that's a good idea

Excerpt 1b reproduces the same excerpt as it was re-transcribed following CA conventions and with the addition of relevant embodied actions.

Excerpt 1b (lower secondary) – Yeah but I start to think that Kim is a guy
```
1      ED:      my: guess is <that she has been> at
2               +u::hm (0.9) mtch- u:::::::h
                +looks up
3               tivo[li.]
4      ANNA:        [>ti]voli.<=yeah.
5      ED:      tivoli.
6               (0.2)
7      ED:      or: <something similar.> ((staccato))
```

```
8    ISA:    >yeah but ↑i start to think that< kim is a guy
9            [because it would]=
10   ANNA:   [yeah because   ]
11   ISA:    =it would really explain +this:: (0.3)
                                      +holds note
12           +no::te,
             +grabs photo from Anna's hand
13           [+and this photo.    ]
             +lifts photo in left hand
14   ANNA:   [and the the (.) photo] over there.
15           (0.3) ((Anna and Isa look at each other))
16   ANNA:   maybe=
17   ISA:    =ye[ah.]
18   ANNA:      [i- ] i- uh
19           [(we can say)]
20   ED:     [+°oh yeah?° ]
             +looks down
21   ISA:    [ maybe it's ] a +girlfriend or some[thing?]
                              +puts down note and photo
22   ANNA:                                       [yeah.]=
23           =+maybe they were (.) there together? (   )
              +Ed nods
24   ISA:    °yeah.°=
25   ED:     °yeah. that's a good idea.°
```

This kind of fine-grained transcription allows for a more detailed analysis of the participants' actions. Specifically, Ed's proposal (that Kim must have been at an amusement park, lines 1–3) is characterized by a word-search, showing his uncertainty in producing the word *Tivoli*. As he delivers this lexical item, Anna recognizes it and ratifies the outcome of the search in line 4. After Ed hedges his epistemic stance, hinting that Kim might have been at a Tivoli 'or something similar' (line 7), Isa disagrees (line 8) with the narrative so far proposed by Ed.

At this point, Isa and Anna simultaneously start developing an account to justify the idea that Kim is a guy (lines 9–10). As Anna withdraws from the overlap (line 10), Isa delivers her account (lines 11–13). In line 14, Anna again displays her alignment with Isa by mentioning the photo in overlap with Isa's turn in line 13. This alignment is triggered by Isa's embodied action of grabbing the photo from Anna's hand (line 12) before even mentioning the artefact; this action is therefore enough for Anna to anticipate where Isa is going with her reasoning. While Isa and Anna are clearly on the same page, as further demonstrated by their mutual gaze (line 15), Ed is looking at the desk where the other artefacts and the instructions are located and eventually produces a delayed *oh yeah?* (line 20), indicating receipt of the talk so far rather than explicit acceptance. In partial overlap with Ed, Isa states that perhaps the photo is of Kim's girlfriend (line 21). While Ed nods (line 23), Anna accepts Isa's idea and further elaborates on the emerging narrative, combining Ed's original proposal with Isa's new idea: probably Kim and his girlfriend were at the amusement park together (line 23). Isa accepts with a soft *yeah* (line 24), while Ed produces a positive assessment (line 25).

Overall, the kind of fine-grained analysis afforded by CA illustrates the close collaboration between Isa and Anna in proposing and elaborating a different take on the narrative. These two participants closely monitor each other's verbal and embodied actions and produce collaborative overlaps (lines 9–10 and 13–14). Throughout this excerpt, Ed has a more peripheral role, though his actions show that he has somehow been following the unfolding interaction (lines 20, 23 and 25).

The conclusion that can be reached with these two kinds of analysis are similar; that is, Excerpt 1 provides an example of student engagement and collaborative interaction. Put another way, the adoption of a CA lens confirms the previous analysis while adding further layers of detail and therefore of evidence, as the CA analysis makes the co-construction of the interaction more apparent.

In the second phase of the project, one more task was designed in a subproject that worked with English: the *Excavation* task. During task design, thanks to the cumulative nature of the project, the research team could build on the findings from the previous phase and use an adaptation of Ellis's (2003) framework that, in its latest version, constitutes the blueprint illustrated in Table 1.3 below. Before discussing the blueprint, however, it is important to briefly describe the *Excavation* task, as the design similarities of this task with *What happened to Kim?* are apparent. The instructions are reproduced in Figure 1.3 below.

```
The excavation - utgrävningen
At an excavation of a cave a person was found together with these
items.
How did this person end up in the cave?
```

Figure 1.3: Instructions for the *Excavation* task.

Here the pupils were asked how a person who was found in a cave with a pair of sunglasses, a Maori necklace, a kiwi fruit, some wool, a boomerang, and a compass had ended up there. In this case, the objects were reproduced in cut-out figures that were given to the pupils together with the instructions.

The *Excavation* task was tested only once in the classroom (with students in the first year of upper secondary school) since it elicited pupils' collaborative interaction in its first implementation and no further revisions were deemed necessary. Indeed, the process (see Tables 1.1 and 1.3) in which the students engaged resulted in the same kind of co-constructed interaction that we had observed in the implementation of *What happened to Kim?*

3.4 Results

At the beginning of the project, we envisioned a list of guiding principles for task design as a relevant and actionable result. Another aim was to explore the use of a framework for task design, namely Ellis's design features (2003), in the Swedish EFL context and in relation to co-constructed oral interaction. Overall, the design features proposed by Ellis (2003) functioned well for task design in our project. They provided the research team with a common vocabulary (cf. Hamza et al. 2018) and a framework of reference during task design and revision. Through the various sub-projects we have produced a series of tasks and, in the latest sub-projects, we have come to rely on a task blueprint (see Table 1.3 below) for open-ended, problem-based tasks such as *What happened to Kim?* and the *Excavation*. In the blueprint, which represents an adaptation of Ellis's (2003) framework, each single design feature is specified in concrete terms.

Table 1.3: Blueprint for open-ended problem-based tasks.

	Design feature	Description
1	Goal	Engage the pupils in oral co-constructed interaction while unraveling a problem by forming hypotheses
2	Input	Short written introduction of problem Artefacts (actual items or paper cutouts)
3	Conditions	Shared information (one set per group) Reasoning-gap task Converging use of information in an open task
4	Procedures	2–3 pupils No planning time
5	Ending	An action that signals task completion
6	Process	'Good interaction'

As Table 1.3 shows, the goal is to engage the pupils in oral co-constructed interaction as they form and negotiate hypotheses while unravelling the problem presented in the instructions. The input should be brief and in writing and should include artefacts. Each group of pupils should get one set of instructions and materials; that is, all groups should share the same information. The convergent use of the information entails that the group needs to find a common solution to the open-ended problem. The gap is similar to what Prabhu (1987) refers to as a reasoning gap in that the pupils should synthesize ideas and form hypotheses. The collaboration in terms of ideas and hypotheses is powered by the 'uncertainty' related to the open task; that is, by the fact that there is no correct answer.

In terms of procedures, we have used groups of 2–3 pupils depending on teachers' preferences and the pupils have not received planning time in any of the subprojects. The ending should entail a clear signal to the pupils that they have completed the task and should not be what we labelled a 'task within the task', such as a written product or a presentation. This last feature differs from Ellis's (2003) framework, where 'product' refers to a predicted outcome. Instead, we prefer 'ending', which refers to an action that signals that the pupils have completed the task.

Finally, we envisage the process as consisting of 'good interaction'; that is, collaborative, co-constructed interaction through which the pupils parse and attend to each other's turns and assess and build on each other's hypotheses. In this kind of process, pupils use and practice their IC (for a more thorough description of the pupils' interactional skills; see Kunitz et al. 2022).

3.5 Dissemination

In line with the guidelines for collaboration specified by STLS (see above), all members of the research team are involved in the dissemination of our findings, as shown by this co-authored chapter. This is to stress that the project is a collaboration from start to finish. Contrary to situations where 'ownership tends to be reclaimed by the researcher at the last stages of the project' (Areljung, Leden, and Wiblom 2021: 471), which risks converting the teachers into objects rather than agents, our project has been represented by both researchers and teachers in co-authored presentations and publications (including this chapter), in both academic and professionally-oriented venues. At the same time, some of the teachers who have participated in our project have started to disseminate the findings in and through their professional practice by designing new oral tasks and by developing criteria for the assessment of oral interaction. These examples evidence the relevance of our findings for the teaching profession as well as the joint ownership resulting from the collaborative research process.

Clearly, this collaborative involvement in the dissemination stage would not have been possible without the support of school organizers and schools in the STLS research environment. In fact, they have encouraged and funded teachers' participation in research conferences and organized opportunities for sharing knowledge and experiences between schools. In writing the present chapter, the authors received funding from the school organizers for a two-day writing retreat.

Contrary to the research community, the teaching profession does not have a well-established organization for reviewing and sharing new knowledge (Andrée and Eriksson 2019; Berggren and Carlgren 2015). In addition, sharing among teachers often entails practical, ready-made products, such as lesson plans, glossaries and exercises, i.e., 'quick fixes'. On the other hand, research (involving theoretical knowledge) is 'slower' in this respect, since the products often need to be transformed and adapted before implementation in practice. The collaborative approach adopted in this research project accelerated this process since the implementation (including the production of relevant instructional materials) is integrated in the methodology. Thus, in disseminating our findings to teacher audiences, we have combined theory and practice, detailing the theoretical foundations and practical implications of our project and sharing its tangible products (tasks). We are currently building a website intended to reach a wider audience; it aims to function as inspiration for teachers who want to design their own tasks for pupil interaction in the classroom. It includes interviews with teachers and researchers, short videos and texts with information about the blueprint for task design (Table 1.3) and IC, as well as copies of the tasks designed in the project.

4 Conclusion

In this chapter we have provided an account of a collaborative project that combines theory and practice. We have described a research process that entailed a collaboration between researchers and teachers grounded in the principles of symmetry and cooperative engineering (Sensevy et al. 2013). In our collaborative endeavour towards our shared research objective (task design for oral interaction), all participants played their part, or 'game' (see Sensevy et al. 2013), by contributing different kinds of expertise that were used to collaboratively solve the pedagogical problem, find answers to the research questions, and disseminate the results. That is, all participants were involved in the production of public and shareable knowledge that resulted from a systematic research process through cycles of task design, implementation and revision, followed by the analysis of interactional data.

Traditionally, in line with the view of them as consumers of knowledge, teachers are charged with the responsibility of implementing and integrating findings from educational research into their teaching. This is often connected to the notion of 'research literacy', defined as the ability to understand, assess and use scholarly/scientific knowledge (Persson 2017), an ability that is rooted in 'a willingness to engage with research' (Waring and Evans 2015: 18). What we have promoted with our work (and what actually has made our work possible) is the idea that responsibilities should be shared and that this willingness should not be one-sided. Rather, researchers should in turn be willing to develop 'practice literacy', which they can gain through a close, symmetrical collaboration with teachers. In a way, then, the reciprocal benefits of the collaboration within our research team lie in the development of research literacy for the teachers involved and of practice literacy for the participating researchers.

Throughout the project, we have worked side by side in a shared process which followed the quality criteria and requirements set by the research community. This entailed that the common path was guided by the researchers, who acted as navigators. One challenge in this respect is to avoid a situation where the collaboration is transformed by any of the participants into a course for the teachers (Andrée and Eriksson 2019; Berggren and Carlgren 2015), where the aim is teachers' professional development and the expectation is that the teachers (as knowledge consumers) learn from the researchers (as knowledge producers). Another challenge concerns researchers' and teachers' potentially different views of what constitutes knowledge, which might lead to a different understanding of the project's results. On the other hand, this helps to explain why collaboration is so important, in that our different lenses provide a multifaceted interpretation of the findings; again, reciprocity is a key outcome of the collaborative process described here, since all actors involved benefit from the inclusion of different perspectives in empirical data analysis.

There can also be practical challenges, like funding and time. In our case, this issue is solved by the involvement of school organizers in the STLS research environment; specifically, participating teachers get half a day per week to take part in the project, and all project meetings are scheduled during that time.

In any case, whichever challenges might need to be faced, they are clearly outweighed by the benefits of creating a synergy between theory and practice. This synergy informs the organizational structure of STLS itself, in that the involvement of school organizers brings symmetry in terms of voices from theory and practice, from the steering group to each sub-project. In particular, the involvement of teachers in the research design guarantees the production of actionable knowledge, which means that 'results will probably become more sustainable than what is normally the case in educational research and developmental work' (Carlgren 2012: 137).

Essentially, the great benefit of conducting educational research as a reciprocal venture, based on the close collaboration between researchers and teachers, is that the problems tackled and the solutions offered are of relevance for the teaching profession and do not need to be 'translated' (Hultman 2015).

References

Andrée, Maria & Inger Eriksson. 2019. A research environment for teacher-driven research – some demands and possibilities. *International Journal for Lesson and Learning Studies* 9(1). 67–77.

Areljung, Sofie, Lotta Leden & Jonna Wiblom. 2021. Expanding the notion of 'ownership' in participatory research involving teachers and researchers. *International Journal of Research & Method in Education* 44(5). 463–473.

Berggren, Jessica & Ingrid Carlgren. 2015. Stockholm Teaching & Learning Studies, En plattform för undervisningsutvecklande forskning [A platform for teacher-driven developmental research]. Working report. Stockholm: Stockholms stad.

Berggren, Jessica, Malin Haglind, Anna Löfquist, Kristina Nyström, Hedvig Anfält, Gunilla Finnson, Johansson Emmeli, Anna Rönquist & Charlotta Wilson. 2019. En språngbräda till bättre undervisning – att använda ett teoretiskt ramverk för att konstruera uppgifter [A springboard for better teaching – Using a theoretical framework to design tasks]. *Lingua* 1. 8–12.

Bulterman-Bos, Jacquelien A. 2008. Will a clinical approach make educational research more relevant for practice? *Educational Researcher* 37(7). 412–420.

Burns, Anne. 2010. *Doing action research in English language teaching*. New York: Routledge.

Burns, Anne. 2013. A holistic approach to teaching speaking in the language classroom. In Mikael Olofsson (ed.), *Symposium 2012 – Lärarrollen i svenska som andraspråk* [Symposium 2012 – The teacher role in Swedish as a second language], 165–178. Stockholm: Stockholms universitets förlag.

Carlgren, Ingrid. 2012. The learning study as an approach for 'clinical' subject matter didactic research. *International Journal for Lesson and Learning Studies* 1(2). 126–139.

Cochran-Smith, Marilyn & Susan L. Lytle. 1990. Research on teaching and teacher research: The issues that divide. *Educational Researcher* 19(2). 2–10.

Ellis, Rod. 2003. *Task-based language learning and teaching*. Oxford: Oxford University Press.

Eriksson, Inger. 2018. Lärares medverkan i praktiknära forskning: Förutsättningar och hinder [Teachers' participation in practice-oriented research: Requirements and obstacles]. *Utbildning & Lärande* 12(1). 27–40.

Hamza, Karim, Ola Palm, Jenny Palmqvist, Jésus Piqueras & Per-Olof Wickman. 2018. Hybridization of practices in teacher–researcher collaboration. *European Educational Research Journal* 17(1). 170–186.

Hiebert, James, Ronald Gallimore & James W. Stigler. 2002. A knowledge base for the teaching profession: What would it look like and how can we get one? *Educational Researcher* 31(5). 3–15.

Hultman, Glenn. 2015. *Transformation, interaktion eller kunskapskonkurrens: Forskningsanvändning i praktiken* [Transformation, interaction or knowledge competition: The use of research in practice]. Stockholm: Vetenskapsrådet.

Kunitz, Silvia, Jessica Berggren, Malin Haglind & Anna Löfquist. 2022. Getting students to talk: A practice-based study on the design and implementation of problem-solving tasks in the EFL classroom. *Languages* 7(2). 75.

Persson, Sven. 2017. *Forskningslitteracitet – en introduktion till att förstå, värdera och använda vetenskaplig kunskap* [Research literacy – an introduction to understanding, evaluating and using scientific knowledge] (Forskning i korthet 1). Malmö: Sveriges Kommuner och Landsting och Kommunförbundet Skåne.

Prabhu, N. S. 1987. *Second language pedagogy*. Oxford: Oxford University Press.

Salaberry, M. Rafael & Silvia Kunitz (eds.). 2019. *Teaching and testing L2 interactional competence: Bridging theory and practice*. New York: Routledge.

Sensevy, Gérard, Dominique Forest, Serge Quilio & Grace Morales. 2013. Cooperative engineering as a specific design-based research. *ZDM Mathematics Education* 45(7). 1031–1043.

Sidnell, Jack & Tania Stivers (eds.). 2013. *The handbook of conversation analysis*. Chichester: Wiley Blackwell.

Sivenbring, Jennie. 2016. *I den betraktades ögon. Ungdomar om bedömning i skolan* [In the eye of the beholder. Young people on assessment in school]. University of Gothenburg: Gothenburg Studies in Educational Sciences 384.

Skogmyr Marian, Klara & Ufuk Balaman. 2018. Second language interactional competence and its development: An overview of conversation analytic research on interactional change over time. *Language and Linguistics Compass* 12(8). 1–16.

Vetenskapsrådet. 2017. *God forskningssed* [Good research practice]. https://www.vr.se/analys/rapporter/vara-rapporter/2017-08-29-god-895forskningssed.html (accessed 17 October 2021)

Waring, Michael & Carol Evans. 2015. *Understanding pedagogy: Developing a critical approach to teaching and learning*. Abingdon: Routledge.

Katherine Mueller, Roswita Dressler, Anja Dressler Araujo,
Frank Moeller and Tanya Ronellenfitsch

2 Improving second language education through Intensive German Weeks: An action research collaboration between teachers and researchers

Abstract: Teachers in Canada's Bilingual Programs recognize the need to design lessons to promote oral language use since students often develop strong listening skills in the target language but are reluctant to speak it. One Bilingual Program in the province of Alberta has introduced Intensive German Weeks at the beginning, middle, and end of the school year to focus on oral language use of K–6 students. This action research over four years brought together the teachers of the German bilingual team and two language education researchers to study their learning about specific pedagogical strategies and to engage in professional learning. The teacher–researcher collaboration resulted in reciprocal learning from the use of strategies from the Neurolinguistic Approach. In this chapter, three teachers from the German Bilingual team and the two researchers reflect on the benefits and challenges of the teacher–researcher collaboration in the first three years of the study. The team developed common understandings around theory and practice, research design and ethics. They managed challenges that emerged around communication, constraints in time and funding, as well as the intrusion of the Covid-19 pandemic. Understandings of language education theory and practice as well as teacher–researcher collaboration have emerged from this study.

1 Introduction

In Canada, there are several models for second language teaching in a school context: Immersion (100% target language instruction), Bilingual (50% target language), and second language (typically 60–100 minutes per week). Since the 1960s, with the introduction of French Immersion, Canada has received international renown for research and innovation in this language teaching approach (Tedick and Lyster 2020; Mueller and Dressler 2022). French Immersion was originally based on the idea that students would pick up French through content instruction, as if by osmosis. From extensive research on the French Immersion model over the past 65 years, we have come to understand that teachers need to design their teaching of any language in a way that deliberately targets the integration of language and content to ensure optimal learning (Lyster 2007, 2016; Tedick and Lyster 2020). On the other hand, focusing too heavily on explicit language instruction is also not an effective way to ensure that students can integrate targeted language features into their developing proficiency. Fortunately, the area of second language pedagogy is a rich focus of pedagogical research and professional learning, and new approaches that merit attention in the classroom are emerging.

Awareness of new approaches comes through pre-service teacher education and in-service teacher professional learning. For those teachers without pre-service teacher education in second language teaching, professional learning is the only avenue toward developing skills in effective, research-informed practice. In the Bilingual Program context, many teachers come to second language teaching with minimal pre-service preparation in second language pedagogy (Dressler 2018). Therefore, they may not know where or how to begin to implement a structured approach to target language development. Scaffolded professional learning through teacher–researcher collaboration can be beneficial for bridging this gap in second language teaching preparation (Dagenais, Moore, and Sabatier 2009), especially as it pertains to fostering oral language use (i.e., production and interaction).

In this chapter, we relay the findings from a study in which the researchers have worked with teachers in a German Bilingual Program in structured professional learning opportunities and training in a second language teaching approach dedicated to enhancing target language use. Through the reflections of teachers and researchers about the study, we highlight the reciprocal benefits and challenges of teacher–researcher collaboration.

2 Literature review

Second language education in Canada falls under provincial jurisdiction. French Immersion is the most widely-known model. Second Language Programs, otherwise known as Core, are similar to language-as-school-subject classes worldwide. Bilingual Programs in non-official languages are the least well-known internationally, but provide a unique context for second language learning in which up to 50% of instruction is provided in the target language at the elementary level. Certain pedagogical approaches are typical for each model:
1. French Immersion generally has three entry points in Canada: *early* (in which students begin in either kindergarten or grade 1), *middle* (in which students begin in later elementary or in middle school), and *late* (in which students begin in grade 7) (Tedick and Lyster 2020). The option to continue

French Immersion is commonly available through grade 12 in many jurisdictions. Over fifty years of research into the French Immersion model has led to valuable insights, most notably through the work of Lyster (2007, 2016) and others who investigate content-based language teaching (Tedick and Lyster 2020; Cammarata 2016). Their work focusing on immersion, in tandem with research in the domain of second-language acquisition that has defined the notion of *focus on form* (Doughty and Williams 1998; O'Connor and Sharkey 2004), has highlighted the importance of integrating language and content to provide an authentic and meaningful context to model language use.

2. Second Language (or Core) programs are those in which the second language is treated as a school subject woven into students' schedules in a variety of configurations. Exposure varies widely, from several times a week, typically from 30 to 80 minutes per class, to daily classes (Masson et al. 2021; Smith 2020). Second language programs have widely varying curricular guidance from province to province, and results for students vary likewise. One approach for teaching French that has emerged from this context and has garnered interest in recent years is Intensive French, based on the Neurolinguistic Approach, hereafter NLA (Germain 2018; Netten and Germain 2004, 2005). It is used to teach French during Grade 5 or 6, for five months of intensive instruction, and is scaffolded before and after the intensive period to provide support to learners.

3. The Bilingual Program model aligns itself more with the French Immersion model, with common entry points being kindergarten or grade 1. Typical pedagogies include immersion pedagogy for the 50% of the time spent in the target language, including content-based language teaching for the subjects assigned to be taught in the target language (Dressler 2018). Perhaps because of its similarities with French Immersion, comparatively little research into the Bilingual Programs has been done beyond initial program evaluations (see Wu and Bilash 2000).

For each of these models, the merits and weaknesses are the subject of research and professional learning discussions across the country. One weakness that causes teachers concern is that learners typically acquire strong receptive skills (reading and listening), but production skills (speaking and writing) often reveal deficits in grammatical accuracy and sociolinguistically appropriate language use (Lyster 2007). These weaknesses emerge partly due to the fact that, without specific curricular guidance regarding approaches, the pedagogy and implementation of strategies are often left to the discretion of the teacher.

We are situated in a school district that has explored and adapted the NLA (Germain 2018) for language teaching to a variety of contexts, including Intensive French, French Immersion, Spanish Bilingual, Mandarin Bilingual and German

Bilingual (Mueller and Dressler 2022). This approach employs a series of strategies to target the development of scaffolded literacy (oral – reading – writing – return to oral). This *literacy loop* provides a structure for implementing an oral modelling sequence that allows students to create authentic, personalized answers in full sentences. Teachers plan a sequence carefully, ensuring that the oral modeling is supported by the reading selection. During the reading phase, the teacher can take the time to delve into sound/letter correspondences and grammatical points that will be important for accuracy, most especially when students reach the writing phase. Using oral language is the focus throughout, during the oral phase certainly, but also as part of the reading discussion (predictions, descriptions) and as the class discusses the writing phase. The literacy loop closes when students share their writing in the target language, discussing with peers and answering questions about their composition. This approach facilitates oral language development in a structured way, in that the teacher can select carefully which oral language the students will need to master.

Our work with the German teachers began as an outgrowth from work Roswita did for her dissertation (Dressler 2012). She was aware of the Bilingual Program and the dedication of the teachers to second language pedagogy, but also some of the challenges they faced since their program was small (the equivalent of one class per grade). Teachers were often hired for their language competency, rather than previous pre-service teacher preparation in second language pedagogy (not required in our context). However, when Roswita's first academic position did not provide the time necessary for classroom-based research, she did not return to the school with research in mind until May 2018. At this point, she desired a more democratic approach than she had adopted when she did her dissertation and came with her own questions, so she invited the teachers to share with her their researchable concerns. After brainstorming, we settled on two related foci: fostering oral language use through pedagogical strategies and documenting the scope and sequence of oral language teaching (what can the students learn over the course of a year and how can teachers in subsequent grades build upon that knowledge?). Katherine, who has extensive training in the implementation of the NLA, and who provides professional learning support to teachers, joined our team and we set out to work together as a teacher–researcher collaboration.

In past teacher–researcher collaborations in the field of second language teaching, teachers and researchers have jointly 'formed questions, developed research designs and instruments, designed class-equal (though differential) participation' (Hawkins and Legler 2004: 340). Teachers have deep knowledge of their teaching contexts (Cloonan, Hutchison, and Paatsch 2019) and researchers bring to this knowledge an overview of the field and the latest trends (Buğra and Wyatt

2021; Dagenais, Moore, and Sabatier 2009). Working together can help teachers overcome the constraints of time and motivation, the most frequently mentioned stumbling blocks in teacher research of their own practice (Lassonde, Israel, and Almasi 2019; O'Connor and Sharkey 2004; Wyatt and Dikilitaş 2016). However, the power imbalances that exist or are perceived have been called into question and need to be front-of-mind to avoid abuse and misattribution of knowledge (Stewart 2006). Teachers and researchers may have different motivations for entering into research partnerships, therefore common understandings are not always present at the outset of collaborations (O'Connor and Sharkey 2004). Over time, common understandings can be developed, but sometimes conflict arises which needs to be resolved; otherwise there is a risk that teachers will leave the team or the group will adjourn in dismay at its lack of productivity (Lassonde, Israel, and Almasi 2019). Despite possible challenges, teacher–researcher collaboration can be the catalyst for change in classrooms as the coming together of teacher and research knowledge, teacher–researcher collaboration, and the systematic investigation of the problem of practice (action research) result in innovation and professional learning.

With the common interest in oral language use in the German Bilingual Program and the commitment to teacher–researcher collaboration, the research question that emerged for our study was: How do teachers encourage oral language use in the target language classroom?

3 Methodology

The participants and co-researchers in this study were a group of second language teachers working in a Canadian elementary German Bilingual Program (kindergarten–grade 6 with children aged 5–12 years). They were supported in their implementation of research by two university researchers. The two researchers and three of the teachers are authors of this chapter. The larger collaboration took place over four school years (2018–2022) and is ongoing at the time of writing this chapter. Data from the larger study involved interviews (year 1), focus groups (year 2) with the teachers, classroom observation (years 1 and 2), and the gathering of artefacts created by the teachers such as lesson and unit plans (years 1–4). Findings from year 1 of the study have been published (Dressler and Mueller 2020, 2022) and will be highlighted here along with findings from years 2 and 3 to provide context for an analysis of individual reflections written by the teachers and researchers.

Action research was our chosen methodology. It allowed teachers to investigate a problem of practice that was ongoing and repeated, but for which the answer was not yet known (McNiff 2002). Importantly, the program of practice emerged from the teachers themselves, rather than being 'imposed on them by someone else' (Mills 2014: 8). Action research is by nature of reciprocal benefit to teachers and researchers. For our research, we drew from Stringer's (2014) action research interacting spiral of LOOK, THINK, ACT. Each year, the teachers designed three sets of Intensive German Weeks (two weeks each in September, January and April/May). During these weeks, certain subjects in English were set aside so teachers could focus on German. Teachers wanted to use these Intensive German Weeks to foster oral language use, so we decided to implement NLA to determine if the approach would facilitate the teachers and students in speaking more German. Three cycles of the action research iterative spiral (LOOK, THINK, ACT) were implemented around these Intensive German Weeks. At the beginning, LOOK involved taking stock of the current situation regarding oral language use; THINK involved professional learning about NLA and designing a unit for the upcoming Intensive Weeks; and ACT involved implementing NLA during those weeks. For subsequent cycles, LOOK was envisioned as having researchers observe teachers during the Intensive Weeks and interview or provide focus groups to ask questions about the implementation. THINK took place during a subsequent meeting as a teacher–researcher team met to debrief the weeks and plan for the next set, including engaging in additional professional learning around NLA. ACT in those subsequent cycles also involved the implementation of NLA, this time with improved understanding from previous cycles. These cycles were interrupted by the Covid-19 pandemic pivot to emergency remote teaching in March–June 2020 (Dressler and Guida 2022; Timmons et al. 2021) and were taken up in a modified way in Year 3, since researchers were not permitted to do classroom observation when teachers returned to in-person instruction with Covid-19 safety protocols. During Year 4, the collaboration resumed as before, this time with a shift in focus as the action research collaboration evolved. While the project is ongoing at the time of writing, this chapter draws on the work of the first three years of the project to illustrate the teacher–research collaboration.

At the end of the third year of the study, teachers were invited to contribute to this chapter by joining the researchers (Katherine and Roswita) in reflecting upon the benefits and challenges of teacher–researcher collaboration. Of the teaching team at the time (seven teachers), three – Anja, Frank and Tanya – responded to the invitation with their perceptions. Katherine and Roswita conducted a content analysis of our collective reflections for indications of benefits and challenges. These benefits and challenges inform our work moving forward in the larger project but also provide insight into teacher–researcher collaboration.

4 Findings

Over the course of the first three years of working together in a teacher–researcher collaboration, the choice of NLA as an approach to foster oral language use in the Intensive German Weeks was versatile and provided teachers with a variety of avenues to support the development of students' oral language. In Year 1, professional learning was focused on the oral modeling sequence as part of the larger literacy loop. Teachers gained familiarity with the sequence and reported that their students developed a comfort level with the expectation to listen and speak German such that subsequent applications of the approach were more and more productive. In Year 2, new teachers were added to the staff, so some review of the approach was needed, which had the added advantage of providing a refresher for seasoned teachers. With the increase in competence among the group of teachers, learning was scaffolded through the pairing of teachers to bring their classes together for aspects of the Intensive Weeks (i.e., buddy classes). The Covid-19 pandemic declaration resulted in the cancellation of the third cycle in Year 2. With the return to in-person instruction in Year 3, it was a challenge for teachers to implement NLA since safety precautions precluded the use of shared materials and close proximity, but they developed some modifications that worked because they built upon their own and their students' familiarity with the oral modeling sequence and literacy loop from previous years. The benefits of NLA observed in Year 1 and reported in Dressler and Mueller (2020, 2022) remained in Years 2 and 3: structure, purposeful planning and collaboration. Additionally, teachers modified NLA for age groups for which it had not initially been designed and explored content-based language teaching supported by NLA. In this way, the examination of the oral modelling sequence of the NLA to foster oral language use has become less of a focus, and a shift in the project toward fine-tuning other aspects of the literacy loop has occurred.

In reflecting on the larger project, teachers voiced their initial concerns about entering into the project. Anja pointed out that when the project started she was a first-year teacher and she felt 'so overwhelmed by teaching' in general. Tanya noted that the beginning was a 'learning curve' in light of a new job assignment. Yet both reported that they and their students 'became more confident' (Tanya) and they 'felt good about teaching German' (Anja). Once past the initial cycle, the way they approached 'planning and teaching of language [had] changed dramatically' (Tanya) and they developed 'strong skills for planning and executing NLA and the literacy loop' (Frank). For some, aspects of the NLA were 'now a daily activity in [the] classroom beyond the [Intensive German] weeks' (Frank). Anja noted that the NLA aligned with what she had 'learned in [her] linguistics degree about how young children learn their native language' and asked 'students to engage with the material according to their own abilities and it has resulted in more confident students and fewer tears!' These reflections underscored the development of teachers' understanding of NLA and supported its ongoing use in the German Bilingual Program. Most importantly, teachers felt that it successfully allowed them to foster more target language oral use.

While the collaborative relationship between teachers and researchers has been 'positive and flexible' (Roswita), the researchers were not without their initial hesitations. Roswita noted that, as is typical in classroom-based research, it was important to clarify the ethical constraints that would guide data collection and classroom observation. We obtained ethics approval at the university level and at the school board level, and adjusted our research design with the input of the teaching team in order to respect both, while honouring the integrity of our research idea. Still, there were times when it was our responsibility to enact the research within those parameters since 'teachers are used to sharing and working collaboratively, not always remembering we are considered "outsiders" by the school board' (Roswita). As outsiders, we were not permitted to know the identity of students, so teachers were expected to refrain from naming students or showing us individual students' work without blinding it first. Another challenge we experienced, especially as the school jurisdiction entered a time of fiscal restraint, was securing the funding necessary to cover teacher release time. As Cloonan, Hutchison, and Paatsch (2019: 230) have indicated, 'support of teachers' participation in the professional learning programme and deployment of material resources' is critical to giving teachers agency over their professional learning. In our case, school leadership was very supportive of the action research project and facilitated the process. Therefore, we were able to work successfully with the teachers on fostering oral language use and looked toward increasing the ways in which that was measured, considering as a next step a move to gathering student data, which would have required a modification in the ethics application.

Support and communication became especially important when the Covid-19 pandemic brought with it first a sudden move to emergency remote teaching and later face-to-face teaching with safety precautions. First, the Covid-19 responses delayed plans to gather student data as researchers were not allowed in the school for the first year after reopening (Year 3 of the study). Second, we also moved all professional learning online for Year 3. All authors missed face-to-face professional learning and found online learning 'a needed but poor substitute' (Roswita). Yet, despite the challenges to the teaching context brought on by the pandemic, the teacher–researcher team showed great resilience.

The action research continued into Year 4. NLA remains a cornerstone of the work teachers do in fostering oral language. Frank noted that at the end of a day during the Intensive German Weeks, 'students were able to successfully produce oral language that they understood'. So, while it took time to learn, 'the time has been well worth it in exchange for the understanding and engagement of students' (Tanya). While we have still had to delay gathering student data, teachers have continued to work with NLA, discovering new aspects for improvement along the way.

5 Discussion

Returning to the research question, we can answer the 'how' in terms of 'by what means'. First, by means of applying the NLA approach to this context (Intensive German Weeks in a Bilingual Program), the teachers continue to perceive the approach as useful and providing 'easy and meaningful structure' (Anja). When we discuss the teacher–researcher collaboration as the means by which teachers were able to learn about how to apply the approach, teachers recognized that the collaboration meant teachers had 'time to plan and evaluate or reflect on their practice as a team, they [had] support and [. . .] a way [. . .] to demonstrate their progress and the progress of their students' (Frank). Both means provide answers to the research question and underscore the value of teacher–researcher collaboration.

As we think about our ongoing work on this research project, we acknowledge that teachers and researchers bring different strengths and challenges to the table, and that it is the act of reflecting on these that can help us to identify a clear path forward in collaboration (Hawkins and Legler 2004). In our case, teachers came to the table with a strong understanding of their students, and thus a clear vision of what the problem of practice was (Cloonan, Hutchison, and Paatsch 2019). Their challenge perhaps was having the beyond-the-classroom vision to see the problem of practice in a broader perspective (Buğra and Wyatt 2021). Another more evident challenge was having the time to investigate their problem of practice in a systematic way (Lassonde, Israel, and Almasi 2019). The researchers came to the project with a good overview of the field, informed by their own research and that of others in the field (Buğra and Wyatt 2021; Dagenais, Moore, and Sabatier 2009). As part of their work, they had ideas for innovations that potentially could address the problem of practice identified by the teachers. Educational researchers need a context within which they can put their ideas into practice, and to enable them to determine whether these ideas are practicable in a classroom setting. Cummins notes that theory needs to be implemented to come to life: 'We should examine the instructional consequences of implementing specific theoretical ideas or propositions; specifically, we should ask, as one evaluative criterion, to what extent a particular construct or claim is useful in promoting effective pedagogy' (Cummins

2021: xxxiv). The promotion of NLA as an effective pedagogy was our shared goal throughout this collaboration.

As part of our collaborative relationship with teachers, we (Katherine and Roswita) have learned much about working reciprocally with teachers. Perhaps first and foremost, we have come to realize that action research is in fact an exercise in team building – a team that includes the researchers, the teachers, the school leadership and even the students. Working together towards a common goal with positivity, flexibility and a sense of humour, having frequent touchpoints in the process and respecting the parameters of the research design has led to a fruitful collaboration. As we have noted above, researchers come to the table with theoretically oriented ideas to explore. It has been critical for the research team to be open-minded and flexible in understanding how these ideas could be implemented within the classroom context. Fortunately, both researchers are former classroom teachers, so we had an understanding of the various challenges presented by the daily school schedule. Even though the changeability of the elementary school schedule was not unanticipated, it was a source of consternation nonetheless. This impacted not only the classroom implementation of the research design, but also teacher–researcher meetings, which were a critical part of the action research cycle. Both the teachers and the researchers worked together to identify the original goals and timelines and continue to communicate clearly to ensure that the project goals are met.

Our understanding of how teachers can promote oral language use in their classrooms was clarified as a result of this study and was due in large part to the fruitful teacher–researcher collaboration. As facility with oral language use increased, our attention has turned to reading, the next phase of the NLA approach. We discovered the need to find appropriate resources to support the reading phase, which we have now decided to work on next. Additionally, we were only recently (and hopefully finally) freed from Covid-19 safety precautions which constrained interaction in the classroom. We feel confident that as we continue to work together in this collaboration new problems of practice will also be surmountable.

6 Conclusion

Addressing a classroom-based problem of practice can be a challenging undertaking, both from the perspective of classroom teachers who perceive that they could finetune their practice, and from the perspective of researchers who seek to find a practice-based solution to a theoretical problem. We have seen that teacher–researcher collaboration brought with it positives and challenges. In the case of our research presented here, it was our effective collaboration as classroom teachers and educational researchers that provided a vibrant context within which both researchers and classroom teachers have been able to attack the problem of practice and overcome challenges. Ultimately, we recognize that the real winners of our collaborative efforts have been the students, which is the goal of educational research.

References

Buğra, Cemile & Mark Wyatt. 2021. English language teachers collaborating in practitioner research and loving it. *Educational Action Research* 29(3). 483–499. https://doi.org/10.1080/09650792.2020.1842778 (accessed 24 May 2022).

Cammarata, Laurent (ed.). 2016. *Content-based foreign language teaching*. London: Routledge.

Cloonan, Anne, Kirsten Hutchison & Louise Paatsch. 2019. Promoting teachers' agency and creative teaching through research. *English Teaching* 18(2). 218–232. https://doi.org/10.1108/ETPC-11-2018-0107 (accessed 24 May 2022).

Cummins, Jim. 2021. *Rethinking the education of multilingual learners*. Bristol: Multilingual Matters.

Dagenais, Diane, Danièle Moore & Cécile Sabatier. 2009. Negotiating teacher–researcher collaboration in immersion education. In Jennifer Miller, Alex Kostogriz & Margaret Gearon (eds.), *Culturally and linguistically diverse classrooms: New dilemmas for teachers*, 234–251. Bristol: Multilingual Matters.

Doughty, Catherine & Jessica Williams (eds.). 1998. *Focus on form in classroom second language acquisition*. Cambridge: Cambridge University Press.

Dressler, Roswita. 2012. *Simultaneous and sequential bilinguals in a German Bilingual Program*. PhD dissertation, University of Calgary.

Dressler, Roswita. 2018. Canadian Bilingual Program teachers' understanding of immersion pedagogy. *Canadian Modern Language Review* 74(1). 176–95. https://www.utpjournals.press/doi/full/10.3138/cmlr.3407 (accessed 24 May 2022).

Dressler, Roswita & Rochelle Guida. 2022. Innovations from the COVID-19 pandemic: Online learning strategies. *Réflexions* 41(1). 29–31. http://hdl.handle.net/1880/114444 (accessed 24 May 2022).

Dressler, Roswita & Katherine Mueller. 2020. Strategies for purposeful oral language use in the second language classroom. *Réflexions* 39(2). 15–17. http://hdl.handle.net/1880/113053 (accessed 24 May 2022).

Dressler, Roswita & Katherine Mueller. 2022. Pedagogical strategies to foster target language use: A nexus analysis. *Canadian Modern Language Review* 77(4). 75–90. https://doi.org/10.3138/cmlr-2020-0084 (accessed 24 May 2022).

Germain, Claude. 2018. *The neurolinguistic approach (NLA) for learning and teaching foreign languages*. Newcastle upon Tyne: Cambridge Scholars Publishing.

Hawkins, Margaret & Lynn Legler. 2004. Reflections on the impact of teacher–researcher collaboration. *TESOL Quarterly* 38(2). 339–343. https://doi.org/10.2307/3588386 (accessed 24 May 2022).

Lassonde, Cynthia, Susan Israel & Janice Almasi. 2019. *Teacher collaboration for professional learning: Facilitating study, research, and inquiry communities*. Hoboken: John Wiley.

Lyster, Roy. 2007. *Learning and teaching languages through content*. Amsterdam: John Benjamins.

Lyster, Roy. 2016 *Vers une approche intégrée en immersion*. Amsterdam: John Benjamins.

Masson, Mimi, Ibtissem Knouzi, Stephanie Arnott & Sharon Lapkin. 2021. A critical interpretive synthesis of post-millennial Canadian French as a second language research across stakeholders and programs. *Canadian Modern Language Review* 77(2). 154–188. https://www.utpjournals.press/doi/full/10.3138/cmlr-2020-0025 (accessed 24 May 2022).

McNiff, Jean. 2002. *Action research for professional development: Concise advice for new action researchers*. United Kingdom: September Books.

Mills, Geoffrey E. 2014. *Action research: A guide for the teacher researcher*. Toronto: Pearson.

Mueller, Katherine & Roswita Dressler. 2022. Explorer les possibilités de la boucle de la littératie pour l'immersion française. *Journal de l'immersion* 44(1). 33–37.

Netten, Joan & Claude Germain. 2004. Developing the curriculum for Intensive French. *Canadian Modern Language Review* 60(3). 295–308. https://doi.org/10.3138/cmlr.60.3.295 (accessed 24 May 2022).

Netten, Joan & Claude Germain. 2005. Pedagogy and second language learning: Lessons learned from Intensive French. *Canadian Journal of Applied Linguistics* 8(2). 183–210. http://www.aclacaal.org (accessed 24 May 2022).

O'Connor, Arlene & Judy Sharkey. 2004. Defining the process of teacher–researcher collaboration. *TESOL Quarterly* 38(2). 335–339. https://doi.org/10.2307/3588385 (accessed 24 May 2022).

Smith, Cameron W. 2020. *Essayons: French as a second language teacher experiences of technology-enhanced practice*. MA thesis, University of Calgary.

Stewart, Timothy. 2006. Teacher–researcher collaboration or teachers' research? *TESOL Quarterly* 40(2). 421–429. https://www.jstor.org/stable/40264529 (accessed 24 May 2022).

Stringer, Ernest T. 2014. *Action research*. Los Angeles: Sage.

Tedick, Diane & Roy Lyster. 2020. *Scaffolding language development in immersion and dual language classrooms*. London: Routledge.

Timmons, Kristy, Amanda Cooper, Emma Bozek & Heather Braund. 2021. The impacts of COVID-19 on early childhood education: Capturing the unique challenges associated with remote teaching and learning in K-2. *Early Childhood Education Journal* 49(5). 887–901. https://doi.org/10.1007/s10643-021-01207-z (accessed 24 May 2022).

Wu, Joe & Olenka Bilash. 2000. Bilingual education in practice: A multifunctional model of minority language programs in Western Canada. *Hawaii International Conference on Education*. http://www.etspe.ca/ecbea/empowering.pdf (accessed 24 May 2022).

Wyatt, Mark & Kenan Dikilitaş. 2016. English language teachers becoming more efficacious through research engagement at their Turkish university. *Educational Action Research* 24(4). 550–570. https://doi.org/10.1080/09650792.2015.1076731 (accessed 24 May 2022).

Anna Elgemark, Alastair Henry and Petra Jansson

3 An affordance-focused approach for working with authentic materials: A practice–research initiative

Abstract: In Sweden it is now recognized that while teaching should be based on research and proven experience, research-based practice is limited in scope, and classroom teaching is not always informed by findings from educational research. To address this problem, and to develop and test sustainable models of researcher–practitioner collaboration, the Swedish Government has introduced a national system of partnership between schools and universities. Here, research projects are initiated not just by academics, but also by teachers. In each school–university partnership, the aim is to develop and test a model that can support sustainable, research-based practice.

The project reported on here addresses one of the major challenges currently facing teachers of English in Sweden, namely the need to create activities that go beyond the textbook, and which students can experience as relevant and meaningful. While the design of activities that enable students to connect content targeted by the curriculum with experiences from informal domains is a challenge for teachers of any subject, for teachers of English the demands multiply. This is because activities need to be modelled in ways that promote the development of linguistic competence.

The authors – two language teacher educators, and an upper secondary teacher of English – carried out a project aimed at enabling primary, secondary, and upper secondary teachers of English in a rural municipality to develop design skills encompassing language awareness. Carried out during a single academic year, the project enabled teachers to work collegially, and in collaboration with the teacher educators. Drawing on experiences from the project, the chapter examines the conditions under which the collaboration took place, the challenges faced, beneficial influences on teachers' practice, and the potential for sustainability.

1 Introduction

In Sweden it has long been recognized that teaching should be based on research and proven experience, and that knowledge feeding into research-anchored practice is best generated in classroom contexts. Teachers are invested with the responsibility for educational quality which, in turn, is attained through professional development (Carlgren 2010, 2018). However, while responsibilities for quality and development may rest with individual teachers, as a professional group, teachers have not been considered the drivers of research-based knowledge. The profession lacks a strong epistemic culture, and teachers have tended to regard professional knowledge 'in terms of practice-based proficiency acquired through personal experience' (Larsson and Sjöberg 2021: 4).

In a national initiative aimed at developing knowledge-based practice through collaborative projects – where insights from practice and theory might intertwine in mutually constitutive ways – the Swedish government introduced a program of practice-based research. With the aim of bridging gaps between theory and practice, the purpose of the ULF programme[1] is to promote collaborative research between universities and schools (see, e.g., Magnusson and Malmström 2022; Nihlfors 2020).

Part of a range of state initiatives aimed at developing professional skills through contextualized and practice-focused research, ULF-financed projects provide a means of practice development that is problem-oriented and theory-driven (Nihlfors 2020). In common with other research–education collaboration described in this volume, in ULF projects there is a need to identify an aspect of practice which is central for students' development, which presents challenges for teachers, and which can be profitably examined through combined practice–research initiatives (Eriksson 2018). The defining features of research funded by ULF are that it is collaborative, reciprocally beneficial, and views the professional knowledge of collaborating partners (academics and teachers) as complementary (Eriksson 2018). Importantly, the results of practitioner–researcher engagement need to be usable in the contexts in which investigations took place and have the potential to find their way into a wider range of classrooms through appropriate methods of dissemination (e.g., Eriksson 2018, 2022; Nihlfors 2020).

While collaborative research is on the rise, and while increasing numbers of teachers and university faculty are involved in investigative joint ventures, there is no guarantee that a project will address the everyday problems of teachers. Projects that fail to establish shared research interests and lack reciprocity run the risk of failing to contribute to a strengthening of the scientific base of the teaching profession (Andrée and Eriksson 2019). Consequently, collaborating researchers have a responsibility to be receptive to teachers' ideas, and to accommodate the *actual* challenges teachers encounter in everyday practice. In addition to the potentially

---

[1] ULF is the acronym for *Utbildning, Lärande, Forskning* (Education, Learning, Research).

differing interests of teachers and researchers, and the difficulty of aligning 'practice' and 'research' challenges, another frequently identified problem involves the scope of the 'problem' to be investigated. More broadly scoped problem definitions described by teachers – for example, 'it is hard to generate motivation', or 'students struggle with grammar' – rarely mesh with narrowly focused formulations that reflect the scientific logic of incremental knowledge construction. It is important, therefore, that these interests are carefully balanced (Andrée and Eriksson 2019).

2 A shared research interest

With these challenges in mind, we sought a research object that would be central to the practice of teaching English, that created recurring and not easily solved challenges, and that could be expected to be encountered across a range of educational settings (and not just in the local context). At the same time, the problem needed to be sufficiently narrow to allow focused investigation. Combining these imperatives and drawing on previous teacher–researcher collaboration between two of the authors, the project focused on work with authentic materials – 'cultural artefacts produced for a purpose other than teaching' (Henry et al. 2019: 254) – and the identification of affordances that might trigger motivation and facilitate the development of linguistic competence.

Two of us (PJ and AH) first met in a research project investigating secondary English teachers' motivational practice (the Motivational Teaching in Swedish Secondary English [MoTiSSE] project; Henry, Sundqvist, and Thorsen 2019). Funded by the Swedish Research Council, in this project ethnographic research was carried out in the classrooms of 16 secondary English teachers identified as successful in designing motivating activities and creating motivational learning environments. Seeking not only to bridge between students' encounters with English within and beyond the classroom, but also to enable students to develop understandings of the forms and functions of language, PJ was one of a handful of teachers in the project who sought to engage students in classroom activities that were meaningful *and* which provided opportunities to develop linguistic skills. Interested in further developing her practice, PJ continued to work with bridging-focused activities, sharing ideas and designs with colleagues in subject meetings and spaces set aside for competence development. On some occasions AH also took part. Loosely structured, and without employer involvement, the collaboration evolved from a shared interest in exploring learning possibilities in spaces where formal and informal engagements with English might coincide.

At the time of the current project, PJ was working as a principal teacher[2] at an upper secondary school. Part of her post involved responsibility for colleagues' professional development. When the municipality's education department decided to focus on English during the 2021/2022 school year, the collaboration moved into a more formal phase and expanded to include a third partner, AE, an English teacher and senior lecturer in English linguistics.

The municipality in which the project was carried out comprised a small central community and a range of village-sized settlements, the total population being just over 15,000 inhabitants. Like colleagues working in other rural areas, the teachers in the municipality found that English was not seen as a particularly important subject. Generally, students did not have extensive encounters with English beyond the classroom, nor was English always viewed as a life asset, or an essential future skill. Teachers experienced that many students lacked motivation and could struggle to develop productive skills (see Olsson 2016 and Sundqvist 2011 for relevant discussions).

Seeking to address these practice challenges, we wrote a proposal for an ULF project that would focus on the use of authentic materials in classroom teaching and would have the aim of developing teachers' skills in identifying motivational and language-developing affordances. Before describing the project's design, in the sections that follow we first consider the topics of motivation and linguistic development from theoretical perspectives.

3 Motivation and language awareness

In a globalizing world where English is often a presence beyond the classroom, students can respond better to classroom activities that involve authentic materials (Gilmore 2007, 2011; Tomlinson 2012). Working with authentic texts can enhance engagement and mean that the English classroom is experienced as a more meaningful place (Gilmore 2007; Tomlinson 2012). In a study from Sweden where secondary teachers were invited to describe activities that generated motivation, authentic materials predominated (Henry et al. 2018). In the ethnographic work carried out in the MoTiSSE project, numerous examples of positive responses to working with authentic materials were documented (Henry, Sundqvist, and Thorsen 2019).

However, as Ushioda (2013) has made clear, working with motivation is only one challenge facing teachers of English in contemporary contexts. Another equally important challenge involves the need to strike a balance between working with

---

2 In Swedish, *förstelärare*.

social and academic proficiency and working to develop fluency and accurate control over form. As Henry, Sundqvist, and Thorsen (2019: 269) make clear, balancing these professional tasks can be demanding:

> [Given] the demands placed on pedagogical and linguistic skills when working with authentic texts, the question to be asked is whether teachers have the necessary time and/or expertise to attune to the affordances of authentic materials in ways that meet the full spectrum of students' linguistic needs (cf. Gilmore 2011). Thus, although the major motivational challenge facing teachers of English in countries where it is being reframed as a general social literacy may indeed be the need to provide activities that students experience as relevant and meaningful, and that connect with their experiences of speaking/using English in informal domains (Ushioda 2013), these activities need also to be modelled in ways that develop linguistic competence. This is no easy task, not least in that teacher education generally fails to provide sufficient knowledge of underlying systems of language and the skills needed to draw students' attention to grammatical features of texts, to identify learner errors, and to provide useful explanations (Svalberg 2012). Consequently, in contexts where students respond positively to activities constructed around authentic texts, an important future direction for English teachers' professional practice is to develop enhanced skills of language awareness. This should be a major priority for both pre-service and in-service programs of ELT education.

In attempting to strike this balance, teachers need to develop the ability to identify and capitalize on the affordances contained within a text. Affordances are features of an environment to which an individual responds and from which a benefit can be gained (Gibson 1979). As Segalowitz (2001: 15) has suggested, developing skills in another language 'involves attuning one's attention system to perceive the communicative affordances provided by the linguistic environment'. From the teacher's perspective, a text or learning activity can be seen as containing a variety of affordances that can facilitate development through enhanced levels of interest and engagement, and through being guided by the teacher to notice and become aware of the function of linguistic forms (Svalberg 2012). Two categories of affordances of central concern are motivational affordances – features of a text that provide opportunities to link content to students' interests, concerns, identities and experiences – and linguistic affordances, which provide opportunities to work with language in context. From an affordances perspective, the challenge when working with authentic materials is to develop sensitivity to the opportunities that exist within the text, and skills in using identified affordances as departure points for activities focused on meaningful interaction and the development of linguistic competence.

3.1 Attuning to motivational affordances: Creating connections

While an authentic text can trigger a range of positive responses – it can be enjoyable, interesting, stimulating and meaningful – a text's inherent qualities are unlikely to promote deeper forms of engagement. For teachers of English, the professional task is to find ways of making connections between the text, its context, and contexts in which the text is meaningful for the students. While there are many ways of understanding this type of 'bridging practice' (Thorne and Reinhardt 2008), the essence lies in identifying possibilities to forge connections (Henry 2019, 2021; Henry and Thorsen 2019). Put another way, as part of the process of selecting a text and designing a lesson around it, the teacher needs to be on the lookout for content features – no matter how peripheral or inconsequential they may seem – which allow connections to be made to contexts that are relevant beyond the text.

3.2 Attuning to linguistic affordances: Teacher language awareness

For the language teacher, it is essential to be 'language aware'. This involves attuning to linguistic affordances and creating engaging, form-focused activities. It involves what Thornbury (1997: x) refers to as Teacher Language Awareness (TLA), 'the knowledge teachers have of the underlying system of the language that enables them to teach effectively'. A teacher who is 'language aware' understands learners' difficulties with language and has a willingness and ability to actively engage with language content (Svalberg 2015). TLA impacts on the ways in which teachers address language-related issues in lesson design (in selecting input and creating activities), and how they handle classroom interactions. This reflects Andrews's (2007) distinction between the declarative and procedural dimensions of TLA, the former referring to the teacher's knowledge of the structures and forms of the language (which is essential for design), and the latter involving the teacher's ability to use that knowledge in pedagogical interactions. For the teacher, bridging between the declarative and procedural dimensions is no easy task. While identifying affordances and planning and designing activities are challenging undertakings, carrying out activities in unpredictable and shifting conditions presents even greater demands.

4 Design and carrying out

In common with other research–education collaborations in the ULF initiative (Prøitz et al. 2022), we had no preconceived model that we attempt to apply. Rather, the project took the form of a further, if more formalized, stage of the collaboration previously described. Like many other ULF partnerships, our collaboration can be understood as having a 'Mode 2' perspective (Gibbons et al. 1994). In a Mode 2 perspective there is an emphasis on research that is need-generated, solution-focused, and where the primary objective is that knowledge should be useable by the participating practitioners (Prøitz et al. 2022).[3]

Having the features of a 'Third Space' – where knowledge from different domains interacts in productive forms – our design involved recognition of equality between the interests and needs of research ('First Space' imperatives) and practice ('Second Space' imperatives) (Moje et al. 2004; Prøitz et al. 2022). Bringing these interests together, the aim was to work in process form, and in a manner where teachers would have the opportunity to develop the practice skills of identifying and capitalizing on motivational and linguistic affordances. Finally, because we had decided to work across the municipality – giving all teachers of English an opportunity to participate – the project's focus was on everyday classroom work.

A key feature of the collaboration was the idea that the development of an ability to attune to and make use of motivational and linguistic affordances was something that could be beneficial for *any* teacher of English, irrespective of the level at which they might teach. Since authentic materials have a place in *all* forms of English teaching, practice skills that involve abilities to create meaningful connections between a text and students' lived experiences, and to identify opportunities to work with grammar in context, are not specific to a particular stage or to particular classrooms; rather, they are relevant across educational levels. Moreover, we reasoned that if students meet an *affordance-focused* approach at an early point, and come to expect engagements of this sort, transitions between educational levels and the classrooms of different teachers are likely to be smoother.

Two further factors motivated an inclusive 'whole municipality' approach. As previously mentioned, the municipality comprised a central community and a range of smaller village-sized settlements. For many of the lower secondary teachers, they were the only English teacher at their schools. Having an opportunity to discuss central aspects of practice with colleagues from other schools and

---

[3] In the Mode 1/Mode 2 conceptualization, Mode 1 is traditional research.

to share ideas and working methods would go some way toward providing a subject-specific professional context. Working across school boundaries was beneficial for both the lower and the upper secondary teachers. As well as providing an opportunity to find out about one another's practice, they had an opportunity to share views about progression. We felt that the project would provide a forum for discussing proficiency attainment at different levels, and ways of effectuating fluid transitions between levels and schools.

The project was designed to take place in a series of phases (see Figure 3.1). The first stage was the introduction of the project where recent research about motivation, authentic materials, LA and TLA were presented. At this stage, the teachers also had the chance to share relevant experiences from their own practice.

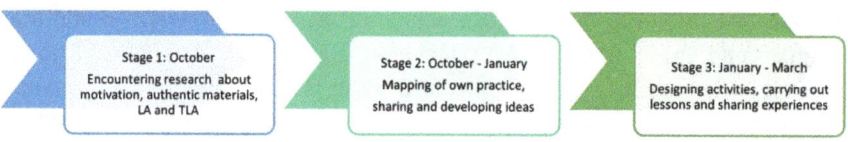

Figure 3.1: Project design.

The second stage focused on the mapping of the teachers' own practice, and the development and sharing of ideas. In this stage, teachers were encouraged to identify meaningful authentic materials, and, bringing such texts into the classroom, to design micro-level form-focused tasks. Throughout this process, the teachers had access to supervision. Having gained TLA skills in this way, in the final stage the teachers were encouraged to design a series of themed lessons based around authentic texts.

4.1 Covid-19

The project took place during a period when Covid-19 was still classified as a contagious disease that threatened public health. Although upper secondary schools were closed for periods during the 2020/2021 academic year, during the 2021/2022 year all schools in Sweden remained open. However, in accordance with guidelines issued by the Public Health Agency, anyone with Covid-related symptoms was required to remain at home. During the winter months particularly, this meant that schools were permanently under-staffed, and teachers had to cover for colleagues who were forced to stay at home. While the municipality had fared relatively well in the autumn, during January, February and early March 2022, Covid cases mounted continuously, and staff absences were extensive. In consequence, non-essential work was either put on hold or cancelled. While the first part of the project had gone according to plan, and many of the teachers had begun to work with authentic materials and had shared their experiences in discussion sessions with the three of us, during the second and the third stages, project work was disrupted. Having to spend periods at home – and at school having to cover for absent colleagues – much of the teachers' time involved catching up. For many, it meant that project work was not a priority. Inevitably, the planning of the collaboration had to be adjusted. The January workshop did not take place. In March, rather than focusing on activities that teachers had been able to carry out, the workshop became a space where the development of affordance-focused skills could continue.

4.2 Generating ideas

As Gilmore (2019: 315) has suggested, issues that involve authenticity and work with authentic materials may be 'best explored locally by practicing teachers themselves, through classroom investigations or action research cycles'. To support efforts to develop an instructional practice associated with the use of authentic materials and the identification of motivational and linguistic affordances, in the March workshop we explored a series of texts. Outlining a model for an affordance-focused practice, we describe a process where, in this workshop, a group of upper secondary teachers drew out the potential for working with motivation and language in an Instagram post. The workshop took place on a Wednesday at the end of March. In preceding days, social media and news channels had been dominated by reports from the Academy Awards ceremony in Los Angeles. During the prize-giving, and in the presence of millions of cable channel viewers, Academy member Will Smith (who won the Best Actor award for his role in the film *King Richard*) walked on stage and assaulted the comedian Chris Rock. In Smith's view, Rock had made disparaging comments about the appearance of Smith's wife (Jada Pinkett Smith), who was suffering from the auto-immune disease alopecia areata. At the time, the event and its aftermath were hard to escape. Opinions were divided about Smith's behaviour; while some took the view that his actions were inexcusable in any circumstances, others praised Smith's support of his wife. The text in focus was an apology that Smith had posted on Instagram the day after the Awards ceremony, and which had instantly gone viral:

> Violence in all of its forms is poisonous and destructive. My behavior at last night's Academy Awards was unacceptable and inexcusable. Jokes at my expense are a part of the job, but a joke about Jada's medical condition was too much for me to bear and I reacted emotionally.

>I would like to publicly apologize to you, Chris. I was out of line and I was wrong. I am embarrassed and my actions were not indicative of the man I want to be. There is no place for violence in a world of love and kindness.
>
>I would also like to apologize to the Academy, the producers of the show, all the attendees and everyone watching around the world. I would like to apologize to the Williams Family and my King Richard Family. I deeply regret that my behavior has stained what has been an otherwise gorgeous journey for all of us.
>
>I am a work in progress.
>
>Sincerely,
>
>Will

While all of us in the room that Wednesday afternoon had come across this text in social media feeds and news reporting, it was the first time we had started thinking about affordances. Recognizing how this was a relevant text (at this particular point in time), and how use of the text would involve a form of bridging between textual environments in and beyond the classroom, we worked on the assumption that the Instagram post would be used the next day in an English 5 class.[4] We began by identifying the linguistic affordances. Then, having considered the potential for working with language, we moved on to consider the motivational affordances.

Linguistic affordances	Noticing activities
Capitalization Academy Awards; Williams Family; King Richard Family;	Why is 'Williams' capitalized? Why is 'Family' capitalized?
Shifting verb tenses My behaviour . . . was unacceptable and inexcusable; jokes . . . are a part of the job; a joke about Jada's medical condition was too much for me to bear and I reacted emotionally. I was out of line and I was wrong. I am embarrassed and my actions were not indicative of the man I want to be. There is no place for violence in a world of love and kindness. I am a work in progress.	What tenses to use in which contexts and why. Why are there shifts in tenses both between and within sentences? 'I am embarrassed and my actions were not indicative of the man I want to be'
Conditionals I would like to publicly apologize to you, Chris; I would also like to apologize to the Academy; I would like to apologize to the Williams Family	Why say 'I would like to' rather than simple present tense 'I like to'? Difference in meaning?

---

4 CEFR B 1.2

(continued)

Linguistic affordances	Noticing activities
Form and function of adverbs I would like to <u>publicly</u> apologize; I <u>deeply</u> regret; I reacted <u>emotionally</u>; <u>Sincerely</u>; a joke . . . was <u>too</u> much for me to bear	Why is the adverb placed before the verb in 'I deeply regret' and after the verb in 'I reacted emotionally'? Adverbs not ending in -ly? Differences between adverb and adjectives: 'publicly', 'deeply', 'emotionally' vs. public, deep, emotional
Genitive forms last <u>night's</u> Academy Awards <u>Jada's</u> medical condition	Why is the apostrophe genitive used for 'last night's Academy Awards' (unmarked usage involves a person possessing something)?
Form and function of prepositional phrases Jokes <u>at</u> my expense are a part <u>of</u> the job, but a joke <u>about</u> Jada's medical condition	Prepositions as parts of set phrases/chunks
Personal idioms I was <u>out of line</u> I am <u>a work in progress</u>	Phrases whose meaning goes beyond the linguistic/literal meaning: How can we understand idioms?
Affixes and vocabulary building My behavior . . . was <u>un</u>accept<u>able</u> and <u>in</u>excus<u>able</u> attend<u>ees</u>	Words formed through affixes: How can words be split into different parts? How can new words be formed by adding these affixes? e.g. 'interviewee' and 'employee' How does the grammatical form (word class) change? 'behavior' vs. 'behave', 'accept' vs. 'acceptable' Why do the similarly formed words 'unacceptable' and 'inexcusable' have different prefixes 'un' and 'in'?
Motivational affordances	**Activities**
'Violence in all of its forms is poisonous and destructive'	Smith begins his post with these words. Why do you think Smith started the post in this way? Is it an effective opening? Why/why not? Are there other events, beyond Hollywood, that might have motivated this choice of opening? – Elicit students' opinions

(continued)

Motivational affordances	Activities
An apology	The Instagram post is an apology, and an acceptance of personal responsibility. Why do you think Smith apologized? Did he have to? What might have happened if he didn't? – Working in groups students share situations when an apology had been necessary but difficult, or when an apology had been necessary but was never made.
Justification?	Was Smith right to apologize? If you had been a personal friend, or maybe Smith's agent or lawyer, what would you have advised? – Write an email to Smith providing advice.
Accepting the apology?	Should the apology be the end of the matter? If you had been the victim, how would you have responded? – Imagine you are Chris. Write an Instagram post with your response.
'I am a work in progress'	What does Smith mean? – Write a letter to your future self. You can describe your hopes for the future, your fears, the person that you are now, and the person that you hope to become.

In the collective process of identifying affordances, the teachers were able to develop an awareness of the linguistic and motivational potential present in the text and, with the application of professional skills, how this potential could be profitably unlocked. As had become clear at the beginning of the project, several of the teachers had noticed how authentic materials could generate positive responses from students, and several had examples of classwork that had revolved around texts 'brought in from the outside'. While designing activities that could build on and add to motivation generated in this way involved a further demand, the opportunity to brainstorm ideas with colleagues meant that the teachers could see how a practice based on motivational affordances could develop.

However, while strategies for unlocking the motivational potential might have been easier to develop, strategies for capitalizing on linguistic affordances created greater demands. While the lead-in of identifying linguistic features was not too difficult, and was a skill that teachers recognized would mature with time, working with grammar 'on the fly' was seen as much harder. Talking about grammatical constructions in relation to identified forms, and supporting students' attempts to identify, describe and generate rule explanations was seen as challenging. While the teachers could readily see the possibilities of working in this way, and possible advantages of also working with grammar (even when the primary focus was on aspects unrelated to accuracy and precision in production), there was the sense that this would place significant demands on their linguistic-didactic competence. In terms of comfort zones and professional security, the tried and tested alternative – working with grammar as prescribed by a course textbook – had clear advantages.

The concerns expressed by these teachers about the feasibility of an affordance-focused approach are echoed by researchers working with grammar. In a recent systematic review of research on explicit grammar instruction, Toth (2022) has emphasized the importance of working with grammar in context. Reviewing accumulated findings, Toth reflects that 'more than ever [this] has convinced me of the importance of developing learners' conscious awareness of how language works for communication, within instruction that centers on personally meaningful L2 activity' (Toth 2022: 29). Yet, like the teachers who participated in the workshop, Toth is left to ponder upon how this can be achieved. As he suggests, 'the question of how best to direct learners' attention to L2 form–meaning–use relationships within the myriad contexts of classroom tasks remains open' (Toth 2022: 8).

Alongside the question of how to integrate a noticing approach in content- and communication-focused teaching, and how best to leverage the language developing potential of working with grammar in context, Toth (2022) raises the further issue of the quality of the explicit information that teachers provide. Reviewing research on guided inductive models – where in sequential stages target structures are presented in narrative texts, the learner's attention is drawn to them, grammatical knowledge is 'co-constructed', and the rule is then practised – he highlights teachers' explanations as a crucial factor, arguing that 'clarity is at least as important as learner involvement in the process of its co-construction' (Toth 2022: 30). Reflecting on what this means for teachers, and the challenges involved in providing contextualized explanations that assist in the process of mastering target forms, Toth draws the conclusion that 'not only must teachers possess a thorough linguistic understanding of the target structure, but they also must be able to adequately shepherd learners' in-the-moment hypotheses toward a shared, linguistically adequate conclusion' (Toth 2022: 30). Meshing these research-based insights with those of the teachers who participated in the workshop, it is clear that identifying motivational potential and directing attention to linguistic forms are the easier parts of an affordance-focused practice. Producing coherent and contextually framed explanations that can support students' understandings is significantly harder.

5 Conclusion

Working with the Instagram post and the other authentic texts, identifying affordances and brainstorming ideas, a space was created where the teachers were able to develop insights into a type of practice that, for many of them, was new. For several teachers, the project was the first time they had the opportunity to engage in development work that was focused on central aspects of their professional task, and that challenged them to draw more fully on linguistic knowledge and didactic skills. Rather than basing teaching around textbook units, the project opened up possibilities to work in a manner that was more responsive, student-focused, and potentially more rewarding (for both teacher and students). Alerted to the possibilities connected to working with authentic texts, and developing a sensitivity to motivational and linguistic affordances, the potential to transform these ideas into enduring aspects of practice is likely to hinge on a teacher's interpersonal and linguistic skills and perceptions of self-efficacy attaching to them. With varying comfort zones – related to activity design and the in-situ construction of grammatical explanations – and variation in willingness to venture into new territory, some teachers are more likely to engage in affordance-focused work than others. At the same time, we are prompted to reflect again on the informal collaboration and reciprocity from which the project initially sprang. Incentivized by personal interest in exploring the possibilities of affordance-focused teaching (rather than any instrumental gain), the collaboration had endured over time. The same may be the case for the participating teachers. For varying and fully understandable reasons, it is likely that some will remain hesitant in embracing an affordance-focused approach. For others, enthusiasm is likely to wane, not least given the additional work and professional responsibilities that the approach entails. However, for some, we suspect that the insights might have hit a chord and triggered an interest for working in this way. With a collegially developed template for working with affordances and having an engaged and informed colleague (PJ) who could function in a hybrid role as a 'third space professional' (Rasmussen and Holm 2012), we hope that more enduring shifts in practice might occur. Indeed, these may be part of the foundations upon which quality might ultimately develop.

References

Andrée, Maria & Inger Eriksson. 2019. A research environment for teacher-driven research – some demands and possibilities. *International Journal for Lesson and Learning Studies* 9(1). 45–55.
Andrews, Stephen. 2007. *Teacher language awareness*. Cambridge: Cambridge University Press.
Carlgren, Ingrid. 2010. Den felande länken. Om frånvaron och behovet av klinisk utbildningsvetenskaplig forskning [The malfunctioning link: On the absence of clinical educational research]. *Pedagogisk Forskning I Sverige* 15(4). 295–306.
Carlgren, Ingrid. 2018. Pedagogiken och lärarna [Pedagogy and the teachers]. *Pedagogisk Forskning I Sverige* 23(5). 268–283.
Eriksson, Inger. 2018. Lärares medverkan i praktiknära forskning: Förutsättningar och hinder [Teachers' participation in practice-close research: conditions and constraints]. *Utbildning och lärande* 12(1). 27–40.
Eriksson, Inger. 2022. Utvecklingsarbete som motor i utbildningsutvecklande forskning [Development work as a motor in education-developing research]. In Inger Eriksson & Ann Öhrman Sandberg (eds.), *Praktikutvecklande forskning mellan skola och akademi: Utmaningar och möjligheter vid samverkan* [Practice-developing research between schools and the academy: Challenges and possibilities involved in collaboration], 294–304. Lund: Nordic Academic Press.
Gibbons, Michael, Camille Limoges, Helga Nowotny, Simon Schwartzman & Peter Scott. 1994. *The New Production of Knowledge: The dynamics of science and research in contemporary societies*. London: Sage.
Gibson, James J. 1979. *The ecological approach to visual perception*. Mahwah, NJ: Lawrence Erlbaum.
Gilmore, Alex. 2007. Authentic materials and authenticity in foreign language learning. *Language Teaching* 40(2). 97–118.
Gilmore, Alex. 2011. 'I prefer not text': Developing Japanese learners' communicative competence with authentic materials. *Language Learning* 61(3). 786–819.
Gilmore, Alex. 2019. Materials and authenticity in language teaching. In Steve Walsh & Steve Mann (eds.), *The Routledge handbook of English language teacher education*, 299–318. Abingdon & New York: Routledge.
Henry, Alastair. 2019. Motivational teaching as a relational practice: Three concepts, three connections. *Lingua* 2. 28–33.
Henry, Alastair. 2021. Motivational connections in language classrooms: A research agenda. *Language Teaching* 54(2). 221–235.
Henry, Alastair, Helena Korp, Pia Sundqvist & Cecilia Thorsen. 2018. Motivational strategies and the reframing of English: Activity design and challenges for teachers in contexts of extensive extramural encounters. *TESOL Quarterly* 52(2). 247–273.
Henry, Alastair, Pia Sundqvist & Cecilia Thorsen. 2019. *Motivational practice: Insights from the classroom*. Lund: Studentlitteratur.
Henry, Alastair & Cecilia Thorsen. 2019. Weaving webs of connection: Empathy, perspective taking, and students' motivation. *Studies in Second Language Learning and Teaching* 9(1). 33–56.
Larsson, Christer & Lena Sjöberg. 2021. Academized or deprofessionalized? – policy discourses of teacher professionalism in relation to research-based education. *Nordic Journal of Studies in Educational Policy* 7(1). 3–5.
Magnusson, Petra & Martin Malmström. 2022. Practice-near school research in Sweden: Tendencies and teachers' roles. *Education Inquiry*. 1–22. DOI: 10.1080/20004508.2022.2028440

Moje, Elizabeth Birr, Kathryn McIntosh Ciechanowski, Katherine Kramer, Lindsay Ellis, Rosario Carillo & Tehani Collazo. 2004. Working toward third space in content area literacy: An examination of everyday funds of knowledge and discourse. *Reading Research Quarterly* 39(1). 38-70.

Nihlfors, Elisabet. 2020. Respekt för varandras kunskaper [Respect for each other's knowledge]. *Pedagogisk forskning i Sverige* 25(4). 112-116.

Olsson, Eva. 2016. On the impact of extramural English and CLIL on productive vocabulary. PhD thesis, University of Gothenburg.

Prøitz, Tine S., Ellen Rye, Jorunn S. Borgen, Kristin Barstad, Hilde Afdal, Sølvi Mausethagen & Petter Aasen. 2022. Utbildning, lärande, forskning Slutrapport från en utvärderingsstudie av ULF-försöksverksamhet [Education, learning, research: Final report from an evaluation of the ULF-initiative]. Universitetet i Sørøst-Norge Skrifterien nr. 87

Rasmussen, Jens & Claus Holm. 2012. In pursuit of good teacher education: How can research inform policy? *Reflecting Education* 8(2). 62-71.

Segalowitz, Norman. 2001. On the evolving connections between psychology and linguistics. *Annual Review of Applied Linguistics* 21. 3-22.

Sundqvist, Pia. 2011. A possible path to progress: Out-of-school English language learners in Sweden. In Phil Benson & Hayo Reinders (eds.), *Beyond the language classroom*, 106-118. Houndmills: Palgrave Macmillan.

Svalberg, Agneta M.-L. 2012. Language awareness in language learning and teaching: A research agenda. *Language Teaching* 45(3). 376-388.

Svalberg, Agneta M.-L.2015. Understanding the complex processes in developing student teachers' knowledge about grammar. *The Modern Language Journal* 99(3). 529-545.

Thornbury, Scott. 1997. *About language*, 2nd edn. Cambridge: Cambridge University Press.

Thorne, Steven L. & Jonathon Reinhardt. 2008. 'Bridging activities,' new media literacies, and advanced foreign language proficiency. *Calico Journal* 25(3). 558-572.

Tomlinson, Brian. 2012. Materials development for language learning and teaching. *Language Teaching* 45(2). 143-179.

Toth, Paul D. 2022. Introduction: Investigating explicit L2 grammar instruction through multiple theoretical and methodological lenses. *Language Learning* 72(S1). 5-40.

Ushioda, Ema. 2013. Motivation and ELT: Looking ahead to the future. In Ema Ushioda (ed.), *International perspectives on motivation: Language learning and professional challenges*, 233-239. Houndmills: Palgrave Macmillan.

Part 2: **Learners as collaborative agents**

Marie Källkvist, Henrik Gyllstad, Erica Sandlund and Pia Sundqvist
4 Reciprocity and challenge in researcher–student collaborative labour in a multilingual secondary school

Abstract: This chapter focuses on challenge and reciprocity in researcher–student *collaborative labour* (Zigo 2001) in a large multilingual secondary school in Sweden. The school was recruited for a larger longitudinal study of classroom language policy. For the purposes of the present chapter, we analysed ethnographic data to shed light on the well-known challenge of recruiting and retaining students to participate in longitudinal research, and on aspects of reciprocity, which was operationalized as benefits that both parties, i.e. students and researchers, needed or desired (Trainor and Bouchard 2013). Results show that of the 43 students who were present in the classrooms studied, 35 (81%) provided written, informed consent to fill in a language-background questionnaire and participate in an interview. Fewer students with low grades consented to participate, but those who did provided data no less rich than that provided by students with top grades. As to reciprocal benefits, the researchers secured the research data needed, but also new knowledge about students' heritage languages and the multilingual territories they had left prior to settling in Sweden. Another benefit relates to empowerment. The researchers were empowered by learning culturally appropriate terminology to use when communicating about multilingual and multi-ethnic territories; and interview data suggest that students were empowered when positioned as experts on their multilingual repertoires and the language ecology in their prior home territories. Finally, the chapter reveals that researchers' stance of reciprocity evolved organically over time through their ethnographic engagement in the classrooms.

1 Introduction

School-based research provides rewarding opportunities to learn from the work that students, teachers and other school staff do. On the way, however, one may encounter considerable challenges such as negotiating access, building rapport and gaining

---

Acknowledgements: We gratefully acknowledge funding from the Swedish Research Council (registration no. VR-UVK 2016-03469). Our deep thanks are due also to the school and to Vincent and his students for generously devoting time to participate in MultiLingual Spaces.

Open Access. © 2023 the author(s), published by De Gruyter. [CC BY-NC-ND] This work is licensed under the Creative Commons Attribution-NonCommercial-NoDerivatives 4.0 International License.
https://doi.org/10.1515/9783110787719-005

informed written consent from participants (Spada 2005; Warriner and Bigelow 2019). In this chapter we elaborate on the well-known challenge of recruiting student participants for classroom research, and on reciprocal benefits for researchers and participating students in a sub-study of MultiLingual Spaces (Källkvist et al. 2022). The school was an urban lower-secondary school where the majority of students had a migrant background. Following prior research in education, we apply the concepts of an *ethical stance of reciprocity* (Trainor and Bouchard 2013) and *collaborative labour* (Zigo 2001) as conceptualizations of reciprocity. Below, we elaborate on these concepts, followed by descriptive quantitative data of student participation. We then analyse ethnographic data, aiming to elucidate reciprocal benefits that emerged over the course of seven months through the researchers' stance of reciprocity.

2 Reciprocity: Conceptualization and prior research

Reciprocity in the researcher–participant relationship has been defined as one 'in which each contributes something the other needs or desires' (Trainor and Bouchard 2013: 986). The contribution *per se* has been conceptualized, for example, as an exchange of goods, labour or money as reimbursement (Trainor and Bouchard 2013; Zigo 2001). In the context of qualitative inquiry like ours, Trainor and Bouchard (2013: 989) advanced a conceptualization of reciprocity as an ethical stance rather than an economics-oriented exchange of goods, describing it as 'a broader and more comprehensive approach to reciprocity throughout the research process'. Prior research has revealed the following as examples of reciprocity in classroom research: contributing to a greater social good (Zigo 2001), empowering the immediate participants by affording them opportunity to express their ideas (Eder and Fingerson 2001), exchange of labour by the researcher also serving as a teaching assistant (Bernstein 2019; Zigo 2001) and exchange of goods (Trainor and Bouchard 2013). We begin our analysis below by attending to the omnipresent need in education research to obtain written informed consent prior to data collection involving human participants.

3 Participants: The need to gain written informed consent

We recruited the school through an e-mail to the City Council, asking for access to a lower-secondary school where there would be a substantial number of students of a non-Swedish-speaking background, typically due to migration. The language of schooling was Swedish, as is the norm in Sweden, but at the time, this particular school was in the process of establishing an English-language profile, offering a fast-track EFL (English as a foreign language) option and a CLIL (content and language integrated learning) option where three content subjects were taught in English. This chapter focuses on two Year 8 classrooms both taught by a lead teacher (*förstelärare*) whom we call Vincent. One class was the fast-track EFL class in Year 8, referred to as *8 FT*. The other was a Year 8 class in which students were studying EFL at the regular pace, here referred to as *8 R*.

In Table 4.1 we present the total number of students in each class, followed by the total number of students from whom we obtained informed written consent to a) fill in a five-page questionnaire on their language backgrounds and current language practices, and, later on, b) to participate in an audio-recorded interview with one of the researchers. These data thus address the challenge reported on in this chapter: securing informed written consent from students, in our case aged 14–15.

Table 4.1: Number of students in each class and number of students consenting to participate.

Class	Number of students in the class	Number of students providing informed written consent		Data collected		
		Questionnaire (five pages)	Interview (audio-recorded)	Number of completed questionnaires received	Number of interviews conducted	Number of lessons observed
8 R	23	17 (74%)	15 (65%)	17 (74%)	10 (43%)	7
8 FT	20	20 (100%)	20 (100%)	16 (80%)	9 (45%)	5
Total	43	37 (86%)	35 (81%)	33 (77%)	19 (44%)	12

Table 4.1 reveals that all students in 8 FT consented to participate whereas in 8 R, 65% consented to both the questionnaire and the interview. The students in 8 R who declined to participate had in common the relatively low grade of D in EFL (the top grade being A). Due to students in 8 FT being absent from some of the lessons, in the end we actually received more questionnaires in 8 R (17) than in 8 FT (16). Fewer students were interviewed, which is common in ethnography (De Fina 2019). The reason we did not interview all students who consented was lack of EFL lesson time at the very end of the semester when the teacher had completed grading. We refrained from interviewing students prior to grading being complete, leaving two weeks during which we asked students to be interviewed individually during an EFL lesson. Table 4.1 also shows that we conducted more lesson observations in 8 R (7) than in 8 FT (5) since our research questions required

data in mainstream EFL classrooms with the normal range of student proficiency levels, here operationalized as their grades (Table 4.2).

With the overall qualitative design, we intended to explore language practices in EFL classrooms in their full complexity, for example in terms of the range of students' prior languages and their varying proficiency levels in English. Thus, ideally, we needed students in the complete range of grades, A–F (A–E are pass grades whereas F equals *fail*). Table 4.2 provides a breakdown of student numbers relative to their grades.

Table 4.2: Grades in EFL in the two classes; A = the top grade; E = the lowest pass grade; F = fail.

Grade	8R		8 FT	
	Number of students receiving each grade	Students consenting to participate	Number of students receiving each grade	Students consenting to participate
A	0	n/a	8	8
B	7	6	12	12
C	4	4	0	n/a
D	11	4	0	n/a
E	1	1	0	n/a
F	0	n/a	0	n/a

As illustrated in Table 4.2, all 8 FT students had top grades (either A or B), which is probably a reflection of them having passed an admission test as an entry requirement for doing fast-track EFL. Data in Table 4.2 suggest there was a relationship between grade and consent to participate in research. In 8 R, virtually all students with a B or a C consented, whereas fewer than 50% of students with a D did. The student in 8 R with the lowest grade (E) stands out as opting to participate despite their low grade. This student was generous with their time and sharing relevant details about their learning of English in the interview despite being very quiet in class.

Due to lack of time to interview all students who consented to being interviewed, we applied criterion selection of students, asking those who were users of a heritage language at home and attending mother-tongue tuition in their heritage language to be interviewed. Tables 4.3 and 4.4 list the students who were interviewed, including details of their language background, choice of language in the interview (English or Swedish) and the duration of the interview. In total, 19 students were interviewed, eight of whom were girls and the rest boys.

Table 4.3 reveals that, across the ten students, they spoke seven different heritage languages and their grades ranged from B to E. Seven were born in Sweden whereas three were born abroad.

Table 4.3: Students interviewed in 8 R.

Pseudonym	Heritage language	Age of first exposure to Swedish	Choice of language in the interview	Grade in EFL	Duration of interview (minutes)
Abdullah	Arabic	1	Swedish	B	23
Masoud	Arabic	10	English	D	34
Lea	Arabic	1	Swedish	D	53
Sagal	Somali	1	Swedish	E	36
Ines	Arabic	1	Swedish	B	44
Hasin	Urdu	4	English	D	29
Fredrik	Greek	0	Swedish	C	22
Yasna	Turkmen	5	Swedish	C	31
Saman	Sorani (Kurdish)	2	Swedish	B	42
Nila	Serbian	1	Swedish	B	38

Table 4.4 provides the same details about students interviewed in 8 FT. It shows that three different heritage languages were represented among the nine students. Four were born in Sweden whereas five were born abroad. They all had top grades, either an A or a B. Four opted to have their interview in English compared to five choosing Swedish. Tables 4.3 and 4.4 also reveal that the interview lasted between 22 and 54 minutes.

Table 4.4: Students interviewed in 8 FT.

Pseudonym	Heritage language	Age of first exposure to Swedish	Choice of language in the interview	Grade in EFL	Duration of interview (minutes)
Rim	Arabic	1	Swedish	A	44
Adnan	Arabic	11	Swedish	B	42
Amir	Arabic	11	English	B	31
Hamid	Arabic	1	English	B	47
Hero	Sorani (Kurdish)	6	Swedish	B	43
Barzan	Sorani (Kurdish)	7	English	B	33
Amir	Arabic	3	Swedish	B	28
Sirwe	Southern Kurdish	1	English	B	54
Jamal	Arabic	1	Swedish	B	31

In sum, the challenge of securing student participants manifested itself in 100% consent to participate in 8 FT, where all students had top grades, and in lower levels of consent in 8 R, where 15 out of 23 students (65%) consented to both the questionnaire and the interview. Among those interviewed, four had low grades: three had a D whereas one had an E. Hence, our data suggest that students with higher grades are more likely to consent to being research participants. Even so, students with Ds and an E did consent to being interviewed, and two of them had long interviews; for example Lea (Table 4.3), a girl in 8 R with the low grade of D, spent 54 minutes being interviewed and Sagal (Table 4.3, 8 R), the only student with an E, spent 36 minutes being interviewed. No student in these two classes had an F (fail), which is due to students with an F in EFL being taught in a separate small group by another teacher. We attribute the high level of consent to participate on the part of the students partly to their teacher, Vincent, who generously explained the value of research to the students at crucial moments in the classroom when we were recruiting for the interviews.

Next, we turn our attention to reciprocal benefits, beginning with benefits gained by the researchers because we have reason to believe that we gained more than the student participants, a finding that we share with Pettitt (2019), discussed also by Zigo (2001).

4 Reciprocity for the researchers through collaboration in labour

The concept of *collaboration in labour* applies here as we sought to position the students as experts at knowing how to use their prior languages as an aid to enhance their communication and learning of English. This, in turn, would narrow the power gap often inherent in youth–adult communication, particularly in institutions like schools (Zigo 2001). In other words, the students' job was to learn English and ours was to understand whether and how they used their prior languages to do so, including the complexity inherent in language-diverse classrooms. Prior research has shown that collaboration in labour can emerge in qualitative research contexts where a researcher is 'present, attentive, and fully engaged as a co-member of the participants' immediate community' (Zigo 2001: 352). Moreover, researchers tend to gain concrete benefits whereas participants' gains are more in the abstract (Zigo 2001).

On entering the classrooms for fieldwork, we began enacting our stance of reciprocity, stating that we were joining classes to learn more about how skilful teachers teach EFL (Vincent being a lead teacher of EFL). Three months later, we felt that we had developed rapport with the teacher and students to the extent that we could go ahead with our data collection plans to the students. We were careful to explain that we were eager to learn from them about whether and how they used their prior language(s) when learning and using English, thus positioning them and their multilingual repertoires as resources. Initially, we communicated this in

English, but when repeating the information later on, Vincent asked us to use Swedish to ensure that all students would understand. We continued in the same vein a further three months later when conducting the student interviews: we positioned students as experts when explaining their language backgrounds and current language practices, including their perceptions of mother-tongue tuition of their heritage language and their need to use a stronger language than English to facilitate their comprehension or learning of English. This provided the benefit that we *needed*, i.e., the research data.

Over the course of the seven months, we also gained knowledge from both the teacher and the students, knowledge that we *desired*, because of our interest in it and because we are EFL teacher educators. We found the opportunity of spending time in classrooms highly rewarding, particularly meeting refugee-background students whom we would otherwise have limited opportunity to encounter, let alone have dialogue with.

We found the interviews particularly meaningful, which is an observation we share with Young Knowles (2019), because we could talk about shared classroom experiences and we could hear students' perspectives in their own words. Qualitative coding (Saldaña 2016) of our fieldnotes and transcribed interviews enabled us to identify topics (themes) about which we had dialogue.

From the classroom observations, we learnt about *the nature of EFL lessons in a multilingual school taught by a young lead EFL teacher*. Seated at the back of the classroom, we were able to view not only Vincent's teaching practices but also students' behaviour. Students addressed us on numerous occasions, usually in English. They were curious as to why we were there; in particular, they were wondering whether we were assessing Vincent's teaching skills. They were careful to let us know that Vincent was a very good teacher.

The interviews were semi-structured and, in addition to providing research data, they afforded the opportunity of asking students follow-up questions about matters we were keen to know more about. At the very end of the interview, students were explicitly provided with time to ask any question that they might have had. Thematic content analysis showed that we learned about the following diverse topics:

Language practices in territories that are multilingual, including intercomprehension of closely related languages, different spoken varieties of Arabic, and *whether English would serve as a lingua franca,* for example in the Kurdish region of northern Iraq, whether speakers of Southern Kurdish and Farsi can understand each other, and whether you can rely on English as a lingua franca when travelling in the Greek archipelago.

Student preferences as to labels of their territorial origins, for example whether a student preferred to be referred to as a Kurd or an Iraqi when coming from Iraqi Kurdistan. The student answered that he saw himself as 'a Kurd from Iraq'.

Students' perceptions of EFL teaching methods, grading, and their attitudes to mother-tongue tuition in their heritage language (for example Somali and Sorani) and *the second foreign languages taught at the school* (French, German and Spanish were on offer).

How the 8 FT students learned English to such a high level and *whether code-switching/translanguaging practices in their daily life were perceived as efficient means of communication*. We now turn to our analysis of what we perceive to be students' benefits from being part of our research.

5 Reciprocity for students through collaboration in labour

Prior interview research has found that reciprocity on the part of children and adolescents may be the *rewarding experience of feeling a sense of empowerment* (Eder and Fingerson 2001) and *a greater understanding of their own life experience as a result of having the opportunity to think through ideas and issues of importance to them by speaking to an interested adult* (Eder and Fingerson 2001; Hammersley and Atkinson 2019). In our research context, an additional benefit may be the opportunity of *interacting in English or Swedish individually with a researcher*. From research in psycholinguistics, we know that input is necessary for language development, that is to say, changes in a language system (Mitchell, Myles, and Marsden 2019). From a sociolinguistic perspective, we believe that students were introduced to new discourse practices, the practices of explaining research and of participating in a research interview, i.e., practices where they normally would not find themselves at age 14–15. Thus, we have reason to believe that the interview provided a context from which learners could potentially learn English through a new discourse practice, and Swedish for those who chose to speak in Swedish. This would be something that students may need and desire.

Our analysis involved thematic content analysis of the 19 interview transcripts to see whether themes emerged that would suggest that students may have felt empowered and shown signs of a greater understanding of their own life experience as outlined by Eder and Fingerson (2001) and Hammersley and Atkinson (2019). Many migrant students are language-minoritized in school when they cannot use their strongest language(s) in the classroom. For example, having an opportunity to speak about the potential issue of being language-minoritized in an interview may engender a sense of empowerment. Content analysis yielded four themes:

'If I am in my home country then it is great for me to use it' – Multilingualism *beyond English and Swedish as a resource*: In connection with asking questions about the use of their heritage language, we often provided comments from our own lives where knowledge of a language in addition to English had been an asset, or else we pointed out to students that their heritage language may be a resource. In Excerpt 1 below, the researcher positioned Ines's command of Arabic, her heritage language, as a resource (original in Swedish, English translation in italics):

Excerpt 1

Researcher	Ja (.) men engelska är (.) det finns något väldigt positivt med engelska *Yes (.) but English is (.) there is something about English that is very positive*
Ines	Ja *Yes*
Researcher	Jag kan tänka mig att det finns något väldigt positivt med arabiska också fast kanske på ett annat sätt *I am thinking that there is something very positive about Arabic too but perhaps in a different way*
Ines	Ja alltså (.) till exempel jag bor ju i Sverige (.) jag kan inte riktigt (.) alltså (.) du vet att alla kan inte arabiska så jag kan inte ha någon användning av det men om jag nu är mitt hemland och så (.) så är det väldigt roligt också att använda det (.) då kan jag hela tiden tala arabiska och det är också bra *Yes ok (.) like I live in Sweden (.) I can't (.) ok (.) we know that everyone cannot speak Arabic so I cannot use it but if I am in my home country like (.) then it is great for me to use it (.) then I can speak Arabic the whole time and that is good too*
Researcher	Ja (.) det är ju fantastiskt för det öppnar upp en stor del av världen för personer som dig *Yes (.) that is fantastic because it opens up a big part of the world for people like you*

This is one of the most obvious examples of what may be interpreted as student empowerment, and the student responded by reflecting on the researcher's comment that Arabic is useful, remembering occasions when she was using Arabic in her previous home country, where everyone understands it.

The most common theme in students' questions was to do with our research – 'Why do you do this?' – the process and benefits of doing research. Of the 19 students, twelve asked questions at the end of the interview whereas seven did not. Excerpt 2 provides Sirwe's (8 FT) question:

Excerpt 2

Sirwe	Why do you do this?
Researcher	We do it because we train English teachers at Lund University and they ask us many questions (.) so one question they ask is (.) is it important when we teach grammar to use Swedish in the classroom (.) for example to explain difficult things like grammar and difficult words (.) it's the most frequent question that I get asked

Other themes emerging through student questions included asking the researcher *How many languages do you speak?* and *the use of English at university*. We now turn to discussing our findings.

6 Discussion and concluding remarks: Challenge and reciprocity in the EFL classrooms

In this chapter, we have brought our data to bear on a challenge well-known in classroom research: gaining a sufficient number of student participants to address research questions. In total, 33 out of 43 (77%) of the students in the two classes provided consent *and* filled in the questionnaire. Of those who did not, six did not consent, whereas the remaining four were absent from class. Due to lack of time at the very end of the school year, fewer (19 out 43, 44%) were interviewed, which is common in ethnography (Da Fina 2019). Fewer students with a low grade consented, although as many as four students with a D or E did participate. Thus, we have data from students in the entire A–E grade range, which we needed as our research questions required data from students of different proficiency levels. However, we do not have data from students with an F, the reason being that students with an F at this school were offered remedial EFL teaching in a small group. Also, most of the participants had a high grade (B), due to one of the classes being a gated, fast-track EFL group. In terms of the overall level of participation, attaining 100% participation among students is unrealistic (cf. Trainor and Bouchard 2013). In 8 FT, where 20 out of 20 (100%) students consented to participate, absence in the final couple of weeks of the semester resulted in questionnaires from 16 (80%) of them. Also, given that interviews had to be carried out in the final two weeks of the semester in order not to remove students from lessons prior to grading being complete left us sufficient time to interview in total 19 (44%) of the students. Analysis of the interviews suggested that, with this sample, we were reaching a level of saturation (Dörnyei 2007: 127), which in qualitative research means that collecting more data would yield similar findings to those already analysed. The 44% participation level may provide sufficient qualitative data to answer MultiLingual Spaces' research questions, given that participants in the grade range of A to E were interviewed and generously responded to the researcher's questions.

Turning now to reciprocity, we drew on the definition of each party contributing 'something the other *needs* or *desires*' (Trainor and Bouchard 2013: 986; our italics) and the conceptualizations of *a stance of reciprocity* and *collaboration in labour*. We had ideas about providing students benefits in return for their participation prior to engaging in our fieldwork, but once we were in the field, we developed a stance of reciprocity of the kind described by Trainor and Bouchard (2013). We believe that we gained more than the participants did in view of the fact that we collected concrete research data, in the longer term yielding research publications, which was our immediate need. What the participants gained was more in the abstract as mentioned by Zigo (2001). When enacting our stance of reciprocity in student interviews, thus trying to benefit our *'immediate* participants' and not only 'a greater good' (Zigo 2001: 352), we positioned their multilingual repertoires beyond English and Swedish as a resource in their present and future lives. Also, we positioned them as a great deal more knowledgeable than us about their heritage languages, the multilingual ecologies of their original home countries and about mother-tongue tuition that they were attending. We believe we killed two birds with one stone: the student was empowered by explaining matters to us, who in turn were learning about languages and countries of origin among the linguistic minorities in Sweden. This knowledge comes in handy not only in our profession as EFL teacher educators, but also in general in social encounters in present-day multilingual Sweden, for example in referring to people of migrant backgrounds in culturally appropriate ways. Thus, we found it useful to learn from Saman (8 R), a native speaker of Sorani (the Kurdish spoken in the Kurdistan region of northern Iraq), that he himself referred to Kurds living in northern Iraq as 'Kurds from Iraq'. Learning about the different varieties of spoken Arabic used among the students interviewed was equally useful, as was learning their perceptions of the mother-tongue tuition they were receiving, which is a topic often debated in Swedish media. The most valuable abstract benefit for us was the encounter and the dialogue we were able to have with young people with whom we rarely cross paths due to housing segregation in Sweden.

As to benefits for the students, we hope they felt empowered by being positioned as having important knowledge of their heritage languages and us taking an interest in language(s) spoken in their countries of origin and attitudes to the teaching of languages in their school. All students present in the classroom were exposed to descriptions and explanations of the research we were doing, including the practice of written informed consent, which we believe was a discourse practice that was new to them. In the interviews, their most frequent questions indeed pertained to our research: why we were interested in their language practices, where we were collecting data and what we were going to do with it over time. As we ended our engagement with them, at the end of the school year, we brought chocolate for them as a concrete token of gratitude and told them to get in touch should they want to study at Lund University. This may serve as an example of a 'stance of reciprocity [that] calls us to become available to our participants' (Trainor and Bouchard 2013: 1000). We stepped into future time, saying that we would be available in the future, engendering a discourse of a prestigious university not far away being interested in seeing them as students.

References

Bernstein, Katie A. 2019. Ethics in practice and answerability in complex, multi-participant studies. In Doris S. Warriner & Martha Bigelow (eds.), *Critical reflections on research methods: Power and equity in complex multilingual contexts*, 127–142. Bristol: Multilingual Matters.

De Fina, Anna. 2019. The ethnographic interview. In Karin Tusting (ed.), *The Routledge handbook of linguistic ethnography*, 154–166. London: Routledge.

Dörnyei, Zoltán. 2007. *Research methods in applied linguistics*. Oxford: Oxford University Press.

Eder, Donna & Laura Fingerson. 2001. Interviewing children and adolescents. In Jaber E. Gubrium & James A. Holstein (eds.), *Handbook of interview research*, 181–201. London: Sage.

Hammersley, Martyn & Paul Atkinson. 2019. *Ethnography: Principles in practice*. London: Routledge.

Källkvist, Marie, Henrik Gyllstad, Erica Sandlund & Pia Sundqvist. 2022. Towards an in-depth understanding of English-Swedish translanguaging pedagogy in multilingual classrooms. *HumaNetten* 48. 138–167

Mitchell, Rosamond, Florence Myles & Emma Marsden. 2019. *Second Language Learning Theories*, 4th edn. New York: Routledge.

Pettitt, Nicole. 2019. Weaving reciprocity in research (with)in immigrant and refugee communities. In Doris S. Warriner & Martha Bigelow (eds.), *Critical reflections on research methods: Power and equity in complex multilingual contexts*, 143–156. Bristol: Multilingual Matters.

Saldaña, Johnny. 2015. *The coding manual for qualitative researchers*. London: Sage.

Spada, Nina. 2005. Conditions and challenges in developing school-based SLA research programs. *The Modern Language Journal* 89(3). 328–338.

Trainor, Audrey & Kate A. Bouchard. 2013. Exploring and developing reciprocity in research design. *International Journal of Qualitative Studies in Education* 26(8). 986–1003.

Warriner, Doris S. & Martha Bigelow. 2019. Introduction. In Doris S. Warriner & Martha Bigelow (eds.), *Critical reflections on research methods: Power and equity in complex multilingual contexts*, 1–10. Bristol: Multilingual Matters.

Young Knowles, Sarah. 2019. Researcher–participant relationships in cross-language research: Becoming cultural and linguistic insiders. In Doris S. Warriner & Martha Bigelow (eds.), *Critical reflections on research methods: Power and equity in complex multilingual contexts*, 85–97. Bristol: Multilingual Matters.

Zigo, Diane. 2001. Rethinking reciprocity: Collaboration in labor as a path toward equalizing power in classroom research. *Qualitative Studies in Education* 11(3). 351–365.

Annamaria Pinter
5 The organic processes of learning in an exploratory collaborative action research (CAR) project

Abstract: This chapter reports on my reflections relating to the reciprocal benefits and challenges documented in a funded British Council project focussed on primary teachers working together with their learners as partners in a collaborative action research project in India. Elevating children to the roles of partners in research is in line with principles advocated in New Childhood Studies and contemporary rights-based approaches to working with children, but so far in applied linguistics such a focus on learners in active roles has not received much empirical attention. The project had two broad aims. Firstly, to explore whether a partnership with children in action research was feasible in schools in India, and secondly, to discover what impact implementing such partnerships in research would have on teachers' professional development over the course of a whole academic year. Reciprocal processes of learning were documented between teachers and learners in classrooms and between teachers and academic facilitators in workshops. Both settings were characterised as democratic and non-hierarchical where joint meaning-making and respecting all voices, including differences in opinion, became the norm. In addition to the positive outcomes, the main challenges of child–adult research partnerships are also discussed.

1 Introduction

This chapter is devoted to my reflections about a British Council English Language Teaching Research Partnerships (ELTRP) project in India, in which two academics (one of them myself), 25 primary and lower secondary English teachers, and more than 800 primary school learners were involved together. This longitudinal, collaborative project entitled 'Children and teachers as co-researchers in Indian primary classrooms'[1] was focussed on the feasibility of involving children in classroom action research in active roles as well as on opportunities of teacher development as a result of participating in the project and working collaboratively with learners.

---

[1] https://www.teachingenglish.org.uk/article/children-teachers-co-researchers-indian-primary-english-classrooms (accessed 10 June 2022).

We were interested to find out whether teachers' classroom practices would become more learner-centred as a result of children's active involvement. With regard to the children's involvement, we were interested to explore the concept of the agentic child borrowed from the Childhood Studies literature (Kehily 2009). The broad aim of the project was to find out whether a focus on children as active participants was at all possible, and if it was, what shape and form such collaboration between teachers and children could take and what kinds of professional development gains the teachers would report.

The focus in the project was first of all on the children and their responses to a new way of working, but we also intended to explore how teachers made sense of the changes that occurred in their classrooms as a result of (re-)conceptualizing learners as 'partners' in research. We all learnt from each other but in particular the teachers' professional development was documented formally through regular reflective interviews. In this chapter, I will mainly focus on the many different ways in which the teachers benefited from this collaborative endeavour. In addition to the benefits, some challenges will also be discussed, especially relating to the ethical dilemmas relevant to promoting innovative practices in schools where teachers are somewhat isolated and where children ultimately need to revert to old ways of working.

I have to emphasize from the outset that this is a reflective account, described through my own lens as one of the academic facilitators of the project. Having been involved in analysing and publishing our findings in various journals and books over the last few years, and due to the fact that I am still in contact with many of the participants, I have come to construct the benefits and the challenges in a way that is highly personal to me.

2 Children as active collaborators in research

The idea of inviting children to work in partnership with their teachers was motivated by a particular perspective on childhood and children. This perspective is related to the 'agentic child' image, originating from Childhood Studies and its associated scholarship that has been around for more than 30 years, influencing research in various disciplines, such as health care education, climate change education, social care research, and others, but without too much impact on research in child second language education.

Childhood Studies, as an approach to studying children, emerged as a result of the criticism that surrounded traditional research assigning children passive roles. Given that developmental psychology promoted the image of childhood as a natural, universal phenomenon, traditionally children used to be seen as small adults in development, i.e., 'becomings' rather than 'beings', always described in deficit terms compared to adults, who are by definition complete, mature and rational (Walkerdine 2009). However, this image of the child and the traditional research methods began to receive more and more criticism and Childhood Studies scholars began to suggest that children should not be condemned to passivity, but instead should be invited to speak up and be studied as unique individuals in their own right.

In 1990 James and Prout, in a milestone publication, argued that childhood was a social phenomenon and children should be studied as active agentic beings. Children were described as capable and resourceful with much to contribute as long as adults were truly willing and able to listen. In contrast to traditional methodologies that suggested experimental methods and observation as the main ways to understand children, scholars interested in children were now encouraged to listen to children, and develop methodological solutions that helped with eliciting children's views about their experiences. Various participatory approaches such as visual and arts-based approaches were promoted as suitable. In this alternative paradigm, where children are treated as experts of their own lives, it becomes the adults' pressing responsibility to engage with them in ways that allow the children to communicate their views and perspectives with ease on all important matters. Adults need to create spaces for open dialogue and engage in what has been referred to as the 'pedagogy of listening' (Rinaldi 2006).

The political impetus behind the emergence of Childhood Studies was bolstered by the publication of the United Nations Convention on the Rights of the Child (UNCRC, 1989), which declares that children are rights-bearing citizens and adults have the important ethical and moral duty to make sure their rights are respected. In particular a few key articles in the UNCRC were identified as relevant to researchers who embraced a new conception of the agentic child. Article 12, for example, proposes that children's views and insights about important matters in their lives were to be listened to and acted on by adults in all contexts, including of course their school experiences and, by implication, any research undertaken with them as participants. This led to a suggestion that research should not be conducted only by adults through an adult lens (the traditional approach) but instead, if and where possible, such research must be complemented by approaches that allow children to be involved in active roles, including roles of collaborating with adults or even undertaking their own research (e.g. Kellett 2005, 2010).

Over the last 30 years, Childhood Studies as an approach to studying children has evolved from a largely sentimental view of celebrating children's perspectives to a more critical approach, questioning the sharp divide between the natural and the social child and emphasizing how children's voices and participation must be interpreted within the web of social, cultural and institutional discourses and power dynamics (e.g., Spyrou 2018). Equally, the UNCRC has been criticized as ambiguous in terms of the key messages about children, open to various interpretations, and biased towards Western childhoods. Nonetheless, the fact remains that children have rights and these need to be taken into consideration by adults when they work with them; and contemporary childhood scholarship has accepted that children will have important insights about most matters that are worth listening to.

How can the image of the agentic child be relevant to second/foreign language education? Can children be conceptualized as experts of their own L2 learning experiences? Can/should children have a voice in research that targets their L2 learning experiences? Generally, we know very little about children's perspectives on L2 learning despite the fact that much research now targets this population (Philp, Oliver, and Mackey 2008; Mourão and Lourenço 2015; Nikolov 2016; Enever 2011; Enever and Lindgren 2017; Garton and Copland 2019). We do not know much about what children think about L2 learning, how they feel, what they find interesting or challenging, and if they were to be invited to be involved in research collaboratively with adults, we do not know what they might be interested in exploring.

Various frameworks have been proposed to explore how children might be involved in research in active roles. The best-known framework is based on Hart's (1992) ladder metaphor, which illustrates increasing levels of participation from tokenistic involvement to taking full responsibility at the top rung. Various other models built on Hart's work, describing opportunities for children's participation in some detail (such as Shier 2001 or Lundy 2007). All these frameworks emphasize that adults can incorporate children's input into continuous decision-making, and where and when children are ready and interested, adults can enable them to take active roles in various stages of the research process, such as asking questions, helping to collect and analyse data, or disseminating findings. Merits of partnership in research and child-led research have been documented (Lundy, McEvoy, and Byrne 2011; Lundy and McEvoy 2012; Kellett 2005) as well as inherent problems and challenges (Barratt-Hacking and Barratt 2009; Lomax 2012; Robinson and Taylor 2013).

At the time when the project was launched we were not aware of any studies that explored the processes of teachers working with children as partners in primary English language classrooms in a longitudinal project, which lasted over a whole academic year, so we embarked on an exploratory study with a genuinely open question: Can such collaboration work, and if yes, what shape could it take?

3 The British Council project: Rationale behind the design

Given the ambitious and somewhat controversial goal, i.e., inviting children to become partners or co-researchers, we, the academic facilitators, were aware that the suggested focus was going to be new and potentially challenging for the teachers. Elevating the children to the role of partners, i.e., important stakeholders rather than just passive receivers of whatever teaching or research was planned, meant that teachers' classrooms were to be shaken up. Looking at things through the children's eyes was a novel approach. Indeed, teachers were sceptical at the start: *It might not work as my children are so young.* In view of this, we decided at the beginning to introduce the agentic child perspective and the concept of the partnership between children and teachers as open-ended opportunities rather than a prescribed set of steps to follow. In fact, each teacher was able to interpret for themselves what this approach could mean, and what was possible to experiment with in their classrooms. All teachers were invited to contemplate which rung on the ladder (Hart 1992) they were able to progress to. The lower rungs included different types of consultation with learners before adult decisions were made, then at the next level shared decisions based on adult-initiated ideas, and finally, at the top of the ladder, shared decisions based on learner-initiated ideas.

The project's backbone was a set of three workshops where all participants (academic facilitators, teachers and some children) came together. Most of the 25 teachers who volunteered to participate had worked with the Indian academic colleague prior to this project and all had several years of experience, with some holding postgraduate degrees in English language teaching. Out of the 25 teachers, 5 started the process of working with children as partners a few months earlier than the other 20 teachers, and these 5 acted as mentors throughout the project, each supporting a group of 4 teachers in the larger cohort.

The first workshop introduced the idea of the agentic child and the possibility of involving children in classroom action research in active roles. We discussed some relevant academic articles, and the 5 teachers who had started the work earlier than the others shared their initial experiences of working with children in collaboration. These presentations included details about how they introduced the idea to the children, what they decided to focus on together, how exactly the children participated, and what they achieved and contributed. The presentations were followed by discussion, questions and comments, debating what worked and why and what did not work so well. Following this, the rest of the workshop was devoted to planning ideas for the first action research cycle. The teachers planned ideas to introduce some kind of collaborative project in their own classrooms. All left the workshop armed with ideas and inspiration for their own plans. For 12 weeks all teachers were experimenting with these new ideas in their classrooms.

In the second workshop everyone gave a presentation about their own project. Some children from the local schools were able to attend the workshop and they presented their work enthusiastically too. Again, both successes and challenges were fully discussed. More reading material was recommended to the teachers and ideas from these were discussed and linked to the teachers' practical experiences. Finally, just like in the first workshop, teachers planned the next steps for the second cycle of the project. Some decided to carry on with the same work, while others took ideas from their colleagues and started something different with a new group of learners; yet others managed to extend their practice to several new classes. Some teachers were not able to incorporate this work into their ordinary English classes because of exam preparation and/or because of the highly prescriptive curricula they had to follow, so they ran extra-curricular research club sessions with interested pupils.

There were a large variety of projects. In one class children decided to create a newspaper about their own lives at school and in the community. Groups of students volunteered to produce different sections of the newspaper. In order to involve everyone, multiple languages were used (L1, L2 and L3), and those who felt unable to contribute to the writing of the articles, were put in charge of creating visuals. The children interviewed teachers, peers and some members of the community about current issues to generate articles on top of the content that was generated in class. In another class the children and the teacher worked with story books. The story books were all stored in a cupboard and when the project started the children chose books for themselves to read. They all wrote some notes about the books they liked. The ones they did not like, they could put back in the cupboard. After a few weeks the class brainstormed questions for a survey to evaluate what had been learnt. The draft survey was piloted by a few learners before the whole class filled it in. A group of children then analysed the responses and the whole class discussed the findings. Each project was unique, and each teacher's journey was different. Some teachers were able to involve the children more actively than others.

In the last workshop, which happened 12 weeks after the second one, all teachers gave a presentation about their experiences in the second cycle and we evaluated our experiences both individually and together. The teachers were keen to put together a handbook with their best ideas about how to involve children in action research, to disseminate via the British Council, but there were also other spontaneous initiatives such as one where a teacher took leadership of editing a book about the teachers' collective experiences for an Indian publisher.

The five mentors took up additional mentoring roles in other projects in India and they gave talks about their work at national conferences.

When planning and conducting the workshops we (the academic facilitators) attempted to put into practice what Zeichner, Payne and Brayko (2015: 125) refer to as 'deliberative democracy' based on the principles of 'horizontal expertise'. Promoting horizontal expertise means working together across boundaries, enriching each other's practices and recognizing the unique knowledge and expertise that each and every person brings to the collaborative effort, thus cultivating reciprocity in learning and meaning-making. We were all learning from each other and no one's knowledge or expertise enjoyed higher status than others. We (the academic facilitators) explicitly talked about this and discussed how all our experiences and expertise (facilitators, teachers and children) mattered, and how we would consciously and explicitly place all these perspectives at the same level of importance. The questions we were exploring were genuinely open and no one knew the answers to them. By interrogating the Childhood Studies literature, we knew that collaborative approaches to research with children could work, but exactly how they might or might not work in these Indian ELT classrooms was unknown to us all. When returning to their classrooms after the first workshop, teachers repeated this message to the children, i.e. that we/they were going to be involved in something exciting that had not been done before. The children were learning new skills such as how to interview peers or how to construct a survey instrument, and the teachers were learning as they listened to the children's insights, observed them take up active roles enthusiastically, and reflected on the links between their day-to-day classroom experience and the workshop discussions.

Jenlink and Jenlink (2008: 314), writing about democratic learning communities following Dewey, suggest that learning communities *include* rather than exclude views, ideas and suggestions by all and they *create* knowledge rather than assume that knowledge is produced by others. In this process it is to be expected that conflict and difference of opinions will be part of the process. We were committed to democratic learning by providing plenty of time and space for engaging in dialogue in the workshops and in between, by staying in touch using a closed Facebook group. In this process we wanted to honour every voice and thus we constructed respectful relationships in the group. We welcomed both successes and challenges, and we never closed any of these debates with a firm 'right' answer. Whenever the teachers returned to their classrooms they were free to continue with what they felt was already working well, or they could just adjust their work based on any new insights. The teachers often commented that despite the clear focus on children as partners, they felt the 'freedom' they had in interpreting the focus was 'liberating'.

4 Teacher learning in a collaborative action research project

Interestingly, the workshops and the deliberate democratic approach we cultivated was explicitly and consciously mirrored by the teachers in their own classrooms, and the way the workshops were run was commented on throughout the project as a source of learning. Teachers often mentioned that they noticed and appreciated that in the 'non-hierarchical environment of the workshop' everyone felt at ease and was able to contribute without 'being judged'. They noticed that we never criticized anyone's project or contribution but aways encouraged everyone, provided academic articles to read relating to the topic but 'never tested' whether everyone had read these or not, and we treated everyone with patience and respect. Teachers commented that they wanted to mirror these principles in their own classrooms. Since children were elevated to the role of collaborative partners in research whose views were to be considered seriously, a similar democratization process to the one they experienced in the workshops was seen as both necessary and desirable in their own classrooms.

A few teachers described transformative changes in their practice (Pinter and Mathew 2017; Pinter 2021) and began to characterize this process of change in contrasting terms, i.e., juxtaposing what they used to do and believe and what they came to believe and do, affirming their new identities as teacher-researchers working in collaboration with their learners.

At the very beginning the teachers' reaction to the project idea was a mixture of excitement and doubt. Looking back on these doubts at the end, teachers articulated that they changed their perspectives and understanding about what good teaching meant:

> *In 25 years of teaching I never thought about handing over to the children. . . . I always thought as a good teacher my responsibility was to find the best activities for my children but I never thought they themselves should find them. I always thought that the learning has to come from me.*

Another teacher said that she discovered that she underestimated the children until she began to change her mind as a result of this project:

> *I hugely underestimated my class, they are my mentors now; they had ideas and they have taken over [. . .]. I learnt that they [the children] are the best teachers who will teach me.*

Following a more democratic and less hierarchical set-up in the teachers' classrooms both peer–peer and teacher–student relationships changed. Children became more active and more confident, and teachers began to use a lot of group work and for the first time allowed the children to organize their own groups.

> *Collaboration is magic. Gone are the days when I was thinking I was the only one teaching them. Teaching is now a collaborative thing, it is a joy.*
>
> *I always put lot of effort into planning. Now we have rules and we help each other and we collaborate and everyone is involved; learners help each other. Every relationship is based on sharing. Good relationships and good rapport. You want to do things for each other.*

Some teachers felt that the original simple but powerful message of listening to children led to the biggest breakthrough in their practice:

> *Looking into my classroom through a different lens, a different angle, I started to listen to the individual voices. Children want to choose something, I say let's do it.*

Some teachers also described how certain 'difficult-to-reach' learners who never used to participate began to participate. In fact, some children enjoyed the new way of working so much that the project was no longer a project, the way of working simply became the norm.

> *My children now will not accept anything ready-made, they want to do things for themselves. In my class the children themselves will not let me stop after this project.*

Even though experiences in the classroom were the main driving force for change, it was evident that the fruitful combination of theory and practice also helped to drive professional development forward. Teachers regularly commented on the usefulness of the workshop discussions, and when someone mentioned a point or argument that was picked up from reading, others felt motivated to read more too. Teachers commented that the academic content complemented their work:

> *I was lacking before in understanding, I did not have [. . .] but with all that reading now and I have started doing things differently.'*

The academic content and theoretical insights that we were able to link to practice were also mentioned; teachers pointed out specifically that they learnt academic terms and formal expressions to help them articulate their experiences:

> *The most important thing for me is whenever I listen to such things whenever I attend a seminar, I feel that I have got words to my expression. Because of the theory I have got some words to my expression.*

The project gave the teachers a great deal of freedom as to how to interpret the image of the agentic child in their own classrooms and what kind of collaborative work they could engage in together, but at the same time everyone developed the discipline of documenting their own practice. This was necessary to help deepen reflections and to record important aspects of ongoing work so that they could share these with their colleagues at the workshops. Documentation was often mentioned as a new skill they learnt:

I was never like, you know, documented consciously documented anything; but now I am definitely I am doing that.

5 Challenges

The project lasted only one year but due to the various extension activities (such as putting together a handbook of ideas, presenting at various conferences, and working on other publications), our discussions and loose collaboration is still ongoing several years after the project was officially completed. The evaluation of the project has been overwhelmingly positive and I am aware that many of the teachers are still working with children in the same way, involving them in decision-making, exploring issues in their classrooms together, providing support and training for children working on interview questions or designing survey instruments to explore various aspects of their L2 learning and beyond.

However, in addition to the many positive outcomes, we have had to grapple with some challenges and ethical dilemmas. One of the most pressing issues was around school support for the project. The teachers came from different parts of India, from different types of schools, and while the learning community we created was a great source of support for all, in between the actual workshops the teachers were rather isolated. Their school authorities all officially supported the project at the beginning (except for one teacher whose case was discussed in Mathew and Pinter 2021), but we noticed that over time this support started to dwindle, and in some cases decreased dramatically due to change of principals, for example. The teachers were facing all kinds of pressures with exams and in some cases parents and colleagues questioning their efforts in experimenting with these innovative ideas in their classrooms. Some teachers were able to cascade what they learnt to interested colleagues who were keen to know more about the project, but others faced resistance and even criticism. Teacher-researchers' struggles to be legitimatized by their colleagues have been documented elsewhere (e.g., Burns 2017) and the fact that their reception in their schools was mixed is not surprising. However, given that the experimentation with children as active partners in longitudinal projects will impact the day-to-day teaching and learning processes in any school in quite a substantial way, it would have been desirable to extend the boundaries of the learning community to everyone in all these schools (Burns et al. 2022). Unfortunately, this was not possible within the constraints of the project.

Looking at the issues from the children's side, some believe that research with children is ethical only if it benefits them directly. But how is benefit interpreted? We have plenty of evidence that the children who participated in these classrooms benefited in many ways (such as gaining new skills in interviewing, collaborating with peers, or learning presentation skills). But when they had to move to another class, for example, or be taught by another teacher, they were often disappointed that they could not continue with their active participation. In this sense the longitudinal design was a double-edged sword. Once encouraged to embrace a more active way of working and collaborating with the teacher, is it ethical to be told to go back to old ways? As one teacher commented:

> When my children went to the secondary school, my colleague phoned me and said these children are different, they seem to want to tell me what to do.

The tension between hierarchical set-ups in schools and projects that take children's views seriously has been documented in the literature (e.g., Leach 2020), and it is a huge challenge to find and navigate that third space where fruitful experimentation can thrive. Even the best intentions of empowering children are ultimately negated by larger forces of hierarchical school systems. As long as schools remain rigid and hierarchical, any attempt to involve children in active roles in teaching and learning processes or in research can only partially succeed and/or have limited impact. Fielding and Moss (2011) suggest that in order to promote child participation we need democratic schools characterized by dialogue, respect, care and inclusivity, where learning is emergent and dynamically shared between learners and teachers. At the heart of democratic education lies the process of empowering students (Collins, Hess, and Lowery 2019), and in democratic schools the idea of children becoming partners in research would fit well.

6 Conclusion

The ultimate ethical question that I had to grapple with is this: Is it ethical to promote a longitudinal project with the active involvement of children against the grain of a rigid hierarchical system? Some might say that it is not, but I am somewhat encouraged by Schostak, Clarke and Hammersley-Fletcher (2020: 192), who suggest that despite the difficulties, experiments in democracy on the 'margins' are worthwhile because they will attract the curious and the committed, such as teachers who can at least create precious pockets of democratic learning. Such pockets of democratic education will continue 'to provide evidence of the irrepressibility of the democratic spirit' (ibid.), and who knows how they might inspire those who enjoyed being even just a small part of it?

References

Barratt-Hacking, Elisabeth & Robert Barratt. 2009. Children researching their urban environment: Developing a methodology. *Education 3-13* 37(4). 371–383.

Burns, Anne. 2017. This life-changing experience: Teachers be(come)ing action researchers. In Garry Barkhuizen (ed.), *Reflections of language teacher identity*, 133–138. London: Routledge.

Burns, Anne, Emily Edwards & Neville John Ellis. 2022. *Sustaining action research: A practical guide for institutional engagement*. New York & Abingdon: Routledge.

Collins, Julia, Michael E. Hess & Charles L. Lowery. 2019. Democratic spaces: How teachers establish and sustain democracy and education in their classrooms. *Democracy and Education* 27(1). Article 3.

Enever, Janet (ed.). 2011. *ELLiE: Early Language Learning in Europe*. London: British Council.

Enever, Janet & Eva Lindgren (eds.). 2017. *Early language learning: Complexity and mixed methods*. Bristol: Multilingual Matters.

Fielding, Michael & Peter Moss. 2011. *Radical education and the common school: A democratic alternative*. London: Routledge.

Garton, Sue & Fiona Copland (eds.). 2019. *The Routledge handbook of teaching English to young learners*. London: Routledge.

Hart, Roger A. 1992. *Children's participation: From tokenism to citizenship*. Florence: UNICEF International Child Development Centre.

James, Allison & Alan Prout (eds.). 1997. *Constructing and reconstructing childhood*, 2nd edn. Basingstoke: Falmer Press.

Jenlink, Patrick M. & Karen E. Jenlink 2008. Creating democratic learning communities: Transformative work as spatial practice. *Theory into Practice* 47(4). 311–317.

Kehily, Mary Jane (ed.). 2009. *An introduction to childhood studies*. Milton Keynes: Open University Press.

Kellett, Mary. 2005. *How to develop children as researchers: A step-by-step guide to teaching the research process*. London: Sage.

Kellett, Mary. 2010. *Rethinking children and research: Attitudes in contemporary society*. London: Continuum.

Leach, Tony. 2020. Democracy in the classroom. In John Schostak, Matthew Clarke & Linda Hammersley-Fletcher (eds.), *Paradoxes of democracy, leadership and education*, 147–158. Abingdon & New York: Routledge.

Lomax, Helen. 2012. Contested voices? Methodological tensions in creative visual research with children. *International Journal of Social Research Methodology* 15(2). 105–117.

Lundy, Laura. 2007. 'Voice' is not enough: Conceptualising Article 12 of the United Nations Convention on the Rights of the Child. *British Educational Research Journal* 33(6). 927–942.

Lundy, Laura & Lesley McEvoy. 2012. Childhood, the United Nations Convention on the Rights of the Child and research: What constitutes a 'rights-based' approach? In Michael Freeman (ed.), *Law and childhood*, 75–91. Oxford: Oxford University Press.

Lundy, Laura, Lesley McEvoy & Bronagh Byrne. 2011. Working with young children as co-researchers: An approach informed by the United Nations Convention on the Rights of the Child. *Early Education & Development* 22(5). 714–736.

Mathew, Rama & Annamaria Pinter. 2021. Teachers and children as co-researchers in Indian classrooms. In Annamaria Pinter & Kuchah Kuchah (eds.), *Ethical and methodological issues in researching young language learners in school contexts*, 206–222. Bristol: Multilingual Matters.

Mourão, Sandie & Monica Lourenço (eds.). 2015. *Early years second language education*. London: Routledge.

Nikolov, Marianne (ed.). 2016. *Assessing young learners of English: Global and local perspectives*. Switzerland: Springer International.

Philp, Jennifer, Rhonda Oliver & Alison Mackey (eds.). 2008. *Second language acquisition and the young learner: Child's play?* Amsterdam: John Benjamins.

Pinter, Annamaria. 2021. 'You gave us a lens to look through': Teacher transformation and long-term impact of action research. *Issues in Educational Research* 31(4). 1195–2012.

Pinter, Annamaria & Rama Mathew. 2017. Teacher development opportunities in an action research project: Primary English teachers working with children as co-researchers. In Eva Wilden & Raphaela Porsch (eds.), *The professional development of primary EFL teachers*, 141–152. Münster: Waxman.

Rinaldi, Carlina. 2006. *In dialogue with Reggio Emilia: Listening, researching and learning*. London: Routledge.

Robinson, Carol & Carol A. Taylor. 2013. Student voice as a contested practice: Power and participation in two student voice projects. *Improving Schools* 16(1). 32–46.

Schostak, John, Matthew Clarke & Linda Hammersley-Fletcher. 2020. Conclusion. In John Schostak, Matthew Clarke & Linda Hammersely-Fletcher (eds.), *Paradoxes of democracy, leadership and education*, 190–195. London: Routledge.

Shier, Harry. 2001. Pathways to participation: Openings, opportunities and obligations. *Children & Society* 15(2). 107–117.

Spyrou, Spyros. 2018. *Disclosing childhoods*. London: Palgrave Macmillan.

United Nations. 1989. *United Nations Convention on the Rights of the Child*. New York: United Nations.

Walkerdine, Valerie. 2009. Developmental psychology and the study of childhood. In Mary Jane Kehily (ed.), *An introduction to childhood studies*, 112–123. Maidenhead: Open University Press.

Zeichner, Ken, Katherina A. Payne & Kate Brayko. 2015. Democratizing teacher education. *Journal of Teacher Education* 66(2). 122–135.

David Little and Déirdre Kirwan

6 Managing linguistic diversity in an Irish primary school: Reciprocal collaboration in practice and research

Abstract: This chapter explores the role of collaboration and reciprocity in the development, documentation and interpretation of one Irish primary school's approach to the management of extreme linguistic diversity – more than 50 home languages among 320 pupils. The approach, which to the best of our knowledge is *sui generis*, has two key features: pupils' home languages played a significant role in the educational process even though they were mostly unknown to the teachers; and pupils from immigrant families successfully transferred their emerging literacy skills in English and Irish to their home language, mostly without benefit of explicit instruction. The chapter begins by focusing on the reciprocal nature of the collaboration between the two authors, the former principal of the school (Déirdre Kirwan) and a researcher (David Little). It then describes what the school's approach looked like in 2014/2015, after some twenty years of continuous development, and refers to some of the theory and research on which we drew to understand and illuminate it. The chapter goes on to explore the complex web of reciprocal collaboration that characterized the successive phases of development. The conclusion argues that without such collaboration it is impossible to maintain the interdependence of pedagogical theory, classroom practice and ongoing exploratory research on which educational progress depends.

1 Introduction

The *Concise Oxford Dictionary* defines reciprocity as 'the practice of exchanging things with others for mutual benefit'. In educational research, collaboration usually means one of two things. Either researchers collect data from teachers and learners in order to test a hypothesis, in which case the benefit to teachers and learners may not be obvious; or else teachers and researchers collaborate to solve some problem of teaching and learning, in which case (assuming a successful intervention) teachers have an easier life and researchers add to their list of publications. In this chapter we describe a different kind of collaboration. Its purpose has been to describe and understand successful practice in ways that link it to major themes in the relevant research literature and provide practitioners in other contexts with a principled basis for replication. In its present form our collaboration began in 2012, but it existed in two different forms at earlier stages in a developmental process that depended on a reciprocal relation between pedagogical theory and classroom practice.

For almost thirty years Déirdre Kirwan (henceforth DK) was principal of the primary school in focus, Scoil Bhríde (Cailíní) (SBC; St Brigid's School for Girls),[1] Blanchardstown, Dublin; her contribution to the collaboration has been a narrative framed by the strongly child-centred Primary School Curriculum (Government of Ireland 1999) and a corpus of qualitative data – video recordings of classroom interactions, examples of pupils' written work, teachers' work plans and monthly reports, accounts of particularly illuminating classroom episodes, interviews with pupils, teachers and special needs assistants. David Little (henceforth DL) has contributed descriptive and analytical tools, notably the theory of language learner autonomy (Little, Dam, and Legenhausen 2017) and the Council of Europe's concept of plurilingual and intercultural education (Council of Europe 2001). The never-ending dialogue of the collaborative process has yielded mutual benefits: for DK, a means of detaching the daily round of teaching and learning from its immediate context and bringing its achievements into sharp relief; for DL, a practical understanding of one version of plurilingual and intercultural education and new insights into (language) learner autonomy. These benefits are, of course, two sides of the same coin.

In the next section we describe Scoil Bhríde's approach in the school year prior to DK's retirement, emphasizing in particular its dependence on collaboration and reciprocity at all levels of the school. We then summarize four stages in the evolution of the approach, and we conclude by arguing that without reciprocal collaboration of the kind we have described, educational research is unlikely to influence classroom practice for the better.

2 Plurilingual education in practice, 2014/2015

2.1 The school

In Ireland primary schooling begins at the age of 4½ and lasts for eight years. The first two years, Junior and Senior Infants, correspond to pre-school in other

---

[1] It is estimated that around 17 per cent of primary pupils and a third of post-primary students attend single-sex schools in Ireland. The tide of opinion, however, is running against single-sex education: no new single-sex school has been established this century.

countries, and they are followed by six grades, known as 'Classes'. In the school year 2014/2015, SBC had 320 pupils ranging in age from 4½ to 12½+; 80 per cent of them came from immigrant families; most of the 80 per cent had little or no English when they started school as Junior Infants; and altogether the school had 51 home languages (HLs) other than English. Some of those languages were present in most classes; others were represented by just one family or a single pupil. Extreme linguistic diversity was matched by very great ethnic and cultural diversity, which served to underline the uniqueness of each pupil (for further details, see Little and Kirwan 2019: 29–30). We use the epithet EAL (English as an Additional Language) to designate pupils from immigrant families whose home language was not English.

2.2 A plurilingual approach to primary education

When immigrant parents enrolled their daughters, the principal emphasized the importance of HL maintenance and explained that SBC encouraged the use of HLs inside as well as outside the classroom. She further explained that this policy derived from the school's commitment to inclusive education: a pupil's HL was central to her identity, and she could not be fully included if her HL had no part in the life of the school. From their first contact with SBC it was made clear to parents that the success of their daughters' education depended on effective collaboration between school and home.

From the beginning of Junior Infants, EAL pupils naturally used their HLs to communicate with those of their peers who spoke the same or a closely related language. Reciprocal communication of this kind continued at all levels of the school, especially during breaks in the school yard. HLs were also used in pair and group work – pupils reported their conclusions to the teacher and the rest of the class in English.

Irish is the obligatory second language of the curriculum from the beginning to the end of schooling. Whether pupils came from Irish or immigrant families, they encountered the language for the first time when they started school. SBC had a tradition of teaching Irish communicatively. Thus, in Junior Infants pupils learned to count, carry out simple calculations, work with colours and shapes, and play action games in Irish as well as English. HLs were also included in these activities, which were performed first in English, then in Irish, and after that in all the HLs present in the class. In this way the willing participation of all pupils was secured, their learning was reinforced, and Irish came to serve as a bridge between English and HLs. Here too collaboration between school and home played an important role. In a school where languages are valued, everyone wants to have at least two languages and preferably more, and some parents, newcomers as well as Irish, asked the school to organize Irish classes so that they could share in their daughters' plurilingual development. The school secretary also took steps to improve her Irish so that she could respond to pupils when they addressed her in Irish.

The Primary School Curriculum is strongly child-centred: 'the child's existing knowledge and experience form the basis for learning' and 'the child is an active agent in his or her learning' (Government of Ireland 1999: 8). This ethos implies that the dynamic of teaching and learning should be dialogic: pupils as well as teachers should have the right to take discourse initiatives. Besides encouraging active participation, the inclusion of HLs in Junior Infants made pupils aware that they could make a unique contribution to the life of the classroom. This helps to explain their subsequent readiness to initiate linguistic comparison and analysis and undertake ambitious language-related projects either individually or collaboratively. The inclusion of HLs constantly fed the reciprocity that is fundamental to effective classroom communication: each class functioned as a community not despite but because of the individuality of each pupil.

Already in Junior Infants pupils are surrounded by print, but they are taught to write in English and Irish from the beginning of Senior Infants, when they are 5½+. In SBC basic writing skills were linked to the pupil's identity. For example, in class they copied from the whiteboard onto a simple worksheet sentences like: 'My school is Scoil Bhríde. My teacher is Miss – ' and drew a picture of themselves and their teacher. They then took the worksheet home and their parents showed them how to add the equivalent in their HL.

Learning to write in Irish was treated as an extension of learning to write in English and involved the same activities. For example, the teacher might devote an Irish lesson to the collaborative production of a simple story: the class agreed on a theme and the pupils suggested each successive sentence, which the teacher wrote on the whiteboard, correcting errors without comment. The pupils copied the story into their notebooks and reinforced their learning of Irish by writing an English version for homework. By Third Class (8½+) pupils from immigrant families began to write versions in their HL too, which they read aloud to the rest of the class. In this way, HLs were further acknowledged and valorized. The texts that pupils wrote in their HLs were no less ambitious than those they wrote in English and Irish – the goal was usually to write *parallel* texts; and when they began to learn French, in Fifth Class, it became another medium of written communication. By the time pupils left SBC, they had acquired age-appropriate literacy in English, Irish, French and (in the case of EAL pupils) their HL (for further details and a wealth of practical examples, see Little and Kirwan 2019: 87–125).

The cultural diversity that EAL pupils brought with them was accepted along with their linguistic diversity. Their pre-school experience, after all, was inseparable from their HL, which had been the medium of their primary enculturation. SBC's approach to inclusive education accepted all cultures as equal. Pupils could not help but be aware of the differences between them; but those differences fed into the reciprocal collaboration that characterized the school's plurilingual approach – visitors to SBC frequently commented on the school's harmonious atmosphere. Certainly, there was no room for the focus on 'otherness' that is central to so much discussion of interculturality.

In addition to the learning outcomes already described, SBC's pupils developed high levels of language awareness stimulated by non-stop cross-linguistic comparison. The school was rated in the top 12 per cent for Irish, and in the standardized tests of English and Maths that its pupils took each year from First to Sixth Class, it performed consistently above the national average.

2.3 The interaction of theory, research and practice

We have tried to make our description of SBC's plurilingual approach as 'neutral' as possible, but even in this necessarily compressed version it is shaped by our ongoing attempt to describe and interpret the school's evolved practice in ways that link it to key issues in theory and research. A handful of examples must do duty for many.

At the beginning of our collaboration we agreed that we needed to determine the functions performed by HLs in the classroom. Common sense suggested and observation confirmed that when HLs were mostly unknown to the teachers, they could be used in three ways: for reciprocal communication between pupils with the same or closely related HLs; for purposes of display – 'This is what we say in my language'; and as a source of linguistic intuition and insight. This is clearly reflected in the structure of our description.

It then became clear that the successful implementation of the three functions depended on the kind of exploratory talk implied by the ethos of the Primary School Curriculum. This suggested a link with work in dialogic pedagogy that has its origins in classroom research carried out in England in the 1970s. One of the leaders of this research was Douglas Barnes, who argued (Barnes 1976) that exploratory talk brings 'school knowledge' (the curriculum) into interaction with learners' 'action knowledge' (the complex of knowledge, skills, attitudes and beliefs that they bring with them). The school knowledge/action knowledge dichotomy proved a fruitful way of conceptualizing the special challenge faced by pupils whose HL is not a variety of the language of schooling. Other work that has offered a useful lens through which to 'read' SBC's pedagogical practice includes Jerome Bruner's work on the language of education (e.g., Bruner 1986),

John Dewey's exploration of the relation between the curriculum and the learner (Dewey [1902] 1990), and Robin Alexander's theory of dialogic pedagogy (Alexander 2020),.

Barnes's argument that it is the task of education to bring the curriculum into fruitful interaction with learners' action knowledge played a central role in the theorization of learner autonomy in classroom learning (Little, Dam, and Legenhausen 2017: 6–9). If education starts from wherever the learners happen to be, it makes sense to engage their action knowledge by having them share responsibility for identifying learning targets, selecting learning activities and managing the learning process. SBC's approach also resonated with other arguments that DL had deployed in his theoretical work on learner autonomy, for example: the key role played by a reciprocal instinct in the earliest stages of child development (e.g., Trevarthen 1992); dialogic theories of language and cognition (e.g., Bråten 1992; Linell 2009); the link between motivation and the human drive for autonomy (e.g., Deci and Flaste 1996; Ryan and Deci 2017). Most of the literature on learner autonomy is concerned with pedagogical approaches that explicitly set out to exploit and further develop learners' inborn capacity for autonomous behaviour. SBC showed that autonomy emerges and develops spontaneously when certain pedagogical conditions are met.

Finally, SBC's policy and practice coincided with the Council of Europe's plurilingual approach, first outlined in the *Common European Framework of Reference for Languages* (CEFR), which seeks to develop 'a communicative competence to which all knowledge and experience of language contributes and in which languages interrelate and interact' (Council of Europe 2001: 4). The undoubted success SBC has achieved allows us to offer detailed guidance on the implementation of a plurilingual approach in schools with linguistically diverse pupil or student populations (Little and Kirwan 2021).

3 The evolution of SBC's approach

3.1 The early years (1994–1999)

In 1994 SBC enrolled its first EAL pupil, an eight-year-old Bosnian girl who was a refugee from the Balkan war. The school had no previous experience of integrating pupils whose home language was not English, and there was general amazement at the speed with which this new arrival learned to speak the language. Two years later, four more Bosnian pupils were enrolled at different levels in the school; they made much less rapid progress. From the mid 1990s, for the first time in its history,

Ireland began to experience large-scale immigration – refugees, asylum seekers, economic migrants. At the beginning of each school year, queues formed outside SBC as newly arrived parents sought to enrol their children, and throughout the school year new pupils continued to arrive. The number of languages, cultures and religious affiliations grew at a dizzying pace; in less than a decade half of SBC's pupils came from non-English/Irish-speaking backgrounds.

In the 1990s the internet was in its infancy and mobile phones were not ubiquitous, so schools lacked today's rapid access to information; and to begin with, they received little official support. In responding to the challenge of integrating its increasingly diverse pupil cohort, SBC was guided above all by two considerations. First, although EAL pupils must become proficient in English if they were to fulfil their educational potential, DK was not convinced that this should happen at the expense of their HLs. In nineteenth-century Ireland, language loss was accelerated by educating Irish-speaking pupils exclusively through English, and it was important that the HLs of SBC's EAL pupils should not suffer a similar fate. DK also feared that loss of home languages would create resentment and impact negatively on social cohesion in the school and in society at large. So besides valuing pupils' languages and cultures, the school set out to encourage HL maintenance and to include immigrant parents in their daughters' learning and the life of the school. At the same time, account had to be taken of the concerns of the autochthonous Irish community, whose environment was undergoing rapid change. DK ensured that SBC's developing policy and practice were regularly communicated to the Board of Management and the Parents' Association, and the newsletters that were sent to all parents invariably emphasized the benefits of being able to use more than one language. Irish and newcomer parents were invited into classrooms to talk about their own experience of school, and from the end of the 1990s newcomer parents were elected to SBC's Board of Management and the committee of the Parents' Association. As regards the curriculum, there was some apprehension that a multilingual pupil cohort could have a negative impact on the learning of Irish. SBC had always placed a high value on the teaching and learning of the language, and in response to rapidly increasing diversity, teachers made a determined effort to use Irish more frequently in all aspects of school life. This meant that all pupils experienced Irish as a living language that was part of everyday communication.

In the early years, then, SBC responded to the challenge of diversity by adopting a policy of mutual respect, collaboration and reciprocity and began to implement pedagogical practices that included HLs and made it possible for Irish to play a key role in subsequent developments. The school's approach evolved gradually over the years, it was greeted with enthusiasm by the pupils, and its impact on learning outcomes was entirely positive. This helps to explain why DK and her colleagues encountered no serious opposition from parents.

3.2 Integrate Ireland Language and Training (2000–2008)

In 2000 DL established Integrate Ireland Language and Training (IILT), a not-for-profit campus company of Trinity College Dublin. IILT was fully funded by the Department of Education to provide intensive English language courses for adult refugees and to support primary and post-primary schools in their efforts to develop the English language proficiency of their EAL pupils and students. In fulfilment of this latter function, IILT published *English Language Proficiency Benchmarks* for both sectors (IILT 2003a, 2003b) together with versions of the European Language Portfolio (ELP; IILT 2004a, 2004b). For primary schools it also published *Up and Away*, a handbook for teachers (IILT 2006), and an assessment kit (Little, Lazenby Simpson, and Ćatibušić 2007). All of IILT's resources were based on the *Benchmarks*, which in turn were based on the first three proficiency levels of the CEFR. Thus, the resources reflected the ethos of the Council of Europe as expressed in the CEFR. In particular, by treating learners as autonomous social agents and language learning as a variety of language use, they encouraged pedagogical methods that sought to develop learner agency and assigned a central role to spontaneous use of English. IILT's work was shaped by collaboration and reciprocity: the *Benchmarks* were structured around thirteen curriculum themes identified by focus groups of practising teachers, and all resources were piloted by teachers who attended IILT's twice-yearly in-service days.

One of the most important responsibilities of a school principal is to lead learning, which often requires new learning on the part of the principal herself. DK decided that she needed to know more about language learning and teaching if she was to encourage, motivate and support her colleagues and pupils and inform the pupils' parents; so she regularly attended IILT's in-service days with two of her language support teachers, and as a result SBC adopted the *Benchmarks* and the ELP. Although IILT was charged with supporting the development of EAL pupils' proficiency in English, the in-service days emphasized the importance of encouraging home language maintenance; this was based on international research findings but also on the human rights perspective that the *Benchmarks* inherited from the CEFR. This helped to validate SBC's emerging policy and practice.

3.3 Déirdre Kirwan's PhD research (2004–2009)

At the end of the 1990s, the Department of Education began to fund two years of English language support for each EAL pupil. In order to maximize the benefits of this provision, it was important to know as much as possible about the relation between language teaching and language learning: how progress was likely to be promoted but also inhibited. Having experienced the research-informed basis of IILT's work, DK decided that she should undertake some research of her own. She approached DL, who encouraged her to register as a part-time PhD student under his supervision. The period of her research coincided with rapid growth in the number of EAL pupils attending the school. In 2003, they accounted for 20 per cent of SBC's enrolment; by September 2004, this had risen to 30 per cent because 50 per cent of the intake into Junior Infants was non-Irish; and in 2005, 80 per cent of Junior Infants were EAL pupils.

DK set out to document the language development and curriculum learning of individual children in four groups of EAL pupils. She used a detailed account of what was happening in one school year (2005–2006) to explore the impact of the school's policy and practice (Kirwan 2009). In the course of her research, she became familiar with DL's work on learner autonomy, which emphasizes the importance of putting the learner's identity and interests at the centre of the learning process. Coinciding with the ethos of the Primary School Curriculum (Government of Ireland 1999), this became the lens through which DK and her colleagues viewed the delivery of curriculum content.

DK shared the successive phases of her research with her colleagues in SBC: key issues raised by her literature review; her approach to data collection and its implications for classroom practice; and her interpretation of the data. In this way, SBC's developing policy and practice were explicitly linked to local and international research concerns. Analysis of the data – samples of pupils' written work and transcriptions of video recordings of English language support classes – confirmed that SBC's inclusion of HLs was beneficial for the learning of all pupils: DK was able to reassure parents that plurilingualism could only enhance their daughters' education. It also became clear that exposure to multiple languages benefited autochthonous Irish pupils.

By the time DK completed her PhD research, SBC had joined the Modern Languages in Primary Schools Initiative and French was part of the curriculum in Fifth and Sixth Class. The school also began to experience three benefits of its approach. First, respect for and interest in the languages of others contributed to social cohesion: collaboration and reciprocity in teaching and learning had a direct impact on the school as a community. What is more, the use of HLs had an obvious impact on pupils' motivation and the quality of their work, and this increased teachers' commitment to SBC's integrated approach to language learning. Secondly, the presence of so many other languages in the life of the classroom caused the status of Irish to rise and its use by teachers, pupils and ancillary staff to increase – many Irish pupils came to think of Irish as their HL. Thirdly, individually and collaboratively pupils began to undertake ambitious language-related projects on their own initiative. This arose from the fact that the pupils rather than the teachers were expert in their HLs and provided a focus for collaboration and reciprocity in the classroom.

Also at this time, the school staff developed language and intercultural policy documents that were approved by the Board of Management and the Parents' Association (Little & Kirwan 2019, Appendix). These documents were not required by the Department of Education, but the staff felt they were necessary as a statement of the school's ethos and for purposes of information. Informally and in interviews conducted by DK, teachers clearly stated that they could never return to the way they taught before adopting SBC's version of the plurilingual approach.

3.4 The beginning of our current collaboration (2012–2015)

In October 2012 DK invited DL to meet her and four Fifth and Sixth Class teachers to talk about self-assessment. While they were waiting for the teachers to join them, DK showed DL some examples of pupils' written work, including parallel texts they had written in English, Irish and their HLs. DL suggested that the wider educational world should be made aware of SBC's approach to the management of linguistic diversity. As a first step he and DK agreed that they would offer a paper to a forthcoming international conference on multilingualism in education. This decision had two immediate consequences. First, it was necessary to summarize SBC's policy and practice in a principled way in order to provide ourselves with a basis for description, interpretation and argument. This was a straightforward task. The school had two overarching educational goals: to ensure that EAL pupils became fully proficient in English as language of schooling and to convert linguistic diversity into educational capital that benefited all pupils. In pursuit of these goals, policy and pedagogy were shaped by an inclusive ethos, an open language policy, and a strong emphasis on the development of language awareness and home language literacy. This summary enabled us to begin to categorize the qualitative data DK had already collected and use it to illustrate our exploration of SBC's approach.

The second consequence of our decision was to impose a clear structure on the collection of classroom data. This required the willing cooperation of pupils as well as teachers. In several classes pupils themselves devised activities and projects to explore particular issues – adjective placement in all the languages present in a class; intercomprehension between closely related languages – so that they effectively became collaborators in the research. Not wanting to be left behind by their EAL peers, some Irish pupils began to learn additional languages from older siblings, neighbours, parents and grandparents – the latter evidently enjoyed reviving skills they thought they had forgotten in order to support their children's or grandchildren's learning. This strand of reciprocal collaboration was greatly appreciated by pupils. In a discussion DK recorded with Sixth Class pupils, one girl said that SBC's inclusion of home languages made it possible for her parents to be fully involved in her education, for which she was really grateful. Her classmates agreed.

Our first joint conference presentation aroused a great deal of interest and we were invited to contribute chapters to two edited volumes (Little and Kirwan 2018a, 2018b). Preparing these chapters, we quickly came to realize that we needed to write a book-length study of SBC's approach (Little and Kirwan 2019), and we began work on this during DK's last year as principal. This brought one final strand of reciprocal collaboration: the teachers on whom we depended for much of our data were powerfully motivated by the thought that their innovative work was beginning to gain international recognition.

4 Conclusion: A never-ending story

Our account of the evolution of SBC's version of the plurilingual approach has brought us back to our starting point in 2014/2015. The implication of a closed circle, however, is misleading. Our collaboration continues, and with each new invitation to contribute a chapter or give a talk, whether individually or jointly, we find new resonances to explore between aspects of SBC's classroom practice and one or another dimension of educational theory or research. This is surely as it should be: reciprocal collaboration finds no final resting point because the interdependence of theory and practice itself reaches towards infinity. Prior to our collaboration, reciprocity was a defining feature of the very different work we were engaged in. As we have explained, DK's first response to the challenge of linguistic diversity was shaped by a perception of the need to develop and exploit reciprocities between home and school, pupils and parents, and the increasing number of languages in the school; and since the 1990s, DL's understanding of the nature and power of learner autonomy has been relational: learners enjoy exercising their autonomy not because it releases them from restraint but because it frees them to become themselves in collaboration with their peers (Little 1991). Both perspectives place a high premium on social capital, and as David Hargreaves has written of school leadership:

> When social capital in an organisation is at a high level, people start to share their *intellectual capital*, that is, their knowledge, skills and experience: as they trust and respect one another, they do not feel the need to protect their intellectual capital and guard it from others. When people offer to share their knowledge and experience, reciprocity is enhanced

along with trust. In other words, as intellectual capital gets shared, social capital rises, and a virtuous circle between intellectual and social capital is stimulated [. . .]. (Hargreaves 2011: 17; italics in original)

These words seem to us an apt description of the impact on SBC of collaboration that emphasizes the reciprocal relation between research and practice. They also encapsulate our view that education itself is a collaborative process whose success depends on reciprocity, and they explain why we doubt the value of educational research that does not insist on the interdependence of pedagogical theory, classroom practice and empirical exploration.

References

Alexander, Robin. 2020. *A dialogic teaching companion*. London: Routledge.
Barnes, Douglas. 1976. *From communication to curriculum*. Harmondsworth: Penguin.
Bråten, Stein. 1992. The virtual other in infants' minds and social feelings. In Astrid Heen Wold (ed.), *The dialogical alternative: Towards a theory of language and mind*, 77–98. Oslo: Scandinavian University Press.
Bruner, Jerome. 1986. The language of education. In Jerome Bruner, *Actual minds, possible worlds*, 121–133. Cambridge, MA: Harvard University Press.
Council of Europe. 2001. *Common European Framework of Reference for Languages: Learning, teaching, assessment*. Cambridge: Cambridge University Press.
Deci, Edward L. & Richard Flaste. 1996. *Why we do what we do: Understanding self-motivation*. New York: Penguin.
Dewey, John. [1902] 1990. *The school and society. The child and the curriculum*. Chicago: University of Chicago Press.
Government of Ireland. 1999. *Primary School Curriculum: Introduction / Curaclam na Bunscoile: Réamhrá*. Dublin: Stationery Office.
Hargreaves, David H. 2011. Leading a self-improving school system. Nottingham: National College for School Leadership. https://assets.publishing.service.gov.uk/government/uploads/system/up loads/attachment_data/file/325890/leading-a-self-improving-school-system.pdf (accessed 11 February 2022).
IILT (Integrate Ireland Language and Training). 2003a. *English Language Proficiency Benchmarks for non-English-speaking pupils at primary level*. Dublin: Integrate Ireland Language and Training.
IILT (Integrate Ireland Language and Training). 2003b. *English Language Proficiency Benchmarks for non-English-speaking students at post-primary level*. Dublin: Integrate Ireland Language and Training.
IILT (Integrate Ireland Language and Training). 2004a. *European Language Portfolio: Learning the language of the host community (primary)*. Dublin: Integrate Ireland Language and Training.
IILT (Integrate Ireland Language and Training). 2004b. *European Language Portfolio: Learning the language of the host community (post-primary)*. Dublin: Integrate Ireland Language and Training.
IILT (Integrate Ireland Language and Training). 2006. *Up and Away*. Dublin: Integrate Ireland Language and Training.

Kirwan, Déirdre. 2009. Language support for newcomer learners in Irish primary schools: A review and a case study. PhD thesis, University of Dublin, Trinity College.

Linell, Per. 2009. *Rethinking language, mind and world dialogically*. Charlotte, NC: Information Age Publishing.

Little, David. 1991. *Learner autonomy 1: Definitions, issues and problems*. Dublin: Authentik.

Little, David, Leni Dam & Lienhard Legenhausen. 2017. *Language learner autonomy: Theory, practice and research*. Bristol: Multilingual Matters.

Little, David & Déirdre Kirwan. 2018a. Translanguaging as a key to educational success: The experience of one Irish primary school. In Piet Van Avermaet, Stef Slembrouck, Koen Van Gorp, Sven Sierens & Katrijn Maryns (eds.), *The multilingual edge of education*, 313–339. London: Palgrave Macmillan.

Little, David & Déirdre Kirwan. 2018b. From plurilingual repertoires to language awareness: Developing primary pupils' proficiency in the language of schooling. In Carolijn Frijns, Koen Van Gorp, Christine Hélot & Sven Sierens (eds.), *Language awareness in multilingual classrooms in Europe*, 169–205. Boston & Berlin: De Gruyter Mouton.

Little, David & Déirdre Kirwan. 2019. *Engaging with linguistic diversity: A study of educational inclusion in an Irish primary school*. London: Bloomsbury Academic.

Little, David & Déirdre Kirwan. 2021. *Language and languages in the primary school: Some guidelines for teachers*. Dublin: Post-Primary Languages Ireland.

Little, David, Barbara Lazenby Simpson & Bronagh Finnegan Ćatibušić. 2007. *Primary school assessment kit*. Dublin: Department of Education and Science.

Ryan, Richard M. & Edward L. Deci. 2017. *Self-determination theory: Basic psychological needs in motivation, development and wellness*. New York & London: Guilford Press.

Trevarthen, Colwyn. 1992. An infant's motive for speaking and thinking in the culture. In Astrid Heen Wold (ed.), *The dialogical alternative: Towards a theory of language and mind*, 99–137. Oslo: Scandinavian University Press.

Part 3: **Collaborative research in professional development**

Tanya M. McCarthy
7 Collaboration, reciprocity, and challenges: Professional development-in-practice

Abstract: This chapter describes a collaborative research initiative conducted in Japan that encouraged the professional development of young researchers. An area of concern was students' lack of experience with real-world contexts in their L2. A scientific research exchange programme was thus arranged to help prepare students for the world beyond their labs. Throughout the initiative, the author gleaned various insights. Five core principles of collaborative research were identified: dynamic relationships, autonomous learning, knowledge transfer, sharing resources, and professionalism. Three distinct partnerships emerged: learner/learner, instructor/learner, and instructor/instructor. The central aspects underpinning all partnerships were the benefits of collaboration and reciprocity, and the challenges faced and overcome. It was found that the collaborative partnerships functioned effectively when collaborators shared problems and devised solutions, made personal breakthroughs, and committed to the collective's as well as the individual's needs. Reciprocity was achieved through dyadic relationships that lasted for a long duration and had a meaningful impact. Challenges overcome were mainly scheduling, trust, and technological issues. The chapter concludes with the thought that as current research trends continue to shift to global collaborative and interdisciplinary initiatives, it is beneficial to provide training programmes for young researchers to prepare them for their professional life.

1 Introduction

Professional development is an essential part of education for young researchers to succeed in academia as well as the professional world. For the most part, it is looked upon as a process that prepares individuals for the job market. Most universities, for instance, have career centres which provide services to assist with job hunting or placement or invite speakers from companies to give promotional talks. However, professional development for young researchers, in the form of gaining practical competencies and real-life experiences, is also required to help them take advantage of any opportunities and understand how to deal with the challenges of international research. In this study, I define professional development as processes and practices that improve knowledge, skills and attitudes and also encourage social, intellectual and metacognitive development.

Although Japan has some of the top scientific graduate programmes in the world, professional development training programmes and services for graduate students in their L2 remain somewhat underdeveloped. The professional development skills of presenting at international conferences to different audiences, responding to critiques of research, or networking with potential collaborators are offered to varying degrees depending on the educational philosophy of the research department. At my university, only the departments which fully embrace a multilingual environment are able to meet the specific needs of young researchers, and multilingual departments are few. Further, in graduate schools, learners have limited opportunities to meet, share research, and network with others outside their labs or cross interdisciplinary boundaries. A scientific research exchange programme was thus arranged to help prepare students professionally for the world beyond their labs. The idea was for students to work collaboratively to practise skills they would need to perform effectively in the real-life scenarios they would face during and beyond their graduate studies. This chapter reports on the insights gleaned after implementing this collaborative research initiative. The first section explores theoretical perspectives underpinning the research, followed by observations of three collaborative partnerships and the perceived benefits gained, and challenges faced, by the collaborators.

2 Research trajectory leading to collaborative research

I have been working as a teacher, researcher, and language learning advisor in L2 learning environments for over two decades. Over the years, my research has gradually taken a trajectory (Figure 7.1) from cognitive constructivism (Piaget and Inhelder 1967; Papert 1980; Brown, Collins, and Duguid 1989) to social constructionism (Vygotsky 1978).

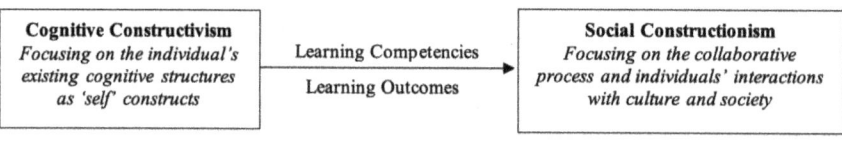

Figure 7.1: Research trajectory.

Essentially, cognitive constructivism focuses on learner constructs, that is, how learners acquire knowledge and create new knowledge and meaning by building on existing knowledge structures. In my early days as a teacher, I was influenced by Benson (2001) and Little (2007) and pursued self-reflexive action research to foster learner development (Noguchi and McCarthy 2009). Through activities focusing on self-discovery and personal reflection, I tried to guide learners to visualize their future selves as they interacted with new learning and built on past experiences. In my role as a language advisor in self-access centres, I tried to help learners develop into independent thinkers by personalizing learning – constructing a deeper understanding about themselves, their experiences, and their learning environment (see Dewey [1938] 1986) and expressing their inner feelings about these experiences in an iterative process. I thus viewed constructive cognitivism as the core component for learners to develop a deeper perspective of their self and the world. I later found myself turning to social constructionism in which Vygotsky theorized learning as being socially situated, with knowledge constructed through social interaction. That is, through a process of collaboration with peers or a tutor, learners are able to experience a deeper level of learning. As I began to work with more advanced language learners (but novice researchers) in the research initiative, I found that although learners benefitted from a continuous process of self-inquiry, learning became more meaningful when they engaged with a real-life environment through collaboration. As the project developed, it aimed not only to teach the fundamental skills for presenting, conferencing and networking through self-inquiry and collaboration, but also to encourage learners to apply and transfer the new knowledge and skills to the real world as a form of professional development. As my focus turned toward collaborative learning, I also noticed that my collaborative partnership with my research colleague deepened, which helped me to broaden my research outlook, question current beliefs about learner development, and approach research with a renewed vigour.

3 Defining collaborative research

The definition of collaborative research varies widely among researchers and within institutions. A basic definition by Bansal et al. (2019: 137) is 'research involving coordination between the researchers, institutions, organizations, and/or communities' which brings distinct expertise to a project. Research collaboration has also been defined as 'the working together of researchers to achieve the common goal of producing new scientific knowledge' (Katz and Martin 1997: 11) or some kind

of tangible outcome. Co-authorship of a paper, for example, is typically considered to be collaborative research in scientific fields, even if researchers have worked independently of each other. Given's (2008: 91) definition however puts the emphasis on research *with* rather than research *on*, thus highlighting the importance of the relationship between stakeholders in a 'shared inquiry of mutual benefit and interest'. It is this notion of a mutually beneficial relationship that defined collaborative research in this project. It was hypothesized that through meaningful, collaborative inquiry, the collaborators would be able to achieve richer results. The process of collaborative research was determined by the following:
- an exchange of meaningful dialogue between the stakeholders – the learners, the instructors, and the institution;
- a co-construction of ideas including the quality and frequency of contributions;
- mutually beneficial division of tasks toward achieving the learning outcome;
- the duration and reciprocal quality of the relationship.

4 Collaborative initiative for young researchers

Between 2019 and 2022, a scientific research exchange programme called *iLearn* (informal learning environment for academics and researchers through networking) was proposed[1] to the instructors' respective universities in response to what they perceived were skills lacking in students after entering graduate or doctoral courses (McCarthy and Armstrong 2021; Armstrong and McCarthy 2021). Essentially, students are required to communicate in English with lab members, participate in international conferences, and practise networking skills which might lead to future collaborative work in their research fields. Typically, Japanese university students must obtain a minimum number of credits for second language learning in their four-year undergraduate courses; however, most students gain these credits in their first and second years. After this, depending on the faculty, many students do not regularly encounter English in everyday situations until they enter graduate school or an international company. This two-year gap significantly hampered the development of language learning skills and many learners lacked self-confidence when they entered the professional industry and research world. In addition, they seemed unable to transfer or apply skills learned in the language classroom to various socially situated learning environments. Especially in the field of science and technology, where projects can be quite complex and

---

[1] Research carried out with the support of a JSPS Grant-in-Aid for Scientific Research <KAKENHI> grant, project number 19K00791.

may require large teams of researchers, (interdisciplinary) collaborative research is encouraged. My own university has established a collaborative research centre in which researchers from private industry, government and wider academia collaborate with the university 'on research subjects of mutual interest in an equal partnership' (SACI 2022). Thus, the concept of collaborative research is integral to this institution.

The participants in the *iLearn* project consisted of learners who were young researchers, mostly in their first or second year of graduate school, and two instructors teaching at different universities in Japan who were collaborators on this project (Table 7.1).

Table 7.1: Summary of project participants.

Learners	Instructors
Young researchers from various graduate schools (Humanities and Sciences), both Japanese and international students, seeking assistance to improve L2 (or L3) conferencing and networking skills. The learners were mostly first- and second-year graduate students with a few first-year doctoral students.	Teachers of general English courses. Provide guidance to graduate and doctoral students to help improve presentation, discussion, and conference skills in the form of workshops, group meetings, one-to-one consultations, and intensive one-week summer courses. Collaborate on project design, development, implementation, and evaluation.

The aims of *iLearn* were to have graduate students improve their research by presenting to both general and specific audiences, learning the conventions of international conferencing, and practising networking skills with researchers outside of their labs. Initially, approximately 60 students signed up to participate in the first summer workshop, which indicated a need for a graduate professional development programme. Forty-two showed up to the first workshop and then partnerships continued over a 14-week semester on a voluntary basis. Student numbers were capped at 30 from the second year and thus there were between 24 and 30 students in the following cycles of the project, with varying rates of attrition. Weekly activities included informal one-to-one meetings to discuss student-generated themes based on immediate research needs. The instructors also arranged a group meeting once a week at lunch time when all students were available. These meetings were held face to face to provide students with opportunities for larger group discussion with others outside of their labs. When pandemic rules and regulations came into effect at the start of 2020, however, research plans had to be adjusted quickly to continue the project and maintain partnerships. Virtual communities had to be built around scientific exchange. This required several meetings between the instructors, who had to acquire new technological skills and make compromises. Students also had to become accustomed to a new online learning environment and learn how to cope with unexpected challenges of online presentations and networking in their L2 without the support structure of their lab. The experiences faced by all participants created a rich collaborative environment which enhanced problem-solving skills, improved communication skills, and provided opportunities for collaborators to recognize individual strengths and learn from each other – skills required for their professional life. At the end of the initiative, the researchers reflected on the core principles or fundamental assumptions that they felt helped the collaborative research project to succeed.

5 Core principles of collaborative research

The instructors first compiled a list of principles from observation of the collaborative partnerships along with personal reflection. In total, five core principles emerged (Table 7.2) and were observed to varying degrees in each partnership. Principles 1 and 3 echo those of Wine et al. (2017: 11), who identified seven emerging themes influencing the collaborative process, and Barnes, Pashby, and Gibbons (2006: 396), who categorized successful collaboration under six themes, among them universal success (e.g., committed relationship, mutual trust, leadership), project management success (e.g., clearly defined goals, adequate resources, and shared responsibilities), and choice of partner (expertise/strengths). The instructors felt that ultimately, these five core principles added value to current educational practices and had significant benefit for the stakeholders. The researchers also agreed that it was the dynamic partnerships that were the driving force behind the success of the project.

6 Dynamic partnerships: Collaboration, reciprocity, and challenges

Dynamic partnerships in this project referred to the involvement of various collaborators from different fields of research, and with different knowledge constructs, experiences, perspectives, and reasons for establishing a connection. There were three distinct partnerships that emerged and developed from the collaborative initiative: The relationship between the instructors, the instructor and the learners, and between the learners themselves (Figure 7.2).

Table 7.2: Principles and partnerships in collaborative research.

Principle	Dyads	Description	Activities
1 Building dynamic relationships	learner/learner learner/instructor instructor/instructor	– Support ongoing collaboration and maintain dynamic partnerships through mutual respect, understanding, trust and reciprocity – Create an environment of meaningful and authentic professional development based on accurate professional models – Acquire specific skills and strategies required for successful professional development – communication skills (formal and informal), critical thinking, negotiation, problem-solving and compromise to avoid possible controversies and challenges	Weekly meetings Networking Workshops One-to-one discussion
2 Facilitating autonomous learning	learner/learner instructor/instructor	– Have the ability to set clear goals, manage time, reflect on the learning process (including an understanding of strengths and areas to improve), and make critical decisions to improve research skills – Understand and clearly articulate roles and responsibilities from the outset and adjust accordingly in response to new situations, changes in learner needs and/or learning outcomes – Evaluate outcomes in an iterative and analytical research process to ensure that learning or programme goals are being met	Organizing Goal setting Planning Scheduling Reflecting Observing Evaluating

(continued)

Table 7.2 (continued)

Principle	Dyads	Description	Activities
3 Creating and transferring knowledge and skills	learner/learner instructor/instructor	– Determine the current needs of learners and extend existing knowledge and skills – Develop and encourage active engagement with learning materials and authenticity in tasks, reflecting real-life scenarios that collaborators will face in international settings – Encourage meaningful connections with the professional world and have a fundamental understanding of how the new skills and knowledge can be readily applied or transferred to various socially situated environments – private industry, governmental agencies, non-profit organizations, and research settings with global audiences	Presentation skills Transfer: conferences; lab meetings; business or research proposals; defending thesis Genre-specific writing transfer: dissertation, research grants, abstracts, CVs, publications
4 Sharing knowledge and resources	learner/learner learner/instructor instructor/instructor	– Involve participants with different knowledge structures, skills and lived experiences in order to establish new understandings and perspectives – Increase the quality of research by encouraging collaborators to critically question the research purpose, method, data analysis, and general research direction – Disseminate findings to various individuals, institutions, communities of practice and organizations, and make accessible in a central repository	Scientific and academic journals Database Emails Weekly discussions Research diary PowerPoint Group learning

5 Promoting professionalism	learner/learner instructor/instructor	– Promote innovative opportunities for professionalism, specifically in understanding the differences in how to communicate with general and specific audiences, in informal and formal scenarios, and how to establish social connections for future collaborative endeavours – Define clear, transparent objectives and responsibilities, as well as ensure that curricula are designed around professionalism education including learning models that emphasize authentic, inquiry-driven learning methods – Promote knowledge exchange that focuses on professional ethics, values and accountability – skills that will be required in life beyond the classroom	Real-life professional models: mock international conference; networking practice Cross-disciplinary professional events Task-based small-group learning

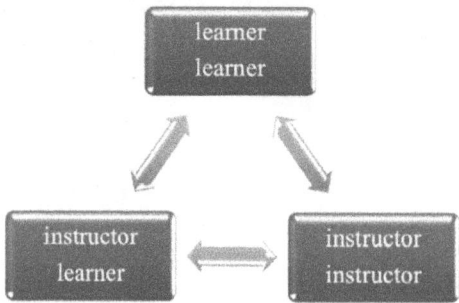

Figure 7.2: Dynamic partnerships in collaborative research.

To establish strong collaborative connections, maintaining dyadic partnerships over the duration of the project was essential. However, the cultural power dimension (Kasuya 2008) and the nature of individualism vs. collectivism in Japan and its potential effect on the collaborative relationship had to be addressed throughout to keep open a path toward reciprocity and shared understandings. That is, although Japan is considered to be a meritocratic society, there remains a strong hierarchical structure in educational and professional settings. This can have a strong influence on the strength and quality of instructor/learner and learner/learner relationships, depending on social classification, level of seniority, and gender. As part of a project that tried to reflect professional realism in international settings, it was important that connections and interactions were made without regard to specific cultural and social norms and that collaborators focused on building relationships that they considered would be mutually beneficial.

Reciprocal learning was viewed as more than just the instructor providing opportunities for interaction between dyads in a classroom environment or learners studying together on a collaborative venture. At its core, reciprocity assumes that individuals within a relationship cooperate to maximize learning through feedback and shared experiences. By encouraging transformative dialogue (formal or informal), partners can reflect more deeply on the task, and possibly alter perceptions or generate new assumptions about themselves. When exploring the term 'reciprocity' in this research context, I focused mainly on the concept of 'reciprocal professionalism' – how it encourages learning that transcends the classroom walls to research and/or industry settings.

Finally, there were many teaching, learning and research obstacles which were overcome by engaging in meaningful discourse. Through dialogic teaching (Alexander 2020), teachers could assist students with challenges encountered, and learners could problem-solve together. Professional discourse between the researchers became the main tool to stimulate discussion, advance understanding, and make informed decisions about how to progress. These ideas of collaboration, professional reciprocity, and the power of dialogue to transform and overcome challenges frame the following discussion of the three partnerships.

6.1 Learner/learner partnership

Collaboration plays a significant role in modern science with breakthroughs being realized through sharing knowledge and resources. Thus, for young researchers there is a great need to become familiar with collaborative research practices (Hafernick, Messerschmitt, and Vandrick 1997). Learners in this research project came from different faculties and countries. Even though a few were conducting research in similar fields, the research content was vastly different. At any given time, they were communicating with general and specific audiences, both peers and professors, in formal and informal situations, and thus had to learn how to adjust tone and delivery accordingly.

As masters and doctoral candidates, the learners for the most part had high levels of knowledge and expertise with the content of their specific research area. Reciprocity was seen in two ways:
1. generating new insights into research methods and transferring knowledge;
2. improving professional skills.

Collaborative partnerships enabled learners to gain a different perspective from peers in different research fields by comparing research practices, exchanging knowledge, and receiving critical feedback on presentation performance. In one partnership, for example, a nurse in training conducting research into human behaviour and a doctoral student studying computer language and artificial intelligence found value in their relationship as they were able to consider how to incorporate ideas from each other's fields into their research. Specifically, the nurse was able to help the doctoral student understand aspects of human behaviour that were lacking in a computer program he was developing. After participating in the programme, he felt his research focused too much on the analysis of large quantities of data and concluded that the dialogic components in the software design could be enhanced by understanding more about how to interpret human communication and write language for the software that the user could more easily connect with. On the other hand, the nursing student came to the realization that nursing seminars lacked knowledge sharing of current studies related to AI and medicine. She was intrigued at the advances in AI and began to question how technology could be used as a tool to support her goal of working for an NGO in developing countries. These two learners were thus able to reconsider their research direction from a unique angle (see McCarthy and Armstrong 2020 for details).

In other partnerships, knowledge transfer (Coulter 2013) occurred as learners from different disciplines shared knowledge of how to improve methods of data collection and analysis, thereby ensuring data reliability and validity. To give an example, in a partnership between a graduate student of marine biology and a doctoral engineer, the biologist gave a brief presentation on his method of collecting ocean samples for a specific experiment. After presenting his methodology, the engineer asked why ocean samples were collected in only one spot when the student was given a research budget to travel across Japan. The young researcher had not considered doing a comparative analysis of ocean samples in different prefectures. Thus, even though learner partnerships were from different fields of study, having to communicate and defend chosen research methodologies to a general audience helped learners to reconsider their research direction. In this way, collaborators went through a process of questioning prior knowledge, co-constructing and internalizing the new knowledge, and then returning to their individual research projects armed with knowledge to make improvements or continue along the same research path. Mutually beneficial professional skills were gained through planning and organizing weekly meetings, negotiating topics for upcoming meetings, group networking sessions, giving formal presentations, offering critical feedback, altering language to suit specific audiences, and giving assistance on CVs and advice about how to prepare for job interviews.

After each cycle of the project, students are asked to reflect on learner partnerships during the project and consider main takeaways or realizations. The following uncorrected excerpts are taken from the surveys:

> It was hard to improve the quality of research structure from the classmate because of our different background, but it was useful to know how to make it easier for the general public to understand the common methods in our field. (First-year master's student)

> XXX asked me if the AI module is equipped with the endoscopy itself. I had no idea from such standpoint, so her question was quite impressing me. (First-year doctoral student)

> I re-learned my research topic. I felt that I had to really truly understand the basics to be able to explain to someone who doesn't know much about my specific field. (Second-year doctoral student)

Another question that students are asked to reflect on is what future action they can take to further their learning. The following excerpt is from a first-year master's student:

> I'll give the information about my research constantly to the persons such as lab-members in English. Waiting the opportunities doesn't bring me any chance to improve. This is what I got through this intensive course.

These short excerpts, reiterated by other students, illustrate the power of reciprocity and dialogue for continued professional development.

Regarding challenges, of the partnerships which developed in the project, only a few collaborators stayed together for the entire 14-week duration of each cycle without changing partners. Other partnerships lasted 6–8 weeks. Research literature has mentioned typical challenges faced in collaborative partnerships such as cultural differences, uneven commitment and reciprocity, and ambiguity in goals or expectations (Given 2008; Sibbald, Tetroe, and Graham 2014; Rycroft-Malone et al. 2016). The main challenges faced in this research were mainly time constraints and trust. In the first place, schedules were set by individual departments and thus it was difficult for students from different faculties to meet due to overlaps in classes and time required in labs to conduct experiments. The only available time for all was during lunch hours which, although not ideal, provided enough time for (mostly online) exchanges. Lack of trust regarding feedback on research and presentation performance was also an issue for some individuals as they did not feel confident in their partner's ability to advise them on research or language acquisition matters. This was solved through dialogue – expanding on advice and suggestions by giving explicit evidence based on scientific research or experts in the field.

6.2 Instructor/learner partnership

As previously mentioned, deeply rooted socio-cultural norms in the Japanese educational system often see the instructors as authority figures who are 'guardians of a sacred body of knowledge' (Furey 1986: 21), while the learner receives the knowledge imparted without question or challenge (see also Becker 1990). Although this created a few challenges along the way, there were more benefits for both instructors and learners. Reciprocity was seen in two ways:
1. The researchers gaining a first-hand perspective on students' lived experiences.
2. Learners engaging with more experienced researchers.

To understand what exactly was required to meet learner goals, a survey was administered before the programme and the results used to design the course. Through this, the researcher gained a first-hand understanding of student life and could fill the gaps in knowledge between what was learned in the classroom and what learners needed to perform effectively in real-life professional settings. Students reported that their undergraduate courses focused on general English and thus they felt somewhat unprepared to conduct research in English in their first year of graduate studies. Second- and third-year graduates and doctoral students reported that they were often required to give presentations in conferences and labs, but there were no specific training sessions. This excerpt sums up the situation well:

> I do not believe that we are given career assistance throughout graduate school. There have not been many professional research conducting opportunities and there are not many international networking events conducted here.

At the beginning of the programme, the teacher negotiated discussion topics to give students more control over the learning process and encourage more self-directed learning. From my position as a researcher/practitioner of learner autonomy, I was able to gain valuable data as the students took a more active role in learning outcomes. The researchers also facilitated discussions and modelled examples of what was expected in real-life situations. The mutual benefit for students was that they were able to see more experienced researchers in action and practise the skills they felt they were lacking in international research contexts. The wider benefit for students was the recognition that they could transfer these skills to their present and future professional lives.

The main challenge faced was the expectations from the instructors and learners. That is, a few students expected one-to-one personal attention from the instructor rather than being expected to invest in the collective. This was solved through ongoing dialogue, setting clear goals, and defining roles from the outset. The instructors expected the learners to be proactive in their research and take full responsibility for self-analysing learning needs and making responsible decisions about their future. After meeting the students, however, we realized that some of them did not have the level of maturity necessary to make these decisions and others had not been exposed to the concepts of learner autonomy or collaborative research partnerships. Accordingly, expectations were lowered and more scaffolding for learner autonomy and opportunities for collaboration were incorporated to help facilitate development. By the end of the programme, the learners viewed the instructors as research colleagues and not only 'professor', as would be the situation in professional settings.

6.3 Instructor/instructor partnership

The most surprising partnership came from the collaboration between researchers. Ellström (2008) recommends that collaborative research partnerships should involve one person with theoretical expertise to collect, analyse and interpret data and the other with practical knowledge to develop curricula and teaching practices which can inform change. Along these lines I, having completed a research-based degree, and my colleague, who had an education-based degree, complemented each other, and could engage in a successful knowledge-building process. We had similar teaching backgrounds and philosophies, but research interests and approaches were at times vastly different. I have been publishing on learner autonomy and dialogue for over a decade, while my colleague publishes on literature in the second language classroom and inclusivity. The collaborative dynamic was apparent from the start, however, as our differences made for a richer research experience. Both of us had previously collaborated on a research paper; however, working on a three-year project required more dialogue-driven decisions, a complete understanding of individual strengths, and clear guidelines about roles and responsibilities. After a few weeks, the collaborative partnership grew stronger as we were equally invested in the research process and outcome and motivated to use this opportunity to improve our teaching and research standards.

Meetings were frequently held online in which we had many lively discussions about how to design surveys, collect and analyse data, and develop the course. My area of expertise was in laying the groundwork for the research and doing qualitative data analysis and my colleague excelled at curriculum design and student-centred learning. We both gained a tremendous amount of knowledge from these discussions as we both brought our own skills, knowledge and experience to the collaborative effort (Kahneman 2003). This enhanced ability to pool resources for mutual benefit was the first area of reciprocity in our relationship. A second benefit was improved communication skills during planning sessions, and when evaluating the outcomes and redesigning the course, but mainly when encountering challenges along the way. This project thus highlighted the importance of dialogue as one of the driving components of collaborative research to maintain a respectful and reciprocal partnership

When the project suddenly had to go online due to Covid-19 restrictions, it was soon made evident that we lacked certain technological skills and know-how to quickly redesign the course. The solution was to look back at the course design and decide how each component could be delivered in an online format and then identify the existing web technological capabilities at each institution. Work was then divided equally according to strengths and interests. If we encountered a situation we were both unfamiliar with, we flipped a digital coin on an app. Professionally, this problem-solving teamwork enabled us to improve as teachers and researchers as we pooled resources, shared knowledge, and taught each other how to use various learning platforms and programmes. Believing that there was a solution to every problem and keeping our focus on the collaborative nature of the programme meant that challenges were always faced and solved together with confidence and conviction.

7 Conclusion

This chapter has introduced several studies from the research literature which advocate the benefits of collaborative research. I have further shown through this study how it can enhance the learning, teaching, and research experience for professional contexts. There were several conclusions that were drawn at the end of the project with regard to what embodied successful collaborative research. To begin with, collaborative initiative was perceived as successful when participants established quality, sustainable, dynamic partnerships and mutually benefitted from the partnership. The quality of the dyadic relationships depended on shared goals, an equal commitment to the project, a clear understanding of roles and responsibilities, and a willingness to trust, respect and support the partner. The collaborative partnership functioned effectively when individuals identified shared problems and devised solutions, made personal breakthroughs, and committed to the collective's as well as the individual's needs. Reciprocity was experienced mostly in dyadic partnerships that lasted for a long time and which had a meaningful impact on each individual. Reciprocity gave rise to successes, and this was the key point in overcoming challenges. A second conclusion drawn was that collaborative research is successful when collaborators build on existing knowledge structures. When knowledge exchange generates new insights, helps collaborators overcome challenges, and results in knowledge application and transfer to both unfamiliar and real-life professional situations, this is further considered to be a success. The final observation was improving professionalism. As current research trends shift to global collaborative and interdisciplinary initiatives, it is beneficial to provide training programmes and enact progressive policies for young researchers to meet research needs and prepare them for the professional life they will experience post-graduation. Encouraging professionalism education in universities through collaborative research initiatives such as this project, is one possible way to ensure that no student is left behind.

After the three-year project came to an end, I was able to continue using the learning materials developed for graduate students in credit-based courses. But there were questions which remained unanswered: What does professionalism education mean to graduate students? Do educational practices at the university prepare students adequately for their professional life beyond the walls of the classroom? What is the gap between language learning in the classroom and language use in the professional world? To answer these questions, the notion of graduate student professional development needs to be unpacked so that students can understand the specific skills, knowledge, and experiences that will be required for research positions, government employment and industry settings. To this end, I have begun a second collaborative initiative[2] involving university professors, graduate students, and industry experts.

To conclude, for the researchers in this project, the simple wish to have learners understand conferencing conventions and become more comfortable with networking and exchanging research for professional development led to mutually beneficial collaborative research for stakeholders and maintained professional relationships that crossed disciplines, nationalities, and cultures. By encouraging collaborative partnerships and especially promoting dialogue, the researchers were able to successfully bridge the gap between learners' classroom knowledge and professional life. In our final reflective discussion as we closed this chapter, we arrived at the conclusion that it is only through building a culture of collaborative research in educational and professional contexts that young researchers can be pushed to think outside of the box, critically reflect on practices and performance, and achieve breakthroughs.

References

Armstrong, Matthew & Tanya McCarthy. 2021. Active participation in a sci-tech community: Collaborative peer review. In Peter Clements, Rick Derrah & Peter Ferguson (eds.), Communities of teachers & learners. *JALT Postconference Publication* 2020(1). 215–223. https://doi.org/10.37546/JALTPCP2020-27 (accessed 24 May 2022).
Bansal, Seema, Saniya Mahendiratta, Subodh Kumar, Phulen Sarma, Ajay Prakash & Bikash Medhi. 2019. Collaborative research in modern era: Need and challenges. *Indian Journal of Pharmacology* 51(3). 137–139. https://doi.org/10.4103/ijp.IJP_394_19 (accessed 24 My 2022).
Barnes, Tina, Ian Pashby & Anne Gibbons. 2006. Managing collaborative R&D projects development of a practical management tool. *International Journal of Project Management* 24(5). 395–404.
Becker, Carl. 1990. Higher education in Japan: Facts and implications. *International Journal of Intercultural Relations* 144(4). 425–447. https://doi.org/10.1016/0147-1767(90)90029-V (accessed 24 May 2022).
Benson, Phil. 2001. *Teaching and researching autonomy in language learning*. London: Longman.
Brown, John, Alan Collins & Paul Duguid. 1989. Situated knowledge and the culture of learning. *Educational Researcher* 18(1). 32–42. https://doi.org/10.3102/0013189X018001032 (accessed 24 May 2022).
Coulter, Janet. 2013. Interdisciplinarity: Creativity in collaborative research approaches to enhance knowledge transfer. In Robert Howlett, Bogdan Gabrys, Katarzyna Musial-Gabrys & Jim Roach (eds.), *Innovation through knowledge Transfer 2012. Smart Innovation, Systems and Technologies* 18, 169–178. Berlin: Springer. https://doi.org/10.1007/978-3-642-34219-6_19 (accessed 25 October 2022).
Dewey, John. [1938] 1986. Experience and education. *The Educational Forum* 50(3). 241–252. https://doi.org/10.1080/00131728609335764 (accessed 24 May 2022).

---

2 Research carried out with the support of a JSPS Grant-in-Aid for Scientific Research <KAKENHI> grant, project number 22K00788.

Ellström, Per-Erik. 2008. Knowledge creation through interactive research: A learning perspective. Paper presented at *The European Conference on Educational Research (ECER)*, Gothenburg, 10–12 September. https://citeseerx.ist.psu.edu/viewdoc/download?doi=10.1.1.525.3250&rep=rep1&type=pdf (accessed 24 May 2022).

Furey, Patricia. 1986. A framework for cross-cultural analysis of teaching methods. In Patricia Byrd & Janet Constantinides (eds.), *Teaching across cultures in the university ESL program*. Washington, DC: National Association for Foreign Student Affairs.

Given, Lisa (ed.). 2008. *The SAGE encyclopedia of qualitative research methods*, vol. 2. SAGE Publications. https://dx.doi.org/10.4135/9781412963909 (accessed 24 May 2022).

Hafernick, Johnnie, Dorothy Messerschmitt & Stephanie Vandrick. 1997. Collaborative research: Why and how? *Educational Researcher* 26(9). 31–35. https://doi.org/10.3102/0013189X026009031 (accessed 24 May 2022)

Kahneman, Daniel. 2003. Experiences of collaborative research. *American Psychologist* 58(9). 723–730. https://doi.org/10.1037/0003-066X.58.9.723 (accessed 24 May 2022).

Kasuya, Michiko. 2008. Classroom interaction affected by power distance. https://www.birmingham.ac.uk/Documents/college-artslaw/cels/essays/languageteaching/LanguageTeachingMethodologyMichikoKasuya.pdf (accessed 24 May 2022).

Katz, J. Sylvan & Ben Martin. 1997. What is research collaboration? *Research Policy* 26(1). 1–18. https://doi.org/10.1016/S0048-7333(96)00917-1 (accessed 24 May 2022).

Little, David. 2007. Language learner autonomy: Some fundamental considerations revisited. *Innovation in Language Learning and Teaching* 1(1). 14–29. https://doi.org/10.2167/illt040.0 (accessed 24 May 2022).

McCarthy, Tanya & Matthew Armstrong. 2021. Overcoming language barriers and boundaries: Video-mediated eTandem. *Bulletin Suisse de Linguistique Appliquée No spécial* 2021(2). 183–202. ISBN 978-1-105-52912-2.

Noguchi, Junko & Tanya McCarthy. 2010. Reflective self-study: Fostering learner autonomy. In Alan Stoke (ed.), *JALT2009 Conference Proceedings*, 160–167. Tokyo: JALT. https://jalt-publications.org/archive/proceedings/2009/E051.pdf (accessed 24 May 2022).

Papert, Seymour. 1980. *Mindstorms: Children, computers, and powerful ideas*. New York: Basic Books.

Piaget, Jean & Bärbel Inhelder. 1967. *The child's conception of space*. New York: W. W. Norton.

Rycroft-Malone, J., Christopher Burton, Joyce Wilkinson, Gill Harvey, Brendan McCormack, Richard Baker, Sue Dopson, Ian Graham, Sophie Staniszewska, Carl Thompson, Stephen Ariss, Lucy Melville-Richards & Lynne Williams. 2016. Collective action for implementation: A realist evaluation of organisational collaboration in healthcare. *Implementation Science* 11(17). https://doi.org/10.1186/s13012-016-0380-z (accessed 24 May 2022).

SACI. 2022. Kyoto University's office of Society–Academia Collaboration for Innovation – Industry–government–academia collaboration program: Collaborative research. https://www.saci.kyoto-u.ac.jp/en/introduction/collaborative/ (accessed 24 May 2022).

Sibbald Shannon, Jacqueline Tetroe & Ian Graham. 2014. Research funder required research partnerships: A qualitative inquiry. *Implementation Science* 9. 176. https://doi.org/10.1186/s13012-014-0176-y (accessed 24 May 2022).

Vygotsky, Lev. 1978. *Mind in society: The development of higher psychological processes*. Cambridge, MA: Harvard University Press.

Wine, Osnat, Sarah Ambrose, Sandy Campbell, Paul Villeneuve, Katharina Kovacs Burns, Alvaro Osornio Vargas & The DoMiNO Team. 2017. Key components of collaborative research in the context of environmental health: A scoping review. *Journal of Research Practice* 13(2), Article R2. https://files.eric.ed.gov/fulltext/EJ1174006.pdf (accessed 24 May 2022).

Gabriele Pallotti, Claudia Borghetti, Stefania Ferrari
and Greta Zanoni

8 Teachers and researchers collaborating to develop effective language education: The project *Observing Interlanguage*

Abstract: This chapter presents an action research project conducted in primary and middle schools in northern Italy. School teachers and university researchers collaborate at all stages and levels. Initially, teachers conduct a needs analysis on their classes using the Interlanguage approach to language teaching, which consists in observing the pupils' competences, processes and strategies in a positive way rather than just focusing on their errors and shortcomings. Didactic activities are then jointly designed to address these needs and to promote an inclusive language education in which all the students are involved regardless of their initial competences and linguistic background, performing numerous collaborative and meta-cognitive activities. Data are also collected at the beginning and end of the school year in order to assess the effectiveness of the intervention in the classes involved. The latter systematically outperform control classes in a number of dimensions, especially those having to do with effective communication and text organization. Both teachers and researchers discuss the results and then publish their findings and reflections in scientific articles and monographs, didactic materials and textbooks for teacher training in order to extend the reach of this approach to other contexts and communities.

1 Introduction

One of the greatest challenges in the field of language education is identifying effective strategies to develop language competences for all students, regardless of whether they are using their first or an additional language. The project presented in this chapter is meant to respond to this demanding task, by means of an action-research teacher training methodology.

The aim of the project *Osservare l'Interlingua/Observing Interlanguage*, started in 2007 in Reggio Emilia (Italy), is to foster effective language education in multilingual classes at elementary and middle-school levels. Its main tenet is that effective teaching practices should be grounded in the teachers' careful analysis of their pupils' needs, competences and learning strategies, that is, in 'observing their interlanguage', seen broadly as any attempt at developing and complexifying linguistic–communicative competences, and thus not limited to L2 acquisition but also including the acquisition of new linguistic skills such as reading and writing.

In order to pursue these goals, *Observing Interlanguage* systematically integrates teacher education and action research. During the former, teachers are trained to analyse their pupils' texts according to the 'interlanguage approach to language teaching' (Pallotti 2017a). As for the latter, they design new pedagogical practices to respond to the learning needs they have identified and carry out the planned activities with their classes for an entire school year. Teachers also monitor the effects of the newly devised teaching materials and procedures along the way, possibly revising them. Each of these actions, though to different degrees and according to each party's competences, is conducted collaboratively between teachers and researchers, who meet every two to three months throughout the school year.

The chapter starts by outlining some key principles of 'interprofessional collaborative action research' which inform the project from a methodological point of view (section 2). Then, it introduces the *Observing Interlanguage* project (section 3), before focussing on its two components, namely teacher training (section 4) and action research (section 5), which are kept separate for descriptive purposes only, as they overlap in many ways. The final sections (6 and 7) report on a preliminary assessment of *Observing Interlanguage* collaborative research and outline future directions for broadening its scope.

2 Interprofessional collaborative action research

The label *action research* (AR)[1] describes a whole family of approaches through which teachers introduce and evaluate new practices in their classes, usually by means of a number of investigative cycles (for general overviews see Altrichter et al. 2002; Kindon, Pain, and Kesby 2007; Mills 2003; Reason and Bradbury 2001; for language education see, e.g., Borg 2010; Burns 2005; Nunan 1992). Action research is a form of classroom research (McKay 2006) in which practitioners

---

1 Some of these sources (e.g., Kindon, Pain, and Kesby 2007) address what is commonly known as 'Participatory Action Research' (see also MacDonald 2012; McIntyre 2008; McTaggart 1997), namely a specific type of action research which, based on poststructuralist discourses, emphasizes the practitioners' ownership of the research processes, values their diverse funds of knowledge, and is explicitly oriented towards social transformation. While *Observing Interlanguage* is not directly inspired by these contributions, they can help define – often by comparison and/or contrast – what action research is.

identify a problem, gather and analyse data, undertake changes in teaching practices according to the obtained results, and test the effects of the modifications implemented. Besides helping teachers find pedagogical solutions which are grounded in their contexts, AR has proved to be useful for teacher education (Burns 2009), mostly because it offers practitioners the opportunity to 'reflect on and improve (or develop) their *own* work and their *own* situations' (Altrichter et al. 2002: 130).

Although in principle action research may be conducted by individual teachers analysing their own practices, it is mostly considered a collaborative activity taking place among colleagues. Collaboration is needed to distribute workload, as AR requires a considerable time commitment (Richards and Farrell 2005). Moreover, it helps achieve greater impact 'as it offers a strong framework for whole-school change' (Burns 1999: 13) and for educational change at large. Finally, collaboration fosters teacher development. Either within the frame of AR initiatives or of 'teacher research' experiences in general (Borg 2010, 2013), the establishment of communities of practice provides teachers with opportunities for professional learning: they share and compare class activities, develop new pedagogical ideas together, experiment with innovative practices in their classrooms, and bring the resulting reflections back to the group for further discussion (Borg, Lightfoot, and Gholkar 2020).

Action research also often implies some kind of collaboration between practitioners and researchers (McKay 2006; Reason and Bradbury 2001). In this sense, it is a form of co-constructed research, where new educational and scientific understandings result from 'interprofessional' partnership: teachers bring their expertise as regards subject matter, curriculum and pedagogy, as well as knowledge about individual learners and the sociocultural context. In other words, they bring the teacher knowledge they develop over time thanks to training, experience and reflection (Freeman 2002; Mann 2005). For their part, academics may share insights about scientific knowledge and research methodologies. This form of collaboration is often embedded in teacher training initiatives, some of which are meant to promote learning for all in multilingual and multicultural classes (as in Dubetz 2005 and Scarino 2014), even when these teaching, research, and training programmes are not explicitly labelled 'action research'. Levels of participation by teachers and researchers can vary significantly according to the project and to the specific stage of the study (identifying the problem, collecting and analysing data, etc.) (Kindon, Pain, and Kesby 2007). Yet, these forms of interprofessional collaboration may contribute to addressing a frequent criticism levelled at teacher research, that is, its lack of methodological rigor and its being seldom made public for the benefit of larger teaching and research communities (Borg 2010). Finally, making action research interprofessional is a way to challenge the belief that action research – and teacher research at large – is necessarily small-scale and qualitative (Burns 1999; Mann 2005), as well as its opposite, that is, that large-scale quantitative studies are necessarily decontextualized and distant from the teachers' and students' needs.

3 The *Observing Interlanguage* project

The *Observing Interlanguage* project consists in a joint collaboration between the University of Modena and Reggio Emilia, Department of Education and Human Sciences, and a network of schools in the Reggio Emilia area. From 2007 to 2019, the Reggio Emilia municipality played a major role as regards practical implementation and networking, a task that is now carried out by the university and some volunteer teachers. The project thus involves a number of professionals who work in different capacities: university researchers, in-service school teachers, teacher trainers, educators, and university students enrolled in the course for prospective primary school teachers. The main assumption guiding the project is that the learning needs found in multilingual classrooms are an opportunity to challenge traditional pedagogical approaches, thus representing a chance for the development of more effective teaching practices for all pupils, regardless of whether Italian is for them a first or an additional language.

Although in the first years only a few schools and teachers were involved, now the project concerns about 10 primary and 3 middle schools, with approximately 20 teachers and several hundred pupils every year. The university contributes with a scientific coordinator (Gabriele Pallotti), 6–7 students doing their internship in the participating schools, mentored by 3–4 expert teacher supervisors (with a 50% employment with the university and 50% of their workload in class). The training group meets every two to three months during the school year in order to plan, implement and revise experimental teaching interventions. Teachers, in some cases with the help of student interns, carry out their lessons in the classrooms and conduct formative assessment on their pupils, based on a careful analysis of their interlanguage. The university team coordinates the training sessions, suggests possible avenues for pedagogical innovations, and performs more large-scale, quantitative analyses to monitor the project's effectiveness on a variety of linguistic aspects. The training and research components of the project are thus tightly intertwined and result in the integration of different roles and funds of expertise.

4 The teacher training component

Several activities developed by the project over the years have been aimed at developing writing skills, which were seen by teachers as a crucial competence needing to be reinforced. Through a process approach (e.g., White and Arndt 1991; Graham and Sandmel 2011), pupils are led to experience and gradually acquire the stages implied in text production: generating and organizing ideas, writing the initial draft, revising, and editing. Writing tasks are carried out cooperatively in small and large groups (e.g., Storch 2013), and they encourage the semiotic mediation of thought by making the writing process more concrete through the use of artefacts such as boxes, envelopes, paper strips, posters (Englert, Mariage, and Dunsmore 2006). Feedback, including peer-to-peer feedback, has always a formative orientation, focussing on learners' strengths and weaknesses, analyzing their strategies, and suggesting ways of developing skills, promoting learners' autonomy and self-regulation (e.g., Andrade and Evans 2013).

The action research teacher-training methodology puts the learning/teaching process at the centre. Teachers are guided in applying research-based tools for observing their school context and consequently set learning goals, develop pedagogic interventions and evaluate the teaching/learning processes, through both a collaborative reflection on their lessons and an analysis of students' performance over time. University researchers assist them in this undertaking and, at some points, collect data for more systematic quantitative analysis, but do not impose their priorities or set the project's agenda based on their need to collect standardized data. This represents an exemplary case of reciprocity as both parties involved, teachers and researchers, contribute by drawing on their pools of expertise and obtain tangible results with a clear bi-directional relationship of mutual advantage.

The project has been running for many years now, and no iteration has been identical to previous ones in a never-ending process of experimenting, discussing and revising. However, on a broad level, a relatively stable feature is that the project's activities may be grouped into three main phases. The first involves needs analysis and goal setting. Teachers conduct systematic analyses of their pupils' oral and written productions, in line with the interlanguage approach (Pallotti 2017b; Selinker 1972). The main goal is to overcome the traditional stance of 'hunting for errors' and seeing learners' productions as defective, incomplete, and instead to be able to appreciate pupils' competences, especially communicative competence, which is often neglected in traditional approaches that almost exclusively focus on formal accuracy. This orientation, and the ability to analyse children's texts accordingly, takes some time to develop. Text-analysis sessions are therefore periodically held as part of the teachers' long-term training. In these sessions, more experienced participants share their way of seeing language productions with newcomers, in a collective effort to strengthen everyone's skills in educational linguistic analysis, which is also part of the course taken by the university students involved in the project.

The second step in the activity cycle consists in planning and implementing the lesson cycles for the following months. Each of these cycles normally takes 8–12 sessions of about two hours each. Learners are guided to work extensively on the same text, so as to have the opportunity to return several times, from different perspectives, to their own productions or those of their peers. This motivates them to refine their work and become experts (e.g., Graham et al. 2012). Learning is mainly viewed as a discovery process, and tasks are structured so that every student can contribute according to their abilities; in other words, teachers do not provide different activities for different proficiency levels. In this way, all students work together, with the same objectives and focussing on the same tasks, so that they can learn from one another, which is especially beneficial for struggling pupils, as teachers have repeatedly attested. Each child is motivated to go through the different phases of the writing process, and experiment with various kinds of learning interactions – with the teacher, in small and large groups – developing a deeper awareness of their own learning processes.

In some years, the whole group tried to converge on a single, shared lesson cycle, obviously adapted to the competences and needs of different age groups. Even in such cases, though, each teacher had the opportunity to select, adapt or fine-tune the overall scheme to their specific context. In other years, teachers were left free to choose one of the previously developed interventions, or to create new ones, in order to promote their agency and their ability to propose further innovations.

The third part includes evaluation of the experience, both from teachers' and pupils' perspectives. Teachers share with the group their experience in the classroom and discuss their findings and how they solved specific problems, with the ultimate aim of defining future learning and teaching objectives and the strategies to attain them. Pupils metacognitively reflect on the learning programme, discussing what they have acquired, what they liked most and least, their difficulties and achievements. This results in diary entries in which pupils report, often in the form of recommendations for themselves or for their peers, what they perceived to be the main take-aways of the didactic activities.

5 The action research approach

After having identified the students' needs in line with the interlanguage approach, and planned pedagogical actions accordingly, teachers and researchers collaborate in data collection. This normally consists in asking pupils to write individual texts both at the beginning and at the end of every school year, to assess their progress over time. Practitioners and academics play complementary roles in this and subsequent stages. Teachers implement the designed pedagogical solutions in their classes, which overall represent the project experimental group. Researchers organize a parallel data collection with classes not involved in the programme (the control group, that is, classes in the same schools or areas whose teachers decided not to take part in the pedagogic experimentation) and perform subsequent quantitative analyses, which allow for comparisons over time and across pupils and classes (section 5.1). When all data have been transcribed and analysed by the researchers and some pre-service student teachers, results are commented on during the periodic discussion sessions among teachers and researchers (section 5.2). This analysis also leads to feedback being given to pupils not in terms of marks or evaluative expressions like *good, fair, well done*, but in terms of individualized recommendations for the future and indications for making classroom work more effective.

5.1 The project studies: An overview

This quasi-experimental research design, with experimental and control classes, is quite resource-intensive, and thus does not take place every year, but every 2–3 years. This has allowed us to gather a considerable amount of data, some of which have already been analysed in some publications, while others are still in progress.

The most extensive study (Pallotti, Borghetti, and Rosi 2021; Pallotti and Borghetti 2019) considers data collected during a school year in seven experimental and seven control classes, in grades 3–5. It looked at the effects of the *Observing Interlanguage* approach on different measures of text quality, including the pupils' ability to divide and organize their texts into paragraphs, to use punctuation marks to divide the syntactic units, or to introduce and maintain entities in discourse through appropriate referential chains. These investigations also aim to evaluate the project's effects on monolingual and multilingual pupils. The main findings are that pupils in experimental classes obtain better results than those in control classes on almost all dimensions assessed. Moreover, multilingual children in the experimental group outperformed both monolingual and multilingual students in control classes on the vast majority of text features, with just a few exceptions.

Other studies focussed only on certain classes and/or specific dimensions of writing. Some concentrate on the use of reported speech in grade 4 (Pallotti, Borghetti, and Ferrari 2019) and grade 5 (Borghetti et al. 2019), based on two experimental and two control classes. Both investigations show that, at the end of the school year, pupils participating in *Observing Interlanguage* increase considerably their use of direct speech to make their texts more lively and expressive; by contrast, this narrative strategy remains largely unused by pupils in the control classes. Ferrari and Burzoni (2018) carried out a holistic examination of the texts produced at the end of the school year in two experimental and two control classes (grade 5). This study was carried out using scales slightly adapted from Kuiken and Vedder (2018) to rate overall functional adequacy. The texts produced in the experimental classes proved to be shorter but more complete, comprehensible, coherent and cohesive than those in the control classes; they were thus more concise, but not poorer in terms of ideas.

5.2 Back to training and education

The studies reported above as well as other project-related investigations (e.g., Pallotti 2017a, 2017b, 2017c) show that *Observing Interlanguage* produces positive results in various areas of language development. These findings help feed the teacher training component of the project (section 4) and encourage a series of initiatives meant to make its methodology public for the benefit of additional teachers and students (section 7).

In the few cases in which systematic studies show that the teaching has not achieved the expected outcomes, researchers and teachers start planning new pedagogical changes for the following school year. These new investigative cycles usually start with academics presenting the obtained results in dedicated teacher training sessions. Then, as a group, all actors formulate hypotheses as to why some specific results are not satisfactory and agree on what changes or additional activities should be foreseen for the future. For example, after having identified that in the 2013–2014 cohort multilingual pupils struggled to maintain verb tense cohesion more than their monolingual classmates (Pallotti and Borghetti 2019), it was hypothesized that this feature might be more directly related to language proficiency than the other dimensions of writing. Therefore, some focus-on-forms activities were integrated within the pedagogical interventions planned for the following school year, in order to support some pupils' language proficiency together with all the other students' writing abilities. Unfortunately, we were not able to collect additional data in the following years in order to analytically assess the effectiveness of these new activities. However, teachers report that they did try them and found them valuable.

6 Assessing the project: Teachers' perspectives

The quantitative data presented in the previous sections show that the approach of *Observing Interlanguage* produces measurable and objective effects on the pupils' writing skills. On the other hand, there are also more qualitative ways of evaluating the effectiveness of an action research project, such as collecting the opinions of those who actively participated. In 2015, at the end of the eighth year of experimentation, individual interviews were conducted with teachers, pre-service student teachers, pupils and some parents. Responses were recorded and transcribed; in the following pages a few excerpts will be presented in English translation.

As pointed out by Borg (2010), working across an action research project often poses challenges related to several contextual constraints that teachers normally face at school, such as time, and the need to follow and complete the school programme and to prepare students for examinations. Both teachers and researchers were aware that at the beginning it takes commitment and time to follow a different approach to teaching writing, based on collaborative and group activities. However challenging this approach may seem at first glance, teachers' perceptions turned out to be extremely positive.

> At the beginning it wasn't so simple, because I thought it was something a little far from what we did practically at school. However, as you begin to work, you understand that you can apply this methodology to many other activities and disciplines.

Respondents highlighted several strengths of the experimental approach, such as the results achieved by the students, the discovery of new materials like audiovisual stimuli, and new pedagogical approaches and techniques for teaching Italian and other subjects.

Teachers recognized the importance of the project in building 'grassroots' skills to deliver practical solutions for improving pupils' competence and overall quality of writing, and showed their interest in continuing to be involved in the experimentation.

> It was a need that I felt for both myself and my students precisely on written production, because I realized first of all that I needed tools for teaching written production, how to teach

> children to write a text. [. . .] What was really useful was to work a lot in such an articulated way on the different phases of written production, which are often dealt with in a hurry.
>
> The project responds to the need for a training placed in the daily teaching experience that it is so difficult to find, and we have exactly found a practical dimension. So we have gradually improved our skills also from the point of view of our professional training.

As stated above, a distinctive feature of the proposed methodology compared to more traditional approaches consists in the attention paid to pupils' productions and the diagnosis of their competencies and needs, going beyond simple hunting for errors. Several teachers became aware of the stages and processes involved in the acquisition of new linguistic skills and how this awareness may impact curriculum design and pedagogy, paying special attention to the diversity of levels, sociolinguistic backgrounds and learning styles.

> The thing that struck me the most and continues to strike me is the idea of dwelling on children's mistakes in a slightly different way; that is to say, trying to see what indications are given to us by pupils' mistakes. This is something that changes the idea of 'error', making it a starting point [for the intervention], not the end point.

Moreover, most teachers perceived the collaboration among pupils to be value-adding and enriching.

> What surprised me the most was the inclusive value of the pedagogical intervention: in each group all participants were essential for the success of the text, so all the students participated actively. Even those who usually experience the process of writing with greater difficulty (for example, kids with specific learning disorders, 'interruptions' generally due to lack of exercise, laziness) were responsible at all stages of the intervention.

The impact of the theoretical principles and practical approaches presented in the action research also emerged in some insights by the student interns. As emphasized in the following comment, students have the possibility to put into practice what they study at the university by means of a simple and attractive methodology. As a result, some students repeated the internship experience for a second year, while working on their master's thesis, to consolidate their teaching skills as well as their ability to collect and analyse the pupils' texts, and to plan focussed teaching activities accordingly.

> Surely there is everything I have read in the books, especially while studying for the exam. Observing the theoretical models of the authors who deal with these techniques, these new strategies, and applying them directly on the field is a wonderful satisfaction, because for the first time I observed what I study at the university and the positive results in practice. Apparently, from what we read in the books, it really seems very difficult to carry it out at school due to deadlines and to the fact that there is never the presence of more than one teacher in class. It seemed impossible to be able to manage a class of twenty children, to satisfy all their

needs and requirements, because they are in any case all different from each other. In practice, it takes very little: it is sufficient to apply these new methods to carry out beautiful work even with small children in grade 2. It was amazing how we were able to create a text, transcribe it, edit it, and do all the activities in small group and large groups.

7 Future directions

The project members have come to realize that the approach taken by *Observing Interlanguage* differs in many respects from standard school practice in Italy, which is also reflected in present-day textbooks. This is why the group has always been concerned with producing teaching materials and activities, which can be drawn upon from both the teacher-authors in later years and from a wider community of professionals across the country, who cannot directly take part in the action research.

Since the very beginning, a website was created containing all the lesson cycles implemented year after year. These are not published as narrative accounts of past experiences, but as descriptions formulated in an atemporal present tense. This is an important point in our opinion – readers should feel that what is proposed by the team is widely applicable and it is not limited to a particular spatio-temporal context, although it is clear that the activities were indeed trialled in real classes by real teachers. The website also contains children's oral and written productions collected in some years, which may be used in several ways, for example to produce new didactic materials inviting for instance pupils to reflect on other children's performance, or to give other teachers the opportunity to practise interlanguage analysis.

However, the quantity of materials produced over the years made browsing the website rather complicated, especially for new users. Furthermore, even more experienced teacher-authors felt the need for more structured resources, accompanying them across the entire school cycle. A syllabus was thus created, containing a selection of the most effective materials, in a progression from the first grade of primary school to the third grade of middle school. The syllabus is an adaptable tool and all the materials are available in an editable format, so that activities can be added, deleted, adapted or enriched according to the class context and the teaching objectives. The units are structured as follows. For every school grade, two 'long' lesson cycles (typically, one on a narrative text and another one on an expository text, but in some cases the focus is argumentative or meta-communicative) are proposed, spanning over several sessions, in which pupils learn how to carefully and slowly craft a text, going through several phases. These are accompanied by a few shorter activities dealing with more formal aspects, always connected to the main communicative orientation of the longer project work. In many cases, both teachers and pupils are asked to reflect on other pupils' production, so that everyone is trained in observing interlanguage.

Currently, some of the most experienced teachers are writing a book, which will appear in a series on language education published by one of the most prestigious Italian educational publishers. The volume will present to other teachers the *Observing Interlanguage* project and, more generally, the principles of a task-based, communicative approach to teaching writing, with a practical, hands-on orientation.

Finally, the whole group of university researchers, teachers and students has embarked on an even more ambitious project, namely a textbook to be used directly in primary school classes and covering all aspects of language education. As mentioned above, many activities of the *Observing Interlanguage* project focus on writing skills, although activities on oral competences have been developed on some occasions. In the coming years, oral communication will receive more attention, as well as receptive skills such as reading and listening, and metalinguistic awareness. This will enable us to propose a complete language education course, to be published open-access and with no commercial profit, which is one of the most effective ways of promoting good practice at school and to further the collaboration among researchers, teachers and university students. The book, in fact, as all the activities developed in the projects, will blend solid theoretical foundations with practical experience, as all activities will be tried out in class before being edited, fine-tuned and finally offered to a wider public.

References

Altrichter, Herbert, Stephen Kemmis, Robin McTaggart & Ortrun Zuber-Skerritt. 2002. The concept of action research. *The Learning Organization* 9(3). 125–131.
Andrade, Maureen Snow & Norman W. Evans. 2013. *Principles and practices for response in second language writing*. New York: Routledge.
Borg, Simon. 2010. Language teacher research engagement. *Language Teaching* 43(4). 391–429.
Borg, Simon. 2013. *Teacher research in language teaching: A critical analysis*. Cambridge: Cambridge University Press.
Borg, Simon, Amy Lightfoot & Radhika Gholkar. 2020. *Professional development through teacher activity groups: A review of evidence from international projects*. London: British Council.
Borghetti, Claudia, Stefania Ferrari, Letizia Lazzaretti, Gabriele Pallotti & Greta Zanoni. 2019. Le voci dei personaggi: insegnare l'uso del discorso riportato alla scuola primaria [The voices of the characters: teaching the use of reported speech in primary school]. *Italiano a scuola* 1. 1–24.
Burns, Anne. 1999. *Collaborative action research for English language teachers*. Cambridge: Cambridge University Press.
Burns, Anne. 2005. Action research: An evolving paradigm? *Language Teaching* 38(2). 57–74.

Burns, Anne. 2009. Action research in second language teacher education. In Anne Burns & Jack C. Richards (eds.), *The Cambridge guide to second language teacher education*, 289–297. Cambridge: Cambridge University Press.

Dubetz, Nancy E. 2005. Improving ESL instruction in a bilingual program through collaborative, inquiry-based professional development. In Diane J. Tedick (ed.), *Second language teacher education: International perspectives*, 231–256. Mahwah, NJ: Lawrence Erlbaum Associates.

Englert, Carol Sue, Troy V. Mariage & Kailonnie Dunsmore. 2006. Tenets of sociocultural theory in writing instruction research. In Charles A. MacArthur, Steve Graham & Jill Fitzgerald (eds.), *Handbook of writing research*, 208–221. New York: Guilford Press.

Ferrari, S. & Giulia Burzoni. 2018. Imparare a scrivere meglio. Un'indagine sperimentale sugli effetti di una sperimentazione educativa sulle classi intere e sugli alunni plurilingui [Learn to write better. An experimental investigation on the effects of an educational experiment on whole classes and on plurilingual pupils]. *Italiano LinguaDue* 10. 308–327.

Freeman, Donald. 2002. The hidden side of the work: Teacher knowledge and learning to teach. A perspective from North American educational research on teacher education in English language teaching. *Language Teaching* 35(1). 1–13.

Graham, Steve & Karin Sandmel. 2011. The process writing approach: A meta-analysis. *The Journal of Educational Research* 104(6). 396–407.

Graham, Steve, Alisha Bollinger, Carol Booth Olson, Catherine D'Aoust, Charles A. MacArthur, Deborah McCutchen & Natalie Olinghouse. 2012. *Teaching elementary school students to be effective writers: A practice guide* (NCEE 2012-4058). Washington, DC: National Center for Education Evaluation and Regional Assistance, Institute of Education Sciences, U.S. Department of Education.

Kindon, Sara, Rachel Pain & Mike Kesby. 2007. Participatory action research: Origins, approaches and methods. In Sara Kindon, Rachel Pain & Mike Kesby (eds.), *Participatory action research approaches and methods: Connecting people, participation and place*, 9–18. New York: Routledge.

Kuiken, Folkert & Ineke Vedder. 2018. Assessing functional adequacy of L2 performance in a task-based approach. In Naoko Taguchi & You Jin Kim (eds.), *Task-based approaches to teaching and assessing pragmatics*, 266–285. Amsterdam: John Benjamins.

MacDonald, Cathy. 2012. Understanding participatory action research: A qualitative research methodology option. *The Canadian Journal of Action Research* 13(2). 34–50.

McIntyre, Alice. 2007. *Participatory action research*. Thousand Oaks, CA: Sage.

McKay, Sandra Lee. 2006. *Researching second language classrooms*. Mahwah, NJ: Lawrence Erlbaum Associates.

McTaggart, Robin. 1997. *Participatory action research*. New York: State University of New York Press.

Mann, Steve. 2005. The language teacher's development. *Language Teaching* 38(3). 103–118.

Mills, Geoffrey E. 2003. *Action research: A guide for the teacher researcher*, 2nd edn. Upper Saddle River, NJ: Prentice Hall.

Nunan, David. 1992. *Research methods in language learning*. Cambridge: Cambridge University Press.

Pallotti, Gabriele. 2017a. Applying the interlanguage approach to language teaching. *International Review of Applied Linguistics in Language Teaching* 55(4). 393–412.

Pallotti, Gabriele. 2017b. Osservare l'interlingua: percorsi di educazione linguistica efficace per ridurre le diseguaglianze [Observing interlanguage: effective language education courses to reduce inequality]. In Massimo Vedovelli (ed.), *L'italiano dei nuovi italiani. Atti del XIX Convegno Nazionale GISCEL*, 505–520. Roma: Aracne.

Pallotti, Gabriele. 2017c. Une application des recherches sur l'interlangue aux contextes d'enseignement. Recherches et applications. *Le Français dans le monde* 61. 109–120.

Pallotti, Gabriele & Claudia Borghetti. 2019. The effects of an experimental approach to writing instruction on monolingual and multilingual pupils in Italian primary schools. *EuroAmerican Journal of Applied Linguistics and Languages* 6(1). 1–20.

Pallotti, Gabriele, Claudia Borghetti & Stefania Ferrari. 2019. Dalla riflessione su oralità e scrittura alla redazione di testi scritti efficaci: uno studio sperimentale [From reflection on orality and writing to the creation of effective written texts: an experimental study]. In Valentina Carbonara, Luana Cosenza, Paola Masillo, Luisa Salvati, Andrea Scibetta (eds.), *Il parlato e lo scritto: aspetti teorici e didattici. Atti del V Congresso della Società di Didattica delle Lingue e Linguistica Educativa (DILLE)*, 91–103. Pisa: Pacini.

Pallotti, Gabriele, Claudia Borghetti & Fabiana Rosi. 2021. *Insegnare a scrivere nella scuola primaria: il progetto Osservare l'interlingua* [Teaching to write in primary school: the Observing Interlanguage project]. Cesena/Bologna: Caissa Italia.

Reason, Peter & Hilary Bradbury (eds.). 2001. *Handbook of action research: Participative inquiry and practice*. London: Sage.

Richards, Jack C. & Thomas S. C. Farrell. 2005. *Professional development for language teachers: Strategies for teacher learning*. Cambridge: Cambridge University Press.

Scarino, Angela. 2014. Learning as reciprocal, interpretive meaning-making: A view from collaborative research into the professional learning of teachers of languages. *The Modern Language Journal* 98(1). 386–401.

Selinker, Larry. 1972. Interlanguage. *International Review of Applied Linguistics in Language Teaching* 10(1–4). 209–232.

Storch, Neomy. 2013. *Collaborative writing in L2 classrooms*. Bristol: Multilingual Matters.

White, Ronald V. & Valerie Arndt. 1991. *Process writing*. London: Longman.

Ofra Inbar-Lourie and Orly Haim

9 Learning to become an English teacher: Collaboration, context and the self

Abstract: This case study explores the first stage of the learning-to-teach process when pre-service teachers (PTs) are in their initial school-based professional experiences implementing pedagogical methodologies, while simultaneously assuming teaching roles and responsibilities. Specifically, this study focuses on the practicum experiences of four TEFL (Teaching English as a Foreign Language) PTs, in an Israeli mentoring school, investigating their clinical practice through participatory reflective research

Building on Opfer and Pedder (2011), the learning-to-teach process is examined through an ecological lens comprising three overlapping systems: the PTs, the school, and the professional development activities. The pre-service teacher system includes prior experiences, beliefs and assumptions about teaching and learning. The school level encompasses the school context, school policy and culture, and interactions with the students, mentor teacher and the staff. The professional learning activities include the assigned tasks and practices the PTs perform. The findings demonstrate the applicability of the ecological framework proposed by Opfer and Pedder. The data uncovered additional reciprocally interrelated dimensions, highlighting the pervasive role of context in the learning-to-teach process. Furthermore, the model has been expanded to include dimensions specifically related to language teaching and learning.

1 Introduction

Language teacher learning is viewed as ranging along an interactive continuum involving the construction of knowledge, skills and professional identity (Varghese 2018). This chapter explores the first stage of the process, when pre-service teachers (PTs) in their initial school-based professional experiences implement pedagogical methodologies while simultaneously assuming teaching roles and responsibilities within a set context (Freeman 2002; Nielsen et al. 2006). The impetus for this study is a collaborative project between an Israeli teacher education college and the mentoring schools serving as venues for the PTs' practicum experience. Each school accommodates a group of students working collaboratively with mentor teachers and school staff on various professional activities, and all stakeholders involved participate in a professional development programme.

Furthermore, collaboration in this programme includes participatory research conducted by the PTs to enhance their professional learning process. The study focuses on the practicum experiences of four TEFL (Teaching English as a Foreign Language) PTs in one of the mentoring schools, exploring the construction of their professional knowledge through their self-conducted research.

2 Literature review

2.1 Learning to teach

The learning-to-teach process is currently viewed as 'socially negotiated and contingent on knowledge of self, students, subject matter, curricula, and setting' (Johnson 2009: 20). Drawing on sociocultural theories, Johnson argues that language teachers' learning in teacher education programmes and throughout their career is intertwined with their contextual surroundings. This ecological approach aligns with Opfer and Pedder's (2011) three overlapping systems, which map the learning development zones of the PTs: the first comprises the PTs, the second the host school, and the third the professional development activities they engage in. The PTs system includes prior experiences, beliefs and assumptions about teaching and learning. The school level encompasses the school context, policy and culture, and interactions with the students, mentor teachers and staff. The professional learning activities include the assigned tasks and practices performed as part of the specialized disciplinary learning process, as in acquiring language teaching skills (Inbar-Lourie 2014).

Yazan (2018) emphasizes the role of community of practice within the situated teaching context and the shared professional community discourse. The notion of communities of practice (Lave and Wenger 1991) has been used to characterize the relationships between PTs and the communities within which they practice in their mentoring schools (Jiménez-Silva and Olson 2012). Attempts to join this professional community are not always successful, however, and Johnson (2016) notes the peripheral position PTs often experience as temporary outsiders in their encounters with the school's community. Yet regardless of whether they are accepted as legitimate members, the interaction with the school community guided by the training programme professionals can have a meaningful impact on the formation of their competencies and professional identities (Akkoç 2016). Moreover, the PTs' common experiences, study goals and school practice may define their own community of practice as an internal professional learning circle. One way of strengthening the cohesiveness of this phenomenon is through engagement in collaborative projects

(Opfer and Pedder 2011), such as participatory collaborative research, which examines their professional development on site within the wider communities of practice in the teacher education institution and mentoring school.

2.2 The clinical practice (CP) practicum model

The practicum experience is considered one of the most valuable elements in teacher education programmes, providing the PTs with ample opportunities to acquire teaching experience (Assadi and Murad 2017), implement the methodologies acquired in their teacher training programme, interact with students and professionals, and position themselves as the 'ideal self' or teacher they wish to become (Thompson 2021). Furthermore, the various activities PTs carry out in the practicum enable them to exercise their agency by making decisions, taking control and self-regulating. Research suggests that this process is contextually bound and inextricably linked to the perceived affordances available in the professional environment where they work (van Lier 2007). Practicum models vary depending on the degree of collaboration with the cooperating schools and the priorities of the teacher education programme.

Currently, the pendulum is swinging towards active partnerships between the teacher education programme and the school, emphasizing the significance of an in-depth experience within schools as complex entities. This approach to the practicum, referred to as clinical practice (CP), perceives the learning-to-teach process as anchored in research-based evidence and judgment, where pedagogical actions are directed by an inquiry and evaluation phase (Alter and Coggshall 2009). Within research-informed CP, the term 'clinical reasoning' has been appropriated from the medical profession and applied to teaching to refer to the professional knowledge and skill-based process which candidate teachers need to acquire as part of their profession (Kriewaldt and Turnidge 2013). Teacher education programmes incorporating a CP approach aim 'to facilitate and deepen the interplay between the different kinds of knowledge that are generated and validated within the different contexts of school and university' (Burn and Mutton 2015: 219). The practicum experience is regarded as particularly challenging since the PTs are required to adjust themselves to the school culture and norms and socialize into the new environment. Discrepancies may, however, occur between the PDs' values, knowledge and beliefs and the school's social values and educational orientations, turning this experience into 'a learning journey that can involve struggle, loneliness, and conflict, as well as excitement and exhilaration' (Trent 2013: 427).

A vital component in CP models is classroom-based research accompanied by reflective analysis. This is often carried out through the inclusion of collaborative participatory research initiatives that allow prospective teachers to engage in research and utilize it for teaching. Willegems et al. (2017: 243) affirm that 'the involvement of multiple actors (e.g., teacher educators, social workers) in a non-hierarchical level (shared inquiry) is the most promising for PTs' learning'. However, they note the scarcity of robust research in this area, which can assist in a better understanding of the complex interactions between the different stakeholders involved in the learning-to-teach process.

With these considerations in mind, we postulated the following research question: How do TEFL PTs in a clinical practice practicum perceive their situated learning-to-teach process within a collaborative teacher education and school partnership?

3 The context

We here describe the two main research contexts, the teacher education college and the mentoring school.

The teacher education college is one of the largest in Israel (approximately 10,000 students and 700 lecturers). It comprises a diverse population of Jewish and Arab students and faculty, and offers BEd and MEd degrees in various disciplines, including teaching certificates for academics. The college has been associated with school-based programmes of professional development for over three decades. Recently, the college established a network with 50 K–12 partnership schools to collaboratively enhance the CP experience in different disciplines, TEFL included. The study was anchored within this macro context and is part of a data set on teacher learning. Within the micro TEFL certification programme, it focuses on a research-based TEFL seminar. The purpose of the seminar was to provide PTs with the opportunity to plan and carry out research in the area of language teaching. The study was conducted in the format of collaborative participatory research, whereby the students and one of the researchers (course instructor) jointly planned and carried out the study including data collection and analysis. Furthermore, the second researcher was involved in the meetings, providing guidance and input. The role of the second researcher was to provide an additional expert perspective regarding the design, implementation and interpretations of the study.

The mentoring school was established in 2002 by parents interested in creating a pluralistic educational framework for their children, cultivating equity, mutual respect and learning. The school includes classes from grade 7 to 10 and is committed to pluralism as a way of life on the personal, social and national level.

Teaching and learning are conducted in diverse environments using varied innovative learning and teaching methodologies.

4 Methodology

Utilizing a qualitative approach, this exploratory case study investigates the professional development partnership, focusing on one participating school. Building on Opfer and Pedder (2011), the learning process is examined through an ecological lens comprising three overlapping systems: the pre-service teacher, the school, and the professional development activities included in the project, as noted above.

4.1 Participants

Four undergraduate PTs (two males and two females) in their final year of the teacher education programme participated in this case study. The PTs were all in their late twenties. Though English was not their mother tongue, they were all highly proficient in English.

Informed consent was collected, and participants' identities are protected through pseudonyms, also used for all other individuals in the two contexts.

4.2 Data sources

Data were generated over a period of eight months during the fall and spring semesters of the academic year 2021/2022. Sources of data were: eight TEFL reflective blog entries of each PT (totalling 32 entries) describing critical incidents throughout the academic year in relation to their ongoing school experiences and dimensions of their professional development; in-depth semi-structured interviews with the four PTs. The audio-taped interviews, developed collaboratively by the PTs and the teacher educators, included questions about the PTs' perceived learning-to-teach process (i.e., aspects of the practicum, professional development activities, relationships with the mentor teachers, impressions about the school context, etc.) based on the literature in the area of teacher development (e.g., Thompson 2021; Woods 1996). The interviews were carried out by the PTs, who interviewed their peers. Additionally, teaching-related artefacts (lesson plans, teaching materials) were used for data triangulation.

4.3 Data analysis

Qualitative data procedures informed by Corbin and Strauss (2008) were utilized to analyse the data. The analyses included three major stages. First, the blog entries were analysed according to the three ecological systems (Opfer and Pedder 2011): the pre-service teacher, the school, and the professional development activities included in the project. Each student selected and self-analysed eight blog entries representing professional development at different points of time throughout the academic year. Based on their analyses, the initial category system was collaboratively established. During this stage, the major themes and sub-themes within each of the three central categories representing the ecological systems were identified. This process involved selecting quotes from the blogs, determining pre-existing themes according to the Opfer and Pedder (2011) framework, and emerging themes sorted into categories. Second, the transcribed interviews were analysed by the students utilizing the same procedures. Third, the analyses obtained from each data source (i.e., the blogs and transcribed interviews) were summarized in a data matrix separately, and eventually in a matrix for the entire data set. After establishing the matrices, patterns and broader categories answering the research question were identified.

The analyses were carried out with the aid of Narralizer software (Shkedi 2004). Triangulation involved comparing and cross-checking the categories emerging in the blog entries, transcribed interviews and the PTs' lesson plans and learning materials. Inter-rater reliability was established by involving all ten students participating in the research seminar; they examined the category system and made changes in cases of disagreement. The category system was piloted and additionally examined by an external TEFL specialist. Based on the pilot phase and the examination, further minor changes were made.

5 Findings

Drawing on the framework proposed by Opfer and Pedder (2011) and sociocultural approaches to researching teacher learning (Johnson 2009), our analyses yielded an extended scheme, aligning with our findings. The scheme consisted of three overlapping intersecting systems. Each level is intimately interconnected with the other two levels, encompassing a number of sub-themes, some of which exist in the original framework, while others emerged from our data. Figure 9.1 presents the extended scheme, depicting both the original elements (in bold) and

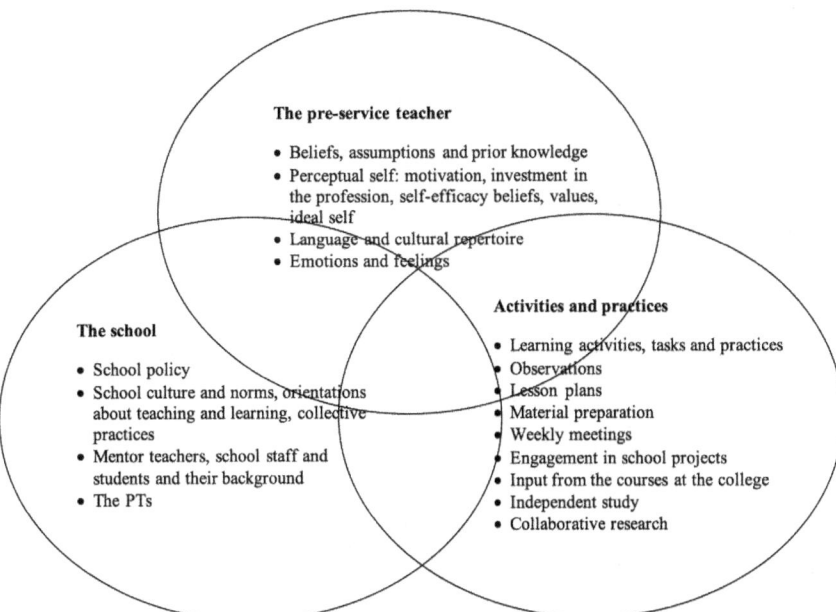

Figure 9.1: The extended nested scheme of themes and sub-themes based on Opfer & Pedder (2011).

the components that have been added. In the following sections, we present the entire scheme organized by the three nested levels.

5.1 The pre-service teacher

Our findings from the blog entries, interviews and language learning materials converge to reveal the following major themes and sub-themes within the level of the pre-service teacher:
1   perceptual self, which includes the following sub-themes: intrinsic motivation, ideal self, self-efficacy, values, and investment in the profession;
2   beliefs about teaching and learning, assumptions and prior knowledge;
3   language and culture repertoire;
4   emotions and feelings.

Perceptual self. As it pertains to motives, our findings point to prominent *intrinsic motives* for choosing the teaching profession, particularly meaningfulness associated with teaching English, given its powerful status as an international language, love of the language and of teaching, altruism, and the desire to contribute to society (Hiver, Kim and Kim 2018). The accounts of the PTs implying that intrinsic motives are prevalent in their choice of the profession, can be explained by the status of teachers in the larger ecological context. Teaching in Israel is not financially rewarding, particularly in the initial years; thus, it should come as no surprise that intrinsic motives were the only driving force for these PTs' choice of the profession (i.e., rather than extrinsic motives), as illustrated in the excerpt below:

> *First, I decided to become a teacher because I had a passion for education; I wanted to influence the next generation and teach them values and manners in order for them to be the best they can. I decided to be an English teacher afterwards, because I felt that many adults hate English and they are afraid of learning the language because of bad experience at school. I wanted to make a change in the next generation's perspective towards English.* (Helen, interview #1)

Concurring with recent research (e.g., Mezei 2014; Thompson 2021), the PTs' 'ideal self' and identity seem to be intertwined with their motivation to teach:

> *I would like to be a source of inspiration for my students. I would like to be an approachable and understanding teacher – with my students and colleagues, but also, with myself.* (Helen, interview #1)

Beliefs about language learning and teaching, assumptions, and prior knowledge. It is widely acknowledged that teaching style is influenced by prior knowledge, past experiences and beliefs, and teachers' orientation towards the learning activities (Borg 2009; Woods 1996). The blog entries depicted the PTs' beliefs, assumptions and dispositions about teaching, some of which were consolidated in the CP experience, based on their observations or activities, as illustrated in this example:

> *I believe that if you prepare well and know what the class is studying, you will not have surprises and the students will treat you respectfully and not just as a visiting teacher.* (Nancy, blog entry)

Moreover, corroborating previous research (e.g., Burns, Freeman, and Edwards 2015; Borg 2009), our analyses demonstrate that the PTs' experiences at school along with their studies at the college, led to the formation of new beliefs, or modifications of pre-existing beliefs based on their past experiences as learners. An interesting theme emerging in their blogs concerned a gap between previous assumptions about English instruction and their classroom observations. Drawing on their accounts, it is plausible to assume that these observed gaps may have facilitated a change in their beliefs and/or adoption of novel insights about teaching and learning, resonating with the notion of 'cognitive conflict or challenge' proposed by Opfer and Pedder (2011). Some of these gaps are described in this example:

> Before I started my practicum this year, I wasn't sure how English teachers in Israel today approach 'Reading' activities in secondary school. It was my assumption that most young teens dislike reading, and [I] was wondering how to overcome this as a teacher. How to inspire students to read books – and not only through book reports and quizzes. Observing Susan (my mentor teacher) showed me a way of achieving it, and also brought with it another important realization – not all native English speakers are good readers. It is important to allow them time to practice their reading skills and expand their vocabulary knowledge. (David, blog entry)

And along similar lines, from Ben's blog entry:

> I was pleasantly surprised to see 'Reading' having a central role in almost every English lesson that I observed; it didn't exactly fit with my assumptions. Also, I found that my assumptions and belief, that when students are allowed to work independently or with their peers they rebel and do not complete tasks, was wrong.

Successful teaching events and episodes often contributed to an increased level of self-efficacy. The PTs reported 'satisfaction' in their ability to carry out their planned lessons, as well as the unplanned lessons required occasionally by the school. Furthermore, our PTs drew on their experiences or skills in their practicum activities, as described by Helen after substituting for one of the English teachers:

> I remember being nervous about a few things, but mostly it was about making sure I was prepared. In these cases I find that, as a pre-service teacher, I rely a lot on my prior experience, even if it's not directly related to teaching. Anything in my bag of tricks from my life experience will be used so that I feel more secure and better prepared when I enter a classroom. (Helen, blog entry)

Language and culture repertoire. The PTs' language repertoire, i.e., perceived competency in English, played an important role in their learning-to-teach process, influencing their investment in teaching, self-efficacy beliefs and perceived interactions with the students. Since the student population in the school includes a large number of English-speaking students and all mentor teachers were native English speakers, some of the PTs, who were L2 English speakers, experienced a lack of confidence in their English and felt a need to invest more effort in lesson preparation, as stated by Ben:

> The school I'm in at the moment has a lot of English native speakers, so I need to use English quite a lot, more than I would use it if the teachers and the students were not native speakers of English. (Ben, interview #2)

Our findings thus imply that the PTs' plurilingual and cultural background interacted with the school's sociolinguistic context, and with how they positioned themselves as professionals during the practicum experience (Burns, Freeman, and Edwards 2015; Ellis 2016; Haim, Orland-Barak, and Goldberg 2020).

Emotions and feelings. The teaching activities and interactions with the students and professionals at school were a source of conflicting emotions and feelings (e.g., enjoyment, disappointment, and tension). In general, the PTs regarded the interactions with the students and teachers as a major source of pleasant emotions. Teaching the lessons successfully and reaching most of their instructional goals elicited feelings of joy and fulfilment. That said, teaching whole classes, particularly at the beginning of the year, was associated with feelings of anxiety, uncertainty and tension. Moreover, instructional events where students struggled to understand the materials used were perceived as challenging. Furthermore, changes in the schedule of the lessons they had planned to teach due to ongoing school events and activities yielded unpleasant emotions, such as frustration and disappointment, as depicted in the following excerpt:

> *Teaching involves a variety of feelings – frightened. I felt like the students were going to eat me alive. Most of my apprehension was concerned with class management and class instructions – with Hillary* [the mentor teacher] *not being in the room with us. Will the students accept us as authority? Will they behave? Will we be able to provide them with correct instructions, and answer their questions? I wasn't sure how it was all going to play out, but by the time I arrived at the high school, I was ready for the adventure and excited for the opportunity to teach a lesson.* (David, blog entry)

5.2 The school level

The school-level system involves the contexts of the school, i.e., the school policy, school culture and norms, orientations about teaching and learning, the mentor teacher and the English staff, the PTs, and the school students. The particular school context powerfully influenced the PTs' learning-to-teach process, optimizing their professional learning conditions on the one hand and creating a sense of confusion (especially at the beginning of the year) on the other. The blogs along with the lesson plans and learning materials developed by the PTs strongly suggest that the unique school culture, as well as its learning and teaching orientations embodied in the school curriculum, afforded learning and teaching opportunities for implementing cutting-edge learner-centred instruction. This occurred within an exceptionally supportive community of practice consisting of the PTs, the mentor teachers, the school staff, the school students, and the pedagogical advisor. The influential role of the school was also evident in the topics and contents of the lessons developed by the

PTs, focusing more on content-based teaching and the use of authentic materials than on the school textbooks. The following excerpts demonstrate the PTs' interpretations of the school context:

> *The unique thing about the school is that their philosophy toward teaching is very special, and it is related to the learner rather than the teacher. This school has no fences, students can come in and out whenever they want, and the teaching is based on trust.* (Nancy, interview #3)

> *First, the atmosphere was very unusual compared to a 'regular' high school, in terms of the intimate surroundings and not many students. Second impression was entering a very small class of students. The class had only 20 students, which is considered a complete paradise for teaching. Third impression was that I witnessed an entire lesson in English, I thought to myself: 'Did I die and reach heaven?!' What is going on? There was no use of Hebrew at all. Fourth impression was that the entire day passes without a bell that rings and informs you when the lesson ends etc.* (Nancy, blog entry)

Although the PTs' approach to the school policy and environment was generally positive, in the initial period some of them felt 'lost' and insecure. The mentor teachers and the community of practice working at the school facilitated the PTs' adjustment into the school context. Concurring with previous research, the mentoring relationship was one of the most meaningful elements of the practicum experience at school (Mena et al. 2016). The PTs reported that the mentor teachers were a source of inspiration for learning about teaching. The personal and professional support provided by them, along with the social support provided by the community of practice, facilitated the PTs' socialization into the school, as shown below:

> Her [the mentor teacher's] *way of thinking and approaching literature is amazing. She has so many unique pre-reading activities, things that I would never have imagined that can be used that way. I felt that the mentors trust me, so I became more confident in what I created and how I performed in the class.* (Ben, interview #4)

> *At the beginning, the experience was really hard. I felt lost. But then my mentor teacher Shani gave me some good advice on how to approach students and especially the struggling ones. I was able to connect with the students.* (David, Blog entry)

5.3 Professional activities and practices

The professional activities in which the PTs took part cast a powerful influence on their learning-to-teach process. The following major categories were identified based on the analyses of the reflective blogs, interviews and language learning materials: *observations, lesson plans, reflections, weekly meetings, engagement in school projects, input from the courses at the college,* and the *collaborative research project.* The activities the PTs carried out at school served as quality learning experiences for acquiring practical knowledge and teaching strategies. In many cases, they also served as an impetus for adopting novel ideas and generating new knowledge (for example, in the use of technological devices), as illustrated in these excerpts:

> Class started with a game in groups using personal cell phones. I am not yet sure what I think about it. On the one hand, I did not like the fact that personal cell phones were part of the lesson. In addition, a few minutes were wasted trying to fix technological issues. On the other hand, the pupils were all engaged, and seemed to have a real interest in the game! They all looked forward to it and were motivated to win so they really pushed themselves to getting the right answers. (Nancy, blog entry).

> As I was looking for materials and ways to teach them, I came to an understanding that I lack knowledge in how to approach students at their age. I can't use techniques that are used in elementary school due to their age. (Ben, blog entry)

Finally, the *participatory collaborative research* afforded the students opportunities to acquire in-depth knowledge about teaching and learning to teach, and about their own professional development. This theme was prevalent in their TEFL reflective blogs, interviews and class discussions (i.e., at the college), accentuating the impact of planning and carrying out a collaborative self-study on their own professional development. The study participants reported that exposure to and analysis of the research literature in the area of teacher learning, along with planning and carrying out the study, enhanced and accelerated their professional development. Furthermore, the collaborative research format served as an additional source of learning and support, as this example shows:

> I like working with another student teacher or even in a small group – I feel that it makes the teaching process more effective and that I learn more about myself and my learning process better. (Ben, interview #4)

6 Discussion and conclusions

This exploratory research set out to examine four TEFL PTs' perceived learning-to-teach process through an ecological analytic lens. Taken as a whole, the findings demonstrate the applicability of the ecological framework proposed by Opfer and Pedder (2011) for the learning process, hence validating the model. Yet our data uncovered additional reciprocally interrelated dimensions to the framework, highlighting the pervasive role of context in a number of ways. Given the interdependence identified within and across the major categories and their components, we discuss the findings holistically, rather than referring to each component as a discrete entity.

The school site presented an unusual experience for the PTs in terms of the composition of its members, but more so in the informal teaching routines and innovative practices. The socialization into this culture was not an easy feat for the PTs, and created ambivalence expressed in favourable or negative reactions, the latter more evident in their initial encounters. Such reactions echo the acculturation difficulties novice teachers often report in their first year of teaching (e.g., Haim and Amdur 2016).

Another dimension strongly influencing the learning-to-teach process concerns the specific discipline of TEFL instruction. Our findings demonstrate that TEFL as perceived by the PTs, permeates all three ecological levels: the pre-service teacher, the school, and the professional activities and practices. Thus, we have expanded the model to include issues specifically related to language teaching and learning, such as the interaction between the PTs' command of English and that of the school community, highlighting the issue of the native/non-native English speaking teachers' conflictual dilemma (Inbar-Lourie 2005). Language and culture in general evoked strong emotions amongst the PTs, who felt less secure in their language skills when attempting to adjust to and meet the norms of the school context. It is worth noting here that though the English language enjoys a prestigious status in Israeli society, the high proficiency level amongst the students and teachers is unique to the mentoring school under investigation. Indeed, these data illustrate the dominant role of the sociolinguistic context on the language teachers' learning-to-teach process (Haim, Orland-Barak, and Goldberg 2020).

Regarding the PTs' ecological level, the accounts point to the centrality of a number of interrelated elements which form what we termed the *perceptual self*, in addition to the dimension of *beliefs, assumptions and prior knowledge* delineated in the original framework. Extending previous research, our findings demonstrate that the individual's interpretations of the affordances provided by the school are linked to his or her sense of agency (Trent 2013; van Lier 2007). Concerning the level of the pre-service activities and practices, it is evident from the data that participatory research allowed for new insights for developing critical understandings about the self, the context and teaching activities through TEFL reflective practice.

Indeed, an important feature of the learning-to-teach process emerging within the ecological systems investigated in the current participatory study is that of reciprocity, i.e., a mutual exchange of ideas, insights and knowledge, which occurred simultaneously among the various stakeholders. The existence of multiple reciprocal relations, which continuously contribute to the knowledge and identity formation of the participating members of the community of practice, is apparent in the data. The PTs reported that the specific contextual framework of the practicum enabled them to *'learn from each other'* and *'from their mentor teacher'* not only ideas and methods about language teaching but also about their perceptual self. Likewise, though from a different angle, the mentor teachers reported that the mentoring process involved *'learning new ideas about English teaching'*, especially in the area of innovative technological media, and also *'insights about themselves as language teachers'*. As it pertains to the participatory study, the PTs reported gaining knowledge and skills about the learning-to-teach process, about themselves as prospective teachers, and also about carrying out teacher research through the situated collaborative process of planning and implementing the study.

In conclusion, this research contributes to our understanding of the multifaceted complexity of the practicum experience as an aspect of the learning-to-teach process, as well as the role of the collaborative partnership between the two institutional contexts, the college of education and the mentoring school. The study offers a comprehensive framework for understanding teacher learning, highlighting the interconnectivity among the various components of which it is composed. We acknowledge the inherent limitation of the findings due to the small sample and call for further research in other contexts to better understand the process of teacher learning.

References

Akkoç, Hatice. 2016. Integrating communities of practice framework into pre-service teacher education. *Proceedings of the Conference of the International Journal of Arts & Sciences*. 271–276.

Alter, Jamie & Jane G. Coggshall. 2009. Teaching as a clinical practice profession: Implications for teacher preparation and state policy. New York Comprehensive Center, National Comprehensive Center for Teacher Quality. https://files.eric.ed.gov/fulltext/ED543819.pdf (accessed 11 July 2022).

Assadi, Nabil & Tareq Murad. 2017. The effect of the teachers' training model 'Academy-Class' on the teacher students' professional development from students' perspectives. *Journal of Language Teaching and Research* 8(2). 214–220. DOI: http://dx.doi.org/10.17507/jltr.0802.02 (accessed 11 July 2022).

Borg, Simon. 2009. Language teacher cognition. In Anne Burns & Jack C. Richards (eds.), *The Cambridge guide to second language teacher education*, 163–171. Cambridge: Cambridge University Press.

Burn, Katharine & Trevor Mutton. 2015. A review of 'research-informed clinical practice' in Initial Teacher Education. *Oxford Review of Education* 41(2). 217–233. DOI: https://doi.org/10.1080/03054985.2015.1020104 (accessed 11 July 2022).

Burns, Anne, Donald Freeman & Emily Edwards. 2015. Theorizing and studying the language-teaching mind: Mapping research on language teacher cognition. *The Modern Language Journal* 99(3). 585–601. DOI: https://doi.org/10.1111/modl.12245 (accessed 11 July 2022).

Corbin, Juliet & Anselm Strauss. 2008. *Basics of qualitative research: Techniques and procedures for developing grounded theory* (3rd edn.). Thousand Oaks, California: Sage.

Ellis, Elizabeth M. 2016. 'I may be a native speaker but I'm not monolingual': Reimagining *all* teachers' linguistic identities in TESOL. *TESOL Quarterly* 50(3). 597–630. DOI: https://doi.org/10.1002/tesq.314 (accessed 11 July 2022).

Freeman, Donald. 2002. The hidden side of the work: Teacher knowledge and learning to teach. A perspective from north American educational research on teacher education in English language teaching. *Language Teaching* 35(1). 1–13.

Haim, Orly & Lisa Amdur. 2016. Teacher perspectives on their alternative fast-track induction. *Teaching Education* 27(4). 343–370.

Haim, Orly, Lily Orland-Barak & Tsafrir Goldberg. 2020. The role of linguistic and cultural background in TEFL novices' induction period. *International Journal of Multilingualism*. https://doi.org/10.1080/14790718.2020.1715412 (accessed 11 July 2022).

Hiver, Paul, Tae-Young Kim & Youngmi Kim. 2018. Language teacher motivation. In Sarah Mercer & Achilleas Kostoulas (eds.), *Language teacher psychology*, 18–33. Bristol: Multilingual Matters.

Inbar-Lourie, Ofra. 2005. Mind the gap: Self and perceived native speaker identities of TEFL teachers. In Enric Llurda (ed.), *Non-native language teachers: Perceptions, challenges, and contributions to the profession*, 265–281. Boston, MA: Springer.

Inbar-Lourie, Ofra. 2014. Knowledge-based language teachers' standards: Who is the good teacher? In Beata Bugajska-Jaszczołt, Joanna Karczewska, Agnieszka Przychodni & Elżbieta Zyzik (eds.), *Kompetentny Nauczyciel Wczesnej Edukacji inwestycjąw Lepszą Przyszłość Vol I*, 151–160. Uniwersytet Jana Kochanowskiego, Kielce Prasa. http://zasobyip2.ore.edu.pl/uploads/publications/a3f147656188f1ee881a8631ada26ea2 (accessed 31 August 2022).

Jiménez-Silva, Margarita & Kate Olson. 2012. A community of practice in teacher education: Insights and perceptions. *The International Journal of Teaching and Learning in Higher Education* 24. 335–348.

Johnson, Karen E. 2009. *Second language teacher education: A sociocultural perspective*. New York: Routledge.

Johnson, David H. 2016. 'Sitting alone in the staffroom contemplating my future': Communities of practice, legitimate peripheral participation and student teachers' experiences of problematic school placements as guests. *Cambridge Journal of Education* 46(4). 533–551 DOI: 10.1080/0305764X.2015.106979 (accessed 24 September 2022)

Kriewaldt, Jeana & Dagmar Turnidge. 2013. Conceptualising an approach to clinical reasoning in the education profession. *Australian Journal of Teacher Education* 38(6). 103–115.

Lave, Jean & Etienne Wenger. 1991. *Situated learning: Legitimate peripheral participation*. Cambridge: Cambridge University Press.

Mena, Juanjo, Marisa García, Anthony Clarke & Tasos Barkatsas. 2016. An analysis of three different approaches to student teacher mentoring and their impact on knowledge generation in practicum settings. *European Journal of Teacher Education* 39(1). 53–76. DOI: https://doi.org/10.1080/02619768.2015.1011269 (accessed 11 July 2022).

Mezei, Gabriella. 2014. The effect of motivational strategies on self-related aspects of student motivation and second language learning. In Kata Csizér & Michael Magid (eds.), *The impact of self-concept on language learning*, 289–310. Bristol, UK: Multilingual Matters.

Nielsen, Diane Corcoran, Arlene Lundmark Barry & Ann Brickey Addison. 2006. A model of a new-teacher induction program and teacher perceptions of beneficial components. *Action in Teacher Education* 28(4). 14–24. DOI: https://doi.org/10.1080/01626620.2007.10463425 (accessed 11 July 2022).

Opfer, V. Darleen & David Pedder. 2011. Conceptualizing teacher professional learning. *Review of Educational Research* 81(3). 376–407. DOI: https://doi.org/10.3102/0034654311413609 (accessed 11 July 2022).

Shkedi, Asher. 2004. *Methodologies of qualitative research: Theory and practice* (2nd edn.). Tel-Aviv: Tel-Aviv University, Ramot (in Hebrew).

Thompson, Amy S. 2021. *The role of context in language teachers' self-development and motivation*. Bristol: Multilingual Matters.

Trent, John. 2013. From learner to teacher: Practice, language, and identity in a teaching practicum. *Asia-Pacific Journal of Teacher Education* 41(4). 426–440. DOI: http://doi.org/10.1080/1359866X.2013.838621 (accessed 11 July 2022).

van Lier, Leo. 2007. Action-based teaching, autonomy and identity. *International Journal of Innovation in Language Learning and Teaching* 1(1). 46–65.

Varghese, Manka, Brian Morgan, Bill Johnston & Kimberly A. Johnson. 2005. Theorizing language teacher identity: Three perspectives and beyond. *Journal of Language, Identity, and Education*, 4(1). 21–44.

Willegems, Vicky, Els Consuegra, Katrien Struyven & Nadine Engels. 2017. Teachers and pre-service teachers as partners in collaborative teacher research: A systematic literature review. *Teaching and Teacher Education* 64. 230–245.

Woods, Devon. 1996. *Teacher cognition in language teaching: Beliefs, decision-making, and classroom practice*. New York: Cambridge University Press.

Yazan, Bedrettin. 2018. A conceptual framework to understand language teacher identities. *Journal of Second Language Teacher Education* 1(1). 21–48.

Part 4: **Collaborative research and national policy**

Batia Laufer
10 From research to a national curriculum: The case of a lexical syllabus

Abstract: The interface between research and policy-making requires sound research-based evidence for informed decisions and accessibility of this evidence to decision-makers. In this chapter I discuss research that should inform the construction of a lexical syllabus, and as a case in point, I report on the lexical syllabus in the new English Curriculum in Israel. The construction of the syllabus involved collaboration between researchers, teachers, textbook writers, curriculum planners, assessment specialists, and education administrators. This collaboration followed the pragmatic model of relations between research and policy-making since both sides' views and expertise complemented each other.

The lexical syllabus consists of vocabulary bands taught at different learning stages. The following research findings and collaborations (in brackets) were behind its design: gaps between learners' lexical knowledge and the amount of lexis necessary for performing language tasks (curriculum designers, researchers, teachers, assessment specialists, ministry administrators); vocabulary treatment in textbooks: amount of exposure and type of activities (researchers, curriculum designers, and textbook writers); challenges in reaching the productive level of word knowledge (researchers, students, textbook writers, curriculum designers); establishing a new word counting unit – the Nuclear Word Family (researchers and curriculum designers); importance and difficulty of multi-word units (researchers, curriculum designers); presentation of words with multiple meanings (researchers and curriculum designers); representation of orthographic patterns (researchers and curriculum designers).

I show how the above findings have been incorporated into the lexical syllabus and how they will be implemented in textbooks and classroom practices.

Acknowledgements: I would like to express my thanks to the following colleagues and students: Dr Tziona Levi, Chief Inspector of English, for her initiative to include a lexical syllabus in the New English Curriculum; Dr Lisa Amdur and Dr Elisheva Barkon, members of the national committee for teaching English, who designed the lexical syllabus; Dr Geke Ravenhorst-Kalovski, my former PhD student, who collected the data on students' lexical size; Ms Cadit Nissan-Zilbiger, my PhD student, who collected the data on vocabulary treatment in textbooks.

1 Introduction

Applied linguistics is a field that identifies, investigates and offers solutions to real-world concerns in which language is a central issue (Brumfit 1997; Davies and Elder 2004). To date, the largest area of applied linguistic research addresses issues in language education. Designing a language curriculum with related language syllabi is a good example of a real task that revolves around language learners and a language to be learnt, and is relevant for educational practice and educational policy. A curriculum is defined as the guideline in planning the academic content of a course or program. It relates to the knowledge and skills that students are expected to acquire, it specifies the underlying philosophy of the guideline and principles guiding task design, teaching practices, and assessment. A syllabus, on the other hand, is a subpart of a curriculum that is concerned with the specification, sequencing, grading, and organization of specific contents (Richards 2001). Thus, the lexical syllabus in the 2020 English as a Foreign Language curriculum for Israeli schools consists of a vocabulary list to be taught throughout the school system, from grade 3 to grade 12, or Pre-A1 to B2 levels in terms of the CEFR (*Common European Framework of Reference for Languages*; Council of Europe 2001). The list is subdivided into several lexical bands intended for different language levels of learners.

In this chapter, I will show how applied linguistic research findings informed the construction of the Israeli lexical syllabus. Furthermore, conducting research that is relevant to syllabus design involves the collaboration of researchers with members of other language-related professions, and the construction and implementation of the syllabus require the collaboration of researchers with stakeholders as well. I will also describe the process of designing the lexical syllabus and the collaborations that contributed to the final product.

2 Decisions behind the design of the lexical syllabus

2.1 Decision 1 – End-of-high school vocabulary size targets

Lexical research has shown that to function in a second language, people need to master certain minimum quantities of lexis. Knowledge of 2,000 most frequent word families may suffice for participating in a simple conversation. To understand simple TV shows and movies, 3,000 most frequent word families are necessary; to read authentic texts with assistance (e.g., dictionary, teacher's guidance) 5,000 word families should be known, at least receptively. In the case of comprehending authentic language without assistance, language users should master 6,000–7,000 word families to understand oral language and 8,000–9,000 to understand written prose (Dang and Webb 2014; Laufer and Ravenhorst-Kalovski 2010; Nation 2006).

Before discussing the vocabulary size that high school graduates should learn in the new curriculum, I needed information on how many words students knew nowadays. This would show what gap we had to narrow between what learners know and what they need. The information became available due to a three-pronged collaboration with college teachers, college administrators, and the Council for Higher Education in Israel.

First, a group of EFL (English as a Foreign Language) teachers in a college agreed to test 760 students who were taking the EFL courses. The students were graduates of Israeli high schools in their first year of college and were, therefore, representative of the range of EFL levels that students achieve. They took the Vocabulary Levels Tests (Schmitt, Schmitt, and Clapham 2000) and Vocabulary Size Test (Nation and Beglar 2007). The results ranged from less than 2,000 to 8,000 vocabulary families. Second, college administrators provided me with their students' scores on the English part of the National Psychometric Test, a national test that students have to take before entering tertiary education. The English part of the test classifies students into several levels of English proficiency (basic, pre-advanced, advanced 1, advanced 2, exemption), and the level, in turn, determines the number of academic hours of English each student has to take during the studies. After matching the students' assigned EFL levels to their vocabulary sizes, I could see what vocabulary was characteristic of each proficiency level. Third, I approached the Council for Higher Education that keeps the records of the psychometric tests taken by all the candidates for tertiary education and received the English test results of all the test-takers in ten years, altogether about 10,000 results. Based on the scores, I calculated the national percentage of students at each proficiency level. As I knew what vocabulary size corresponded to what proficiency level (see previous stages of the process), I could now calculate the percent of students in the country with particular vocabulary sizes. Table 10.1 presents these results.

Table 10.1: Vocabulary size of Israeli high school graduates.

Level	Percent of students	Vocabulary size (in word families)
Exemption	15%	6,000–8,000
Advanced 2	23.5%	5,000
Advanced 1	24.5%	3,000–4,000
Pre-advanced	16%	2,000
Basic	21%	<2,000

The results show that ~62% of high school graduates do not have enough vocabulary to read authentic prose, e.g., newspapers, even with a dictionary, as they know less than 5,000 word families. Unassisted reading is possible only for 15% of graduates. I presented this information to the Ministry of Education administrators and the curriculum planners and tried to convince them to set the target lexis at 8,000 word families. However, their experience with teachers and learners led them to decide to adopt a more modest target of 5,400 word families that would still improve the present state of affairs.

The collaboration cycle that led to the final decision involved researchers seeking information and cooperation from teachers, administrators, and assessment specialists (Figure 10.1). The information was needed to find out how many words Israeli high school graduates knew, as opposed to how many words they should know to understand authentic language. Based on the data, the researchers made recommendations to the curriculum planners and the ministry administration. The final decision was a compromise between the position of the researcher and the curriculum planners who were familiar with the views of the Ministry of Education and education professionals in schools.

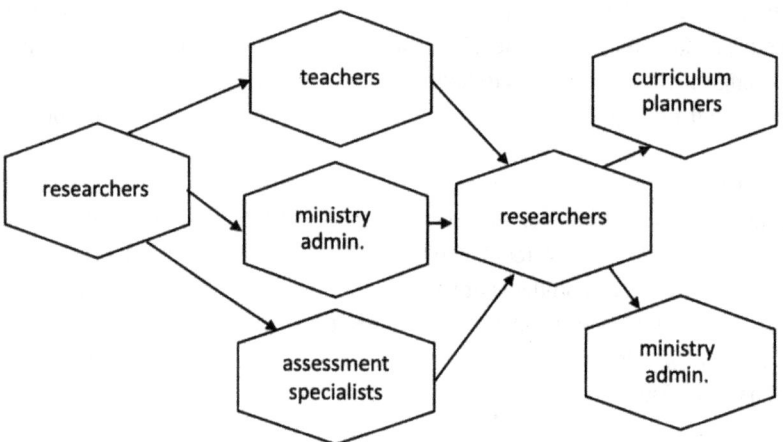

Figure 10.1: Collaboration cycle leading to final decision.

2.2 Decision 2 – Word counting unit: 5,400 lemmas, or word families?

Word lists are usually organized by either lemmas or families. A lemma is a unit that includes the base word and its inflections. Thus *read, reads, read* (past), *reading* (verb) is one lemma. *Reading* (noun) is another lemma. Additional related lemmas are *readable, unreadable, readability*. Lists organized by lemmas take into account each lemma's frequency. As a result, related words like *quick/quickly, beauty/beautiful* are listed and taught at different stages of learning. However, if we organize word lists by word families, the five lemmas of *read* above will constitute one word family that includes a base word, its inflected and derived forms. The advantage of an organization by families is that related words will be taught together. However, a word family may include words that are infrequent and not very useful for school pupils, as, for example, in the word family of *center*. The family includes *center, central, centrally, centrality, centralization, centralize, decentralize, decentralization, centrist, centralism*. The examples show that the target vocabulary of 5,400 word families will include more items than 5,400 lemmas. Both the researcher and the curriculum designers discussed the advantages and disadvantages of the two types of organization. Research suggests that learning related words, e.g., *avoid/avoidable* requires less teaching and learning effort than learning unrelated words, e.g., *avoid/respectable*. Hence, it made no sense to separate words that could be learnt with little effort. On the other hand, it made no sense to invest time and effort in infrequent word family members, e.g. *decentralize*. The researcher also suggested that learning related words will develop awareness and, consequently, the acquisition of morphological patterns. For example, having been exposed to *unbearable, unreadable, unbelievable* together with the respective base words, *bear, read, believe*, learners will most probably recognize *unavoidable*. The researcher suggested a new unit for organizing word lists, a 'nuclear family'. Unlike the 'extended family' that includes all possible derived words which appear in huge corpora of about 300,000,000 words, like COCA (Corpus of Contemporary American English) and BNC (British National Corpus), the nuclear family includes only the most frequent and useful derived words. The idea seemed sensible and practical and was, therefore, accepted by the curriculum designers. (On the construction and validation of nuclear families, see Cobb and Laufer 2021).

A question related to counting and listing words was about words with multiple meanings, polysemes and homonyms. A polyseme is a word with related meanings, e.g., *head* of a body and *head* of state, family, company. A homonym is a word form with unrelated meaning, e.g., *lie* – not tell the truth, and *lie* as in *lie down*. Sometimes one meaning can be frequent and another infrequent, e.g., *solution* in *solution to a problem* as opposed to *saline solution*. Most frequency lists do not separate different meanings, but the EVP (English Vocabulary Profile) and the WFF (Word Family Framework) do. I suggested listing polysemes in the same entries in the lists and homonyms as different entries. However, curriculum designers decided to follow the example of EVP and WFF and separate most of the word meanings when they had different frequencies.

Hence, the target vocabulary was set at 5,400 nuclear families. These families are small at the beginning stages of learning, and may consist of one member, and expand later, as learners' proficiency develops. The curriculum designers decided on the items included in the syllabus by consulting various frequency lists, e.g., COCA, AWL (Academic Word List; Coxhead 2000), the EVP, WFF and several other lists. Additionally, they exercised their expert judgment regarding the usefulness and relevance of the vocabulary items for the learners. To sum up, decision 2, which was to organize the syllabus lists by nuclear families, was reached through an exchange of ideas between the researcher and curriculum planners and by pedagogical consideration regarding the advantages and the disadvantages of the different options of organizing the lists.

2.3 Decision 3 – Not only single words

Most existing frequency lists include single words only. Yet, a large part of English is formulaic, i.e., many words appear in fixed, or semi-fixed patterns. According to Erman and Warren (2000), 58.6% of speech and 52.3% of writing is formulaic. Some examples of such patterns, also called multi-word units (MWUs) or chunks, are fixed expressions like *as a matter of fact, by and large, to say the least*; collocations, e.g., *take place, submit an application*; phrasal verbs, e.g., *let down, look up*; idioms, e.g., *at the drop of a hat*.

The question posed by the curriculum planners was whether there were criteria for the inclusion of specific MWUs in the syllabus. I was not aware of any established criteria for the selection of MWUs for general learning lists. If learnability is a criterion to consider, then there is ample research evidence that phrasal verbs and collocations are problematic for language learners (Hasselgreen 1994; Laufer and Eliasson 1993; Nesselhauf 2005; Paquot and Granger 2012; Peters 2016). Yet their number, particularly of collocations, is extremely large. The existing lists of phrasal verbs, collocations, and other MWUs (e.g., Martinez and Schmitt 2012; Shin and Nation 2008; Pearson's Academic Collocations List) follow different inclusion criteria and consequently consist of very different items. Therefore, I could not provide any objective criteria for including MWUs.

The curriculum designers decided to consult the available lists of MWUs and select the chunks that were related to the words in the lists and were considered most useful to the learners. For example, *in addition, let down, stay in touch, as a matter of fact* were listed after *addition, let, touch*, and *matter* respectively. Furthermore, they added around 30 phrases for beginners that they call 'stepping stones to conversation', e.g., *How are you? Are you ready? What time is it?*

2.4 Decision 4 – Additional inclusion criteria: Orthographic patterns and 'online culture' terms

The curriculum planners made sure that the words included in the syllabus for the elementary school covered the basic orthographic patterns of English, e.g., silent *e* as in *plate*; *a* pronounced as *æ* as in /*sad*/, *ei* as in *late*; consonant digraphs *th*, *ch*, *sh*; an unaccented shwa sound as in *around*, *again*; and other basic patterns. This decision followed the advice given by researchers working on spelling, word decoding and reading (Kahn-Horwitz 2015).

Finally, the curriculum planners decided to include twenty words that are used online though they may not yet appear in the available corpora with high frequency, e.g., *blog, avatar, selfie, emoji, user-friendly*.

Except for the inclusion of 'online culture' terms, decisions 2, 3, and 4 involved a two-way flow of information and ongoing discussions between researchers and curriculum planners, as in Figure 10.2:

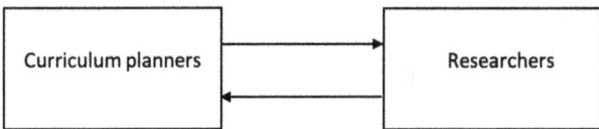

Figure 10.2: Collaboration cycle leading to Decisions 2, 3, 4.

2.5 Decision 5 – Level of knowledge, receptive or productive?

The learner can know a word receptively, i.e., comprehend it in reading or speech. They can also know a word productively, i.e., retrieve the form and use it with the appropriate grammatical and semantic word features and in the appropriate combinations with other words. The questions posed to the researcher by the curriculum planners were how many words of the 5,400 target nuclear families should be taught to the productive level of knowledge, and whether the textbooks used in school provide the necessary training for productive knowledge.

Regarding the productive vocabulary size, there are no studies on lexical thresholds of productive knowledge. West (1960) suggests that 1,200 word families are the minimum adequate vocabulary for speech, but to my knowledge there are no studies to relate productive vocabulary size to the quality of speech or writing. The curriculum planners decided to set the productive vocabulary size target at 3,000 nuclear word families.

The answer to the question of vocabulary treatment in textbooks required the collaboration of textbook writers and a student who mapped the textbook vocabulary. I asked for information about 260 words that appeared in one of the textbooks for grade 9. These words had been included in the old vocabulary bands for junior high school. Before designing a new syllabus, and subsequently new textbooks, it was important to find out how textbook writers treated words that students had to learn. The textbook writers provided the exact page numbers where each word appeared either in a text or in an exercise. This information was essential for a PhD student of mine, who created a 'word profile' for each word. The word profile indicated the number of occurrences of each word in the book, the spacing pattern (whether most appearances were close to each other, whether they were evenly spaced, whether most of them were much later after the first exposure), and task type, i.e., whether and how each word was practised. Among other things, the 'task type' feature of the profile indicated whether each instance of practice targeted comprehension or production of the practised words. Word profiles showed that comprehension was targeted five times as much as production. Each target word was practised productively once or twice. Furthermore, there was no principled approach to the number of occurrences of the words and spacing them. These results showed that before the lexis of the new lexical syllabus is incorporated into the new textbook, textbook writers should be made aware of the importance of productive practice (Figure 10.3).

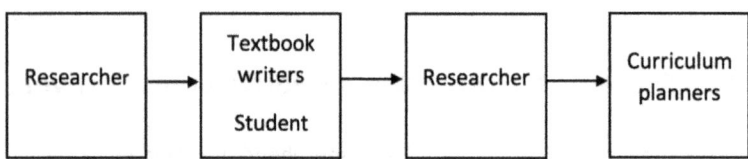

Figure 10.3: Collaboration cycle leading to Decision 5.

3 The resulting lexical syllabus

The various collaborations described above led to decisions about target vocabulary size, the word counting unit, criteria for inclusion of vocabulary in the lists, and the level of vocabulary knowledge. These resulted in the design of a new lexical syllabus for elementary, junior high and high schools in Israel. Table 10.2 presents the lexical targets by school grade and the corresponding CEFR levels of knowledge.

Table 10.2: Lexical targets in the English curriculum 2020.

Level	Pre-basic user Pre-A1	Basic user A1	Basic user A2	Independent user I & II B1 and B2	
Grades	3–6		7–9	10–12	
Receptive per level	200	1200	2000	900	1100
Productive per level	200	1000	800	500	500
Cumulative receptive	200	1400	3400	4300	**5400**
Cumulative productive	200	1200	2000	2500	3000

(Adapted from English Curriculum 2020)

3.1 Future implementations: Vocabulary treatment by textbooks, syllabus evaluation, teacher development

Textbooks are the teachers' primary teaching materials in terms of selection of texts, grammatical and lexical explanations, and exercises that practise what is being taught. The English inspectorate therefore expects the textbook writers to incorporate the new lexical syllabus into the textbooks. Decisions will have to be made regarding the minimum number of exposures of the new words, their dispersion throughout the book, and the type of tasks that provide the necessary practice. Two decisions have already been made by the curriculum designers. One is to introduce the new vocabulary in the first three-quarters of the books. This decision followed a survey of school teachers that asked how much of the textbook material they managed to cover in a school year. Almost nobody taught the entire textbook. Therefore, all the new vocabulary should ideally be introduced in the material that can be completed. The second decision is to include more exercises targeting productive knowledge of words. This decision followed the analysis of the existing textbook tasks described earlier, in section 2.5.

To assess whether a curriculum or a syllabus is effective in promoting an improvement, all relevant information should be collected and analysed (Brown 1995; Marsh 2004; Nichols et al. 2006). The new lexical syllabus will be evaluated against broader teaching goals – to improve learners' vocabulary size (see present size figures in section 2.1) and consequently their overall language proficiency and the scores on the English section of the university entrance exam.

Finally, teachers will receive workshops on the rationale underlying the increased lexical requirements and on the implementation of the syllabus in the classroom. Later, they will be asked to participate in the evaluation of the syllabus in their classes. According to Lieberman (1986), when teachers become active researchers in their classrooms or collaborate with researchers, teacher development often occurs.

The future implementation of the lexical syllabus will depend on a collaborative effort of several partners. Curriculum designers will provide the textbook writers with the requirements for incorporating the target lexis into the textbooks. Textbook writers will try to carry out these guidelines. Researchers will analyse the textbook tasks in terms of effectiveness for language learning and may ask textbook writers for modifications. Teacher trainers will provide teachers with the necessary explanation and training regarding the new syllabus. In the assessment stage of the syllabus vis-à-vis lexical and overall language proficiency targets, collaborative efforts will be required as well. Learners will be asked for input regarding perceived lexical knowledge and lexical needs, assessment specialists will suggest assessment tests, teachers will administer them, researchers will interpret the results in terms of language knowledge levels, and ministry administrators will judge the extent to which the goals of the syllabus have been achieved.

4 Summary and concluding remarks

In the preceding sections, I discussed research that informed the construction of the lexical syllabus in the new English Curriculum in Israel. The construction of the syllabus involved collaboration between researchers, teachers, textbook writers, curriculum planners, assessment specialists, research students, and Ministry of Education administrators. The lexical syllabus consists of vocabulary bands taught at different learning stages. The following research findings and collaborations (in brackets) were behind its design:
- Gaps between learners' lexical knowledge and the amount of lexis necessary for performing language tasks (curriculum designers, researchers, teachers, assessment specialists, ministry administrators)
- Vocabulary treatment in textbooks: amount of exposure and type of activities (researchers, curriculum designers, textbook writers)
- Challenges in reaching the productive level of word knowledge (researchers, students, textbook writers, curriculum designers).
- Establishing a new word counting unit, the Nuclear Word Family (researchers, curriculum designers)
- Importance and difficulty of multi-word units (researchers, curriculum designers)
- Presentation of words with multiple meanings (researchers, curriculum designers)
- Representation of orthographic patterns (researchers, curriculum designers)

The new lexical syllabus is an example of a successful partnership between research and policy-making as it fulfils two basic requirements suggested by Grimm et al. (2018). First, sound research-based evidence relevant to the lexical syllabus was available to the decision-makers. Second, this evidence was made accessible, i.e., complex data and research results were translated into implementable policy recommendations.

The partnership resulted in reciprocal benefits for the various partners. Class teachers who administered vocabulary size tests received information on their learners' lexical knowledge from the researchers, and could take this information into account in selecting teaching materials. Researchers benefited from this information in two ways. They related the data to the theoretical notions of lexical coverage and thresholds that were of interest to other researchers of lexis and reading. They also used the data of lexical size tests together with the national psychometric results to calculate the national lexical sizes at various language proficiency levels. This particular information was submitted to the Ministry of Education, and it showed the gap that the new syllabus had to bridge, or to narrow, between the desired lexical sizes and the lexical sizes of the learners. The syllabus designers used the data on the gaps in their decisions regarding the lexical targets in various class grades. The discussions that I (the researcher) had with syllabus designers about productive vocabulary, nuclear word families, multiple meaning, and multi-word units, benefited us all. I exposed the syllabus makers to relevant research findings, and learnt about pedagogical considerations and limitations in implementing research in classrooms.

The future implementation of the syllabus will also yield reciprocal benefits. The analysis of word treatment in textbooks that the syllabus designers received will be used to suggest changes in future materials. Textbook writers will, in turn, benefit from this analysis to learn about the shortcomings of the current materials and will, consequently, introduce changes in new textbooks. In the syllabus assessment stage, teacher-researchers will collect input data from learners and administer vocabulary tests. In the process, the teachers will improve their understanding about lexical acquisition, syllabus designers will gain insight into the successes and challenges of the new lexical targets, and researchers will continue learning about the pedagogical considerations that mediate the application of research in teaching.

The collaboration between various partners followed the pragmatic model of relations between research and policy-making (Grimm et al. 2018) since both sides' views and expertise complemented each other. According to the pragmatic model, researchers and policy-makers constantly engage and communicate with each other and contribute knowledge from their respective spheres. Sometimes researchers' recommendations dominate, as in the case of selecting the nuclear family as the unit of counting in the syllabus. Sometimes policy-makers' views dominate, as in the case of separating the meanings of polysemes in the syllabus. I believe that the construction of the lexical syllabus was a collaborative success. As for the future implementation, I can only hope for a similar experience.

References

Academic Collocation List. Pearson. https://www.pearsonpte.com/teachers/academic-collocation (accessed 20 May 2022).
Brown, James Dean. 1995. *The elements of language curriculum: A systematic approach to program development*. Boston: Heinle & Heinle.
BNC (British National Corpus). https://www.english-corpora.org/bnc/ (accessed 20 May 2022).
Brumfit, Christopher. 1997. How applied linguistics is the same as any other science. *International Journal of Applied Linguistics* 7(1). 86–94.
Cobb, Thomas & Batia Laufer. 2021. The Nuclear Word Family List: A list of the most frequent family members, including base and affixed words. *Language Learning* 71(3). 834–871.
COCA (Corpus of Contemporary American English). https://www.wordfrequency.info/top5000.asp (accessed 19 May 2022).
Council of Europe. 2001. *Common European Framework of Reference for Languages: Learning, teaching, assessment*. Cambridge: Cambridge University Press.
Coxhead, Averil. 2000. A new academic word list. *TESOL Quarterly* 34(2). 213–238.
Dang, Thi Ngoc Yen & Stuart Webb. 2014. The lexical profile of academic spoken English. *English for Specific Purposes* 33(1). 66–76.
Davies, Alan & Catherine Elder (eds.). 2004. *The handbook of applied linguistics*. Malden, MA: Blackwell.
English Curriculum. 2020. State of Israel, Ministry of Education Pedagogical Secretariat, Language Department Inspectorate for English Language Education.
EVP (English Vocabulary Profile Online – British English). https://www.englishprofile.org/wordlists/evp (accessed 19 May 2022).
Erman, Britt & Beatrice Cecilia Warren. 2000. The idiom principle and the open choice principle. *Text* 20(1). 29–62.
Grimm, Sven, Mareike Magdalena Gensch, Johanna Hauf, Julia Prenzel, Nitja Rehani, Sarah Senz & Olivier Vogel. 2018. The interface between research and policy-making in South Africa: Exploring the institutional framework and practice of an uneasy relationship. Discussion paper 19/2018. Bonn: German Development Institute. https://www.econstor.eu/handle/10419/199539 (accessed 27 October 2022).
Hasselgreen, Angela. 1994. Lexical teddy bears and advanced learners: A study into the ways Norwegian students cope with English vocabulary. *International Journal of Applied Linguistics* 4(2). 237–258.
Kahn-Horwitz, Janina. 2015. 'Organizing the mess in my mind': EFL teachers' perceptions and knowledge of English orthography. *Reading and Writing: An Interdisciplinary Journal* 28(5). 611–631.
Laufer, Batia & Stig Eliasson. 1993. What causes avoidance in L2 learning: L1–L2 difference, L1–L2 similarity, or L2 complexity? *Studies in Second Language Acquisition* 15(1). 35–48.

Laufer, Batia & Geke Ravenhorst-Kalovski. 2010. Lexical threshold revisited: Lexical text coverage, learners' vocabulary size and reading comprehension. *Reading in a Foreign Language* 22(1). 15–30.

Lieberman, Ann. 1986. Collaborative research: Working with, not working on . . . *Educational Leadership* 43(5). 28–32.

Martinez, Ron & Norbert Schmitt. 2012. A phrasal expressions list. *Applied Linguistics* 33(3). 299–320.

Marsh, Colin, J. [1997] 2004. *Key concepts for understanding curriculum* (3rd edn). London & New York: Routledge Falmer.

Nation, Paul. 2006. How large a vocabulary is needed for reading and listening? *Canadian Modern Language Review* 63(1). 59–82.

Nation, Paul & David Beglar. 2007. A vocabulary size test. *The Language Teacher* 31(7). 9–13.

Nesselhauf, Nadja. 2005. *Collocations in a learner corpus*. Amsterdam & Philadelphia: John Benjamins.

Nichols, Beverly, Sue Shidaker, Gene Johnson & Kevin Singer. 2006. *Managing curriculum and assessment: A practitioner's guide*. Worthington, OH: Linworth Books.

Paquot, Magali & Sylviane Granger. 2012. Formulaic language in learner corpora. *Annual Review of Applied Linguistics* 32. 130–149. http://doi.org/10.1017/S0267190512000098 (accessed 19 May 2022).

Peters, Elke. 2016. The learning burden of collocations: The role of interlexical and intralexical factors. *Language Teaching Research* 20(1). 113–138.

Richards, Jack. 2001. *Curriculum development in language teaching*. Cambridge: Cambridge University Press.

Schmitt, Norbert, Diane Schmitt & Caroline Clapham. 2001. Developing and exploring the behaviour of two new versions of the vocabulary levels test. *Language Testing* 18(1). 55–88.

Shin, Dongkwang & Paul Nation. 2008. Beyond single words: The most frequent collocations in spoken English. *ELT Journal* 62(4). 339–348.

West, Michael. 1960. *Teaching English in difficult circumstances*. London: Longman.

WFF (Word Family Framework). London: British Council. https://www.teachingenglish.org.uk/article/word-family-framework (accessed 19 May 2022).

Karita Mård-Miettinen and Anne Pitkänen-Huhta

11 Tensions in collaborative research with teachers in the context of language education policy change in Finland

Abstract: Schools in Finland faced a major policy change in language education at the beginning of 2020, when the age to start learning the first foreign or second domestic language was lowered from third to first grade in primary school. With the aim of examining how practices are formed in this new situation, we planned a case study with one school. The outbreak of Covid-19 forced us to change our original plans in order to maintain contact with the school, and our perspective on the emerging new practices was broadened by including the language teachers' collegial network in online interviews. In this chapter, we analyse these interview data. By paying specific attention to the researcher–practitioner collaboration as it was realized in the interviews, we identified different strategies that the teachers and researchers used in points where tensions in the interviews seemed to arise.

1 Introduction

The context of this chapter is the major policy change in language education that schools in Finland faced in 2020, when the starting age for second/foreign language learning was lowered from the third to the first grade in primary school. The decision challenged schools in many ways. First, the policy decision was made exceptionally rapidly, leaving only a short time for schools to plan their implementation. Second, two new lesson hours were included in the schedule of grades 1–2 in primary schools to be used for language teaching, meaning that schools needed to rethink their teaching resources (Inha and Kähärä 2018). Third, the main policy objective was to broaden the language repertoire of Finnish school children, and schools were encouraged to offer several languages to choose from in grade 1 (Pyykkö 2017). Fourth, the implementation of the decision challenged the premises for language teaching in Finland and raised questions regarding the best qualifications for teaching languages to grade 1–2 students (Hahl and Pietarila 2021).

With the aim of examining how this new and challenging situation influenced the formation of teaching and learning practices, we planned a collaborative case study with one primary school. In this chapter, we will analyse the interview data collected within this project and focus on the tensions that potentially arise in them.

2 The Finnish language education context

In Finland, education policy is carried out both nationally and locally (Vitikka, Krokfors, and Hurmerinta 2012). National education policy is formulated by the Ministry of Education and Culture, which decides which subjects should be taught in Finnish schools and determines the minimum number of lessons for each subject. The national body responsible for policy implementation is the Finnish National Agency for Education, which designs the national curriculum guidelines. However, within the framework of the national core curricula, the local education providers have considerable freedom: they draw up local curricula and can also decide how to allocate lessons for individual school subjects each year.

Regarding language education, until the end of 1990s Finland was known as a country where language learning began early and many languages were studied compared with other European countries. While many other countries in Europe lowered the starting age for languages to 6–7 years or younger in the 2000s, in line with the recommendation in the Framework strategy for multilingualism of the European Commission (2005), until 2020 Finland remained a country where language education began most often at the age of 9–10, i.e., in grade 3 of primary school. As early as the 1990s local decisions were made to introduce languages in grade 1, or even in pre-primary education, but this happened mostly in schools in bigger cities (Peltoniemi et al. 2018; Skinnari and Sjöberg 2018).

The language programme in Finnish schools consists of the compulsory learning of two languages, both introduced in primary school. By far the most common compulsory languages are English and Swedish, which is the second national language in Finland (EDUFI 2019). In addition to these, primary school students may also choose an optional language. These languages continue to be learnt in secondary school, where an additional language can be learnt as an elective subject. The minimum number of languages in the language programme of a Finnish basic education student is thus two and the maximum is four. However, the majority of Finns only study the two compulsory languages (EDUFI 2019). This is due to several reasons: beliefs that language studies are demanding and that it is not advantageous to know several languages, and schools not offering optional and elective languages (EDUFI 2019; Pyykkö 2017). This has resulted in a worrying narrowing of interest in language learning at school.

In 2017 growing concern about the declining interest in language learning in Finland resulted in the Ministry of Education initiating an investigation into the current state of Finland's linguistic capital and its language needs both inside and outside the education system. However, this chapter discusses only the central education policy measure that was suggested to strengthen the country's linguistic capital, i.e., lowering the starting age for language learning for all students. It was suggested in the report (Pyykkö 2017) that 1) language learning should start in grade one in primary school at the age of 6–7 years; 2) an addition to the minimum number of lesson hours for languages should be made to facilitate the earlier start; 3) language learning should start, as a rule, with a language other than English; and 4) the voluntary language in primary school should begin in third grade (at the age of 9–10 years) and should normally be English. As an alternative to all schools starting with a language other than English, it was suggested that all education providers should at least be required to increase the opportunities for students to study languages other than English in primary school.

A rapid decision-making process followed publication of the results of the investigation at the end of 2017. Already at the beginning of 2018, the Finnish Government decided that every primary school in Finland would be required to introduce the first optional language in grade 1 from January 2020 and recommended that it should be a language other than English (Inha and Kähärä 2018). To support this, the Finnish National Agency for Education offered project funding to schools so that they could pilot early language learning (Inha and Kähärä 2018). Many schools took this opportunity, and their experiences were highly positive (Skinnari and Sjöberg 2018). The decision also resulted in changes in the Decree on the distribution of lesson hours in basic education (Government Decree 793/2018): two hours of language lessons were added to grades 1 and 2. Furthermore, the National Curriculum guidelines were updated for language teaching in grades 1 and 2 (EDUFI 2020).

This national education policy decision also challenged teachers and the teaching profession in Finland. Both class teachers and subject teachers may teach languages in primary school, also in the first grade. All teachers from primary school to upper secondary school must have a master's degree. Class teachers major in education, and they are qualified to teach all subjects in grades 1–6. Teachers in secondary and upper secondary school are subject teachers and they specialize in teaching one or more subjects. They major in one subject, for example English, and have another subject, for example German, and pedagogical studies as their minors. Class teachers may also specialize in language subjects and study them further so that they gain qualifications to teach those subjects in secondary school; in other words, they are double-qualified (Hahl and Pietarila 2021). The challenge is, however, that subject teachers in Finland are trained to teach children who are literate, and first graders are not necessarily literate yet. On the other hand, class teachers are trained to teach young learners, but they are not specialized in teaching languages even though they are eligible to teach any primary school subject. To overcome the challenge, the Finnish National Agency for Education granted state subsidies to municipalities to develop tutoring practices, and in-service training was arranged in methods to teach languages to young learners (Hahl and Pietarila 2021).

3 The study

In this chapter, we analyse interview data collected in this new language policy implementation context. Our particular focus is on possible tensions arising in researcher–teacher collaboration in a study that focused on how one school set out to implement the new early start to foreign language learning in their day-to-day practices. The school (a small primary school) was recruited through a mentoring network in a rural municipality. Due to the relatively small number of pupils, the school has combined classes with first and second graders in the same class. A few pre-schoolers were also integrated into the same class except for the lessons of English. The original goal was to engage in close collaboration with the school for the first three years of teaching English to first graders. The stakeholders involved included the subject teacher (specialized in languages), learners, and parents. The study was planned as cycles of classroom observation, stakeholder interviews and questionnaires, and classroom activities developed in teacher–researcher collaboration.

After starting to build trust with the school in three classroom observations, the outbreak of Covid-19 forced us to change plans in order to maintain contact with the school. This meant that instead of the researchers observing and collecting data in the English classroom, the school took responsibility for it, and any data collection meetings with the teacher and students had to take place online. As we were not able to be present in the school, we broadened our perspective on emerging practices by including other stakeholders in the school; at the same time, we had to drop the idea of including parents more extensively as online interviewing proved to be too difficult to arrange. As the school's head teacher (a class teacher by training) gained a more prominent role in teaching English alongside the subject teacher, we also interviewed them via an online platform. To gain a deeper understanding of the collaboration taking place among practitioners, we also included the subject teachers' collegial network in online interviews. This network was part of a tutoring programme, funded by the National Agency for Education, in which subject teachers of English tutor class teachers who have no or limited prior experience of language teaching (see section 2).

4 Method

For the purposes of this chapter, we analysed interview data with the subject teacher, the head teacher and the teachers in the collegial network, including both the subject teacher and class teachers. As the two researchers, we are involved in teacher training at the university, but mainly with subject teachers specializing in languages. These different participant roles may potentially give rise to tensions in the interviews.

When giving examples from the interviews, we refer to these as subject teacher interview, head teacher interview, and group interview. In the interview transcripts, R1, R2 = researchers, ST = subject teacher, HT = head teacher, and CT1, CT2 = class teachers. We conducted four interviews with the subject teacher, one interview with the head teacher and one group interview with three teachers in the network, including our focal teacher. The examples from the interviews are translated from Finnish by the authors. The translations focus on the content of the turns and thus no pauses or nonverbal behaviour, for example, are marked. Commas are added in the examples for ease of reading. Words in square brackets are explanatory text when the direct translation alone would not have been transparent.

In analysing the interviews, we approached them as interactions between the researchers and the teacher(s), i.e., we paid systematic attention to how the teacher(s) reacted to the researchers' questions and prompts, on the one hand, and on how the researchers reacted to the teachers' responses, on the other hand. In our analysis, we were able to identify specific strategies that both parties used, and we analysed these thematically (Braun and Clarke 2006). We found out that in addition to the teachers talking about their own strengths and expertise, many of their accounts included responses in which the teachers appeared sensitive and self-conscious and seemed to assume they were being criticized and tried to explain their actions. As our focus in this chapter is on tensions that may potentially arise from the researcher–practitioner relationship in this participatory research setting, we address only these responses in our analysis. The responses were categorized into four themes: *explaining actions, expressing inadequacy, expressing lack of knowledge, counterarguing*. In the findings section, we will give examples of each of these and discuss the researcher accounts that precede and follow the teachers' responses.

5 Findings

5.1 Explaining actions

When talking about their classroom practices in the new situation, the teachers appeared to feel a need to explain their choice of practices at length. Their explanations were often connected to the use of certain materials and teaching methods, but they were also related to the timetable or the learners (e.g., age, skills).

In example 1 from the group interview, the researcher (R1) asks whether the teachers (CT1, CT2) have used textbooks in their teaching. Textbooks have a fairly prominent role in language teaching in Finland (e.g., Luukka et al. 2008), but the national core curriculum for language teaching in grades 1–2 (EDUFI 2020) emphasizes oral language and the use of varied teaching materials. There are also new textbooks designed for early language learners, following the national core curriculum and therefore giving the class teachers a backbone for teaching languages. This is also pointed out by CT1 in example 1, who explains using the book and the attached material even when there is a stronger focus on action-based methods. However, CT1 is anxious to emphasize that the learners do not have a book. This may be because the researchers are known to be teacher educators of subject teachers and subject teaching relies heavily on textbooks, so the teachers may assume that the researchers expect the use of textbooks in early language teaching as well. However, R1 also seems to be eager to reinforce the teacher's view that textbooks are not necessary in early language learning.

(1) Group interview
    R1: have you, CT2 and CT1, had any textbooks in use or how has the teaching been [organized]
    CT1: so I've had, just for myself, the go-book [*book title*] and its digital material, but last year I perhaps used it more, but this year less, but let's say it's there, but the children don't have a book
    R1: hmm, what did you, when you said you used it more last year and less now, so is it like your own decision, is it like your experience that you don't need it after all
    CT1: yeah, maybe I have like become, but well, there's been a lot of all kinds of needs for support in my group and such, so it's been more like playing and singing, but it's still good to have it available anyway, but I haven't actively worked on it now
    R1: yeah, have the pupils asked about it in any way
    CT1: nooo
    R1: no, yes it's funny that sometimes older pupils seem very conservative with the textbooks, so that we go through everything in the book, so it's nice if the younger pupils think that the book doesn't matter, that you can learn languages in many ways
    CT1: yeah, nooo

In addition to explaining their own, the teachers even defend each other's practices. Example 2 relates to a situation where the head teacher (a class teacher) has started to teach one additional lesson of English on top of the one hour that the subject teacher teaches. The two class teachers in the group interview have previously explained that they are integrating English in other subjects, and the researcher (R1) asks the subject teacher (ST) whether the head teacher does the same in their school now that the head teacher is engaged in language teaching along with the subject teacher. This question leads to a lengthy response, where ST gives reasons for the head teacher's actions. First, ST indicates that there is not much contact between the teachers, as the subject teacher does not have a clear picture of what the head teacher does with the learners. Then ST goes on to explain how demanding the head teacher's job is and that English is probably not a top priority.

(2) Group interview
R1: have you noticed in your school where the class teacher now teaches one lesson, so has English been somehow, you know, do you know if it's included in teaching other [subjects]
ST: well I don't really have a very good picture of how well [*name of head teacher*] has done, so they haven't really been able to do that, [*name of head teacher*] has such a group, both pre-schoolers and first and second graders, and the head teacher tasks on top of that, so I know that English is not like that for them, so that they do it because they have to give that one extra lesson to all of my groups, so well well so, I think that they may sometimes take [English along with other topics], I have given her a calendar board that we always use at the beginning of the lesson, where there are days of the week and dates and weather and such, and I think that they [*head teacher*] may use it sometimes, and sometimes they use songs that I have first taught the pupils, and then they sing them again with [*name of head teacher*], but it must have been quite small scale with that group
R1: yeah it is indeed, there are indeed many kinds of aims, and English is of course not the only aim there
ST: yeah, yeah

After listening to ST's lengthy account, R1 confirms it partly by repeating ST's justifications.

5.2 Expressing inadequacy

Another theme connected to tensions was the teachers expressing inadequacy. In example 3 from the group interview the inadequacy is related to class teachers not having any specific training (referring to qualifications) to teach languages. What is interesting here is that the researcher (R1) merely asks whether this is the first time the class teachers have taught languages. This prompt triggers a response when CT1 first explains that this is not the first time and CT2 continues about having taught Swedish a long time ago, but not having any training (or qualifications) to teach languages. R1 acknowledges this with a minimal response (*yes*), and then CT1 continues by explaining about studies in German years ago but having no experience of teaching English. As the researchers are language teacher trainers, they focused on experiences in their question rather than on the issue of qualifications. They also appear to try to remain neutral in their stance and resort to minimal responses (*yes, hmm*) when the teachers bring up their feelings of inadequacy as to qualifications.

(3) Group interview
    R1: have you taught before, is this like the first time you started teaching languages or teaching English, have you had foreign languages to teach before
    CT1: no we haven't, we haven't had
    CT2: well I have taught, many many years ago, English and Swedish for [special class] ninth graders, but not otherwise, and I don't have any training for that, but last autumn we had training for early language teaching in [*name of city*], so that was really very good, but now I teach English for third and sixth graders in my own [school]
    R1: yeah
    CT1: I have a little language –, I have long ago, so I have studied German like after teacher training, like I've been interested in languages so that I have studied until intermediate studies like donkey's years ago, but I don't really have such experiences of English, and I don't really have [taught] German, except for single workshop type events related to German
    R1: hmm
    CT1: such experiences I've had
    R1: yes yes
    CT1: long ago during my studies, I've taught Swedish for the longer period in a secondary school, so such [experiences]

Example 4 is from the head teacher's (HT) interview. In this extract, HT expresses feelings of inadequacy in English pronunciation and thus not being a good example for the learners. Interestingly HT contrasts class teachers and 'professionals'.

Professionals means here the teacher of English with a subject teacher training. The researchers (R1, R2) remain in the background and appear to be reluctant to take any specific stance to the deprecatory talk.

(4) Head teacher interview
    R1: Mmm, but that then means of course that the English teacher has to be on the same map of what's going on in there, yes sure, but here it must be, I don't know if you have seen it so that if it could be a class teacher in your school [who teaches English], but you of course have the challenge that you only have three teachers, but if you had an ideal opportunity that you had a class teacher who would teach English, so do you think it would be better or different, or somehow
    HT: well, if it were a class teacher who would teach it, so they would know better what they've done and they would use the words more, so it would be good, yes, but on the other hand there's the fact that it's just this kind of class teacher like me [*an especially deprecatory expression in Finnish*] who is always afraid of pronouncing something wrong or something, so if there's the professional who definitely knows how it goes
    R2: right
    HT: is it me the class teacher teaching English like so and so, they [the pupils] always pick up something, there are of course these recordings so that they learn words properly too
    R1 and R2: yeah, right

Teachers' feelings of inadequacy were not only connected to their teaching and expertise but also to the researcher–practitioner collaboration itself. In example 5 the researcher (R1) initiates a discussion on the collaboration. R1 highlights the researchers' incompetence in early language teaching when asking the question about the collaboration. The teacher (ST) continues in similar deprecatory manner when talking about the researchers' benefitting from the collaboration.

(5) Subject teacher interview
    R1: we could still ask you at the end how you've liked these discussions of ours, how you've experienced this, this talking with ignorant outsiders
    ST: well, it's been easy, because there's been no need to prepare myself in any way for these, or at least I haven't had time to prepare, so I

	don't know if you've got anything logical out of my stream of consciousness, I've just told you anything that comes to my mind
R2:	hmm
ST:	I haven't thought about before [our meetings] what they might ask about and what I should reply
R2:	it's good that you haven't, that wasn't the intention
ST:	so that, I hope that you have got something out of this
R2:	yes, we have, we'll start going through these
R1:	yeah this has been very, very interesting for us, because we haven't had any connection there and this new early start to languages has been such a big thing, so it's been very important that we've had a chance to get to understand what's going on there

ST's accounts that signal inadequacy result in R1 giving a lengthy response that emphasizes that the teacher's contributions have been interesting and highly important in understanding the implementation of the national policy of an early start to foreign language learning in the day-to-day practices.

5.3 Expressing lack of knowledge

The third theme of potential tensions in the interviews is teachers expressing lack of knowledge in relation to various issues in their novel situation of early teaching and learning of English. This is not unexpected as the implementation of the policy was done quickly and the teachers were not given systematic training prior to it. Their feelings of lack of knowledge concerned, among other things, materials and methods they used for teaching, parents' engagement in their children's learning, the learning of English and the learners' overall skills.

In example 6, the researchers (R1, R2) and the subject teacher (ST) talk about parental support for the learning of English in the class. When asked whether some of the learners are not supported from home, ST expresses lack of knowledge due to not knowing the learners well enough to answer the question. R2's reaction to the teacher's account is to express understanding by referring to the fact that a subject teacher meets the learners much less frequently than a class teacher. In this way R2 may indicate that the original question was not fully relevant.

(6) Subject teacher interview
R2: so have you noticed, like with some pupils, that there's never any like, or do you suspect that there's someone who doesn't get any support from home

ST:	well I don't really know them that well yet, so that I could say, but there are always some, but I can't say anything precise about these
R2:	hmm, and it is indeed difficult if you only meet once a week, so you won't get that kind of sustained contact

The researchers frequently appeared to attempt to formulate their responses so as to show understanding, as in example 6 above, or empower the teachers with comments like 'It [that a learner doesn't want to sing in the English lessons] may be a more general characteristic which isn't connected to the English language' when the teachers expressed lack of knowledge.

5.4 Counterarguing

The final theme we identified in the data was counterarguing. Often the teachers explained their actions quite indirectly in the interviews, as shown in the previous sections. However, sometimes they were very direct in expressing clear counterarguments to researcher prompts. In example 7, from the head teacher (HT) interview, the researcher (R1) asks a question related to integrating English with other subjects, first seeking confirmation that HT has taught English as a separate lesson, and then instead of asking the teacher directly, R1 makes the assumption that English has not been embedded in other subjects. This leads to HT affirming that the assumption is correct and R1 confirming the answer. R1 starts to continue, but HT interrupts and says it is obvious what the researchers are looking for and uses the technical term 'integrated'. HT thus reacts to R1's assumption about HT not integrating English with other subjects and shows that the concept of (content and language) integration that is mentioned in the renewed national core curriculum (EDUFI 2020) is a familiar concept to them. The fact that it is a curricular concept makes HT assume that it is a practice preferred by the researchers. HT adds apologetically that integration has unfortunately not been implemented in her own early language teaching.

(7) Head teacher interview

R1:	so, when you had that one lesson, so you had it as a separate lesson, you didn't put it into some other subjects
HT:	I didn't put, it was a separate lesson there
R1:	right, so that, so that it's been such that
HT:	yes, now that I know that you're looking for how much it's been integrated there, they've been separate lessons and

R1:	yes, okay
HT:	it, unfortunately I haven't been able to
R1:	there's nothing unfortunate about it
R2:	noo, it's not like, yeah, it's just interesting what kinds of practices are formed

R1 seems to attempt to mitigate the tension by saying that there is nothing unfortunate about the situation. R2 also appears to be anxious to explain that they as researchers are just interested to see how practices develop and to confirm that they do not know whether integration is good or bad.

6 Conclusions

In this chapter, we have shown some examples of the challenges in researcher–practitioner positions and in building trust between researchers and teachers when doing research on the implementation of a new language education policy in Finland. The delicacy of the relationship shows how sometimes mutual (mis)interpretations of the purposes of the other party may lead to tensions which then call for mitigation of one's own argument. The study identified strategies that the teachers used when reacting defensively to the researcher prompts and questions and the researchers' reactions to them.

As regards the teachers, the results show that they appear to feel the need to explain their position. In this study, the explanations by the teachers were connected to feelings of insecurity as teachers of languages to young learners, i.e., there appears to be underlying uncertainty in the new situation, as for example Hahl and Pietarila (2021) also show. In this new situation they feel that their professionalism is being questioned or at least put to the test, and they have to defend their actions to the researchers, who are teacher educators. For the researchers, it is important to build trust to gain the practitioners' view of the new situation. It seems that the researchers sometimes recognize an arising tension in the interviews and try to mitigate the situation in different ways. This shows in the researchers' attempts to align themselves with the teachers by showing that they agree. Sometimes the researchers appear to see a need either to empower the teacher by pointing out crucial factors or to detach themselves from the situation and not to affirm or reinforce certain feelings.

Overall, the study confirms that the research relationship is full of tensions: researchers and teachers are professionals in their respective functions, interested in the same phenomenon but approaching it from two different positions. Even though there is common understanding on the surface, the delicacy of the relationship is revealed by detailed examination of the interaction. Both parties experience considerable underlying insecurity and uncertainty regarding their respective roles.

References

Braun, Virginia & Victoria Clarke. 2006. Using thematic analysis in psychology. *Qualitative Research in Psychology* 3(2). 77–101. Doi: https://doi.org/10.1191/1478088706qp063oa (accessed 6 June 2022).

EDUFI (Finnish National Agency for Education). 2019. *What languages do pupils study in basic education? Statistics on language learning and teaching in Finland*. Facts 1C/2019. https://www.oph.fi/sites/default/files/documents/factsexpress1c_2019.pdf (accessed 6 June 2022).

EDUFI (Finnish National Agency for Education). 2020. *Amendments and additions to the National Core Curriculum for Basic Education 2014 regarding the instruction of the A1 language in grades 1–2*. Helsinki: Finnish National Agency for Education.

European Commission. 2005. *Communication from the Commission to the Council, the European Parliament, the European Economic and Social Committee and the Committee of the Regions. A framework strategy for multilingualism*. Brussels: European Commission. https://eur-lex.europa.eu/LexUriServ/LexUriServ.do?uri=COM:2005:0596:FIN:en:PDF (accessed 6 June 2022).

Hahl, Kaisa & Maija Pietarila. 2021. Class teachers, subject teachers and double qualified: Conceptions of teachers' skills in early foreign language learning in Finland. *International Electronic Journal of Elementary Education* 13(5). 713–725.

Inha, Karoliina & Topias Kähärä. 2018. *Introducing an earlier start in language teaching: Language learning to start as early as in kindergarten*. Ministry of Education and Culture & Finnish National Agency for Education. https://www.oph.fi/sites/default/files/documents/introducing_an_earlier_start_in_language_teaching.pdf (accessed 6 June 2022).

Luukka, Minna-Riitta, Sari Pöyhönen, Ari Huhta, Peppi Taalas, Mirja Tarnanen & Anna Keränen. 2008. *Maailma muuttuu – mitä tekee koulu? Äidinkielen ja vieraiden kielten tekstikäytänteet koulussa ja vapaa-ajalla* [The world changes – how does the school respond? Mother tongue and foreign language literacy practices at school and in free time]. Jyväskylä: University of Jyväskylä.

Peltoniemi, Annika, Kristiina Skinnari, Karita Mård-Miettinen & Sannina Sjöberg. 2018. *Monella kielellä Suomen kunnissa 2017: Selvitys muun laajamittaisen ja suppeamman kaksikielisen varhaiskasvatuksen, esiopetuksen ja perusopetuksen tilanteesta*. [In many languages in Finnish municipalities 2017: A national survey on large-scale and small-scale bilingual education in ECEC, pre-primary education and basic education in Finland]. Jyväskylä: University of Jyväskylä. http://urn.fi/URN:ISBN:978-951-39-7391-9 (accessed 6 June 2022).

Pyykkö, Riitta. 2017. *Multilingualism as a strength. Procedural recommendations for developing Finland's national language reserve*. Helsinki: Ministry of Education and Culture. https://okm.fi/documents/1410845/5875747/Multilingualism_tiivistelm%C3%A4.pdf/be86bffa-d55f-4935-bff4-2fd150c82067/Multilingualism_tiivistelm%C3%A4.pdf?t=1513075341000 (accessed 6 June 2022).

Skinnari, Kristiina & Sannina Sjöberg. 2018. *Varhaista kieltenopetusta kaikille. Selvitys varhaisen ja vapaaehtoisen kieltenopetuksen tilasta sekä toteuttamisen edellytyksistä kunnissa*. [Early language learning for all. A national survey on the state and the premises for early and optional language teaching in municipalities]. Jyväskylä: University of Jyväskylä. https://www.jyu.fi/hytk/fi/laitokset/solki/tutkimus/julkaisut/pdf-julkaisut/varhaista-kieltenopetusta-kaikille.pdf (accessed 6 June 2022).

Vitikka, Erja, Leena Krokfors & Elisa Hurmerinta. 2012. The Finnish National Core Curriculum: Structure and development. In Hannele Niemi, Auli Toom & Arto Kallioniemi (eds.), *Miracle of education: The principles and practices of teaching and learning in Finnish schools*, 83–96. Rotterdam: Sense Publishers.

Camilla Bardel and Gudrun Erickson

12 National graduate schools in language education: Dimensions of collaboration and reciprocity

Abstract: According to the Swedish Education Act, all education should be based on scientific knowledge and documented experience. Since 2008, the Swedish government has acted on this by funding national graduate schools to enable teachers and teacher educators to undertake educational research leading to an academic degree. In this chapter, we describe and discuss two such schools in language education. One brought ten lower and upper secondary teachers to a licentiate degree; the other is bringing nine language teacher educators to a PhD. The design of both programmes entailed collaboration at various levels, between Swedish universities – four in the first programme, three in the second – and between the participants in the research schools and national and international colleagues attached to the programmes as readers and discussants. A characteristic aspect of the two graduate schools that the chapter pays special attention to, highlighting benefits for the parties involved, is the reciprocity embedded in the pedagogical model used, which encompasses graduate students, researchers, schools, teachers and pupils, universities, and educational authorities.

1 Introduction

Since 2008, the Swedish government has funded national graduate schools for teachers in order to develop teachers' research skills (SFS 2007:753). In 2017, a similar investment was made in research schools for teacher educators (Utbildningsdepartementet 2021). The fundamental purpose is to enhance quality in the Swedish school system by contributing to the implementation of a regulatory statement in the Swedish Education Act, namely that all education should be based on scientific knowledge and documented experience (Sw. 'Vetenskaplig grund och beprövad erfarenhet'; Skollag 2010:800 § 5, Skolinspektionen 2019).

In this chapter, two such graduate schools in the field of language education will be described and commented on with regard to their research aims and methodologies and with a special focus on the collaborative and reciprocal aspects of their organizational and pedagogical approaches. The first graduate school involved ten language teachers in lower and upper secondary school aiming for a licentiate degree,[1] and ran from 2012 to 2015 (see Bardel et al. 2017, Bardel et al. 2021); the second, leading to a PhD, is ongoing and involves nine language teacher educators. The two programmes have the same basic structure, with overarching research themes, common and individual courses, and joint seminars with presentations and discussions of work in progress. National and international collaboration characterizes both programmes. Typical of both graduate schools is the thematic and methodological diversity of the students' research projects, not least regarding the variety of research participants (learners of different ages and teachers in various contexts). We will briefly touch upon different projects, focusing on processes as well as products, including evaluative and long-term aspects of the two programmes. In our discussion, we will pay special attention to the collaborative and reciprocal elements embedded in the pedagogical model used, highlighting benefits as well as challenges for the parties involved: graduate students, researchers, teachers and pupils, schools and universities, all of them, directly or indirectly, also relating to the curriculum level, i.e., to national educational policy.

It seems appropriate to mention that we, the authors of this chapter, have been and still are involved in both graduate schools as applicants for their funding, members of their steering groups, and supervisors. Hence, our perspective is that of insiders and our reflections are to a large extent based on our personal experiences and communication with colleagues and students in the two groups.

2 Setting the scene

2.1 The Swedish context

The Swedish educational system may to some extent be perceived as structurally contradictory. On the one hand, powers are devolved to the municipal level as regards, for example, planning, employment and finances. With 290 municipalities in the country, organized into regions, this local autonomy creates a certain diversity regarding administrative as well as content-related issues. On the other hand, there are a national education act, national curricula for the different stages of education within the school system, including subject-specific syllabuses, and an extensive, collaboratively developed assessment system that provides formative support and

---

[1] In Swedish higher education, a licentiate degree is an option available in some disciplines. It comprises two years of doctoral studies and a short thesis.

exercises summative control (Erickson, Borger, and Olsson 2022).[2] Decentralization has been a topic of heated political discussion since its development and implementation in the 1990s, with firm opinions on both sides. Currently opinion tends to favour moving towards a greater degree of central governance in the future (Lärarnas Riksförbund 2022).

2.2 The intended scientific basis for teachers' and teacher educators' research

As already mentioned, the Education Act (§ 1.5)[3] states that all education should be based on scientific knowledge and documented experience; this also includes education at tertiary level, for example teacher education (SOU 1999: 63). The concepts 'scientific knowledge' and 'documented experience' are not defined in the law but clarified and commented on in various documents addressed to schools by the educational authorities, for example, the National Agency for Education (NAE; see Skolverket 2012, 2020). The importance of critical thinking, analysis, interpretation, and active use of findings is emphasized in relation to 'scientific knowledge', while 'documented experience' requires a systematic approach and a focus on collegial as well as individual experience. Compliance with this regulation has been subject to scrutiny by the National Schools Inspectorate, who concluded that a majority of schools and school organizers do not live up to what is required and also that the concepts themselves need considerably more definition and discussion (Skolinspektionen 2019). One of the problems highlighted concerns what is characterized as uncritical attitudes in the choice of methods, accompanied by a clear tendency to follow current trends without adequately analysing various sources or considering possible criticisms of different approaches (pp. 5, 29). A recurring theme in the Inspectorate's analysis was the lack of coordination and collaboration between different levels in the educational system. One observation was that contacts between schools and universities were fairly frequent, but that some teachers pointed out that this collaboration should be more reciprocal, hence focusing equally on the interests of both parties (p. 17).

Despite the regulatory documents' emphasis on the need for a scientific basis and documented experience, most teachers in schools do not add a research degree to their basic qualification in teacher education. The same is true for a considerable

---

[2] Further information at https://www.skolverket.se/andra-sprak-other-languages/english-engelska (accessed 28 October 2022).
[3] https://www.riksdagen.se/sv/dokument-lagar/dokument/svensk-forfattningssamling/skollag-2010800_sfs-2010-800 (accessed 28 October 2022).

number of teacher educators. Various university-based platforms and projects as well as modules provided by the NAE inform teachers and teacher educators about recent research findings and enable them to engage in research activities. However, usually such activities do not lead to a degree as is the case with national research schools.

2.3 Fundamental concepts in educational research

At a general level, a number of basic questions need to be addressed in educational research, focusing on researchers' aims and methods, their decisions regarding agency and use of methods and results, and, crucially, the consequences of the decisions and actions they take. In addition, and importantly, aspects of content have to be taken into account. Institutionalized education normally rests on a more or less explicit definition of the knowledge or competences required in a particular context, often referred to as the construct. This is commonly summarized in curricula and syllabuses for the level of education in question, comprising descriptions both of content and expected attainment levels, the latter sometimes referred to as performance standards or criteria. These documents play a crucial role in education and need to be constructed and implemented following a conscious plan. Thus, curriculum theory is of obvious relevance in educational research, where van den Akker's (2003) distinction between the intended, implemented and attained curriculum is an example of a useful tool in analysing relationships between different levels and actors in education.

In addition to these more general and structural perspectives, aspects of the individual and the pedagogical levels need to be added. This entails a number of domain and subject-specific issues, not least regarding strong and reciprocal relationships between aspects of the pedagogical process, reflecting principles of constructive alignment, i.e., a consistent and visible relationship between objectives, learning, teaching, and assessment practices (Biggs 1996; Council of Europe 2001, 2020; Erickson, Borger, and Olsson 2022). Such issues may be both internally and externally related and encompass epistemological perspectives as well as learners' and teachers' attitudes and beliefs concerning, for example, construct as well as method and agency-related aspects. In this, language, being a medium of communication, affects learning as well as teaching and assessment, for teachers as well as learners (Schleppegrell and Christie 2018). Furthermore, the human capacity for bi- and multilingualism and the presence of multilingualism in schools as in the rest of society (see, e.g., Bonnet and Siemund 2018), makes the thematic orientations of our two research schools highly relevant for educational research.

We will now describe the two research schools in more detail.

3 Two examples: FRAM and SEMLA

The two graduate schools FRAM[4] and SEMLA[5] were both funded by the government through the Swedish Research Council, the first offered to language teachers in schools and leading to a licentiate degree, the second offered to language teacher educators and leading to a PhD. Both schools were coordinated by Stockholm University and run in collaboration with other universities in Sweden.

3.1 FRAM

The licentiate graduate school FRAM for teachers of English and Modern languages[6] in lower and upper secondary schools focused on three content domains: aspects of language learning from an individual perspective, ICT in learning and teaching languages, and forms of assessment in language studies. These domains and how the individual projects related to them are briefly described below (4.1); see also Bardel et al. (2017) and Bardel et al. (2021).

FRAM was a collaboration between four Swedish universities, Linneaus University, Lund University, Stockholm University, and the University of Gothenburg, and comprised five terms of study.

At the beginning of 2012, ten student positions were announced. Some fifty applicants showed an interest in the graduate school; about half of them wanted to specialize in English as target language. The applications of forty of the candidates, including previous academic texts and research plans, were assessed by two potential co-supervisors within the field of language studies and language education. The authors of the seventeen most highly rated applications were interviewed by the steering committee, partly in the candidate's target language. After

---

4 FRAM (VR 729-2011-5277) is an acronym derived from the Swedish name of the graduate school: *De främmande språkens didaktik. Forskarskola i språkdidaktik med inriktning mot engelska, franska, italienska, spanska och tyska* ('The teaching and learning of foreign languages. Graduate school for teachers in language education with a focus on English, French, Italian, Spanish and German').
5 SEMLA (VR 2017:06048) is an acronym derived from *Learning, teaching and assessment of Swedish and English. Multilingualism as an asset and a challenge – PhD program for language teacher educators*.
6 While English instruction starts no later than school year 3, it is possible (though not mandatory) to study a Modern language from year 6 (at the latest) in Swedish compulsory school. Pupils can normally choose between French, German and Spanish. In upper secondary school, other language options are available, depending on students' choice of study programme (Bardel, Erickson, and Österberg 2019; Erickson et al. 2022).

this, the committee agreed on the ten most suitable candidates, based on their ability to discuss their research plan, the role of the researching teacher, and their attitudes to collaboration. Proficiency in their target language was also considered. Eventually, it turned out that five of the successful candidates had chosen English as their target language, one French, one German, one Italian, and two Spanish.

The FRAM students continued to serve in their schools one day per week during their studies. The schools participated in the collaboration by endorsing the teacher's application and co-financing their research, as the grant covered only 75% of their salaries. The students were distributed between the four participating universities according to a) their choice of thematic strand and b) their choice of target language, taking into account the specialization of the supervisors affiliated to the different universities. Three students registered with Stockholm University, three with the University of Gothenburg, three with Lund University, and one with Linnaeus University. The students followed the internal PhD programmes at their respective universities, but throughout the programme they also participated in courses and seminars that were compulsory for all ten students and organized by the participating universities. Thus, the group travelled and participated in joint activities for the whole period of their studies.

3.2 SEMLA

While FRAM comprised schoolteachers, SEMLA offered PhD studies to language teacher educators. It was planned as a four-year research programme on language education in a multilingual setting, targeting especially the main language Swedish and the foreign language English and recognizing multilingualism as a societal and pedagogical challenge, an educational goal and an asset for language learning.[7] In the research programme, learning, teaching and assessment are seen as the three fundamental components of language education (Council of Europe 2001, 2020) and they correspond to the three main strands of the research programme.

The SEMLA application to the Swedish Research Council involved the universities of Gothenburg, Stockholm and Umeå. The project was approved in the academic year 2017/18, and planning and recruitment started immediately. Students were

---

[7] For an analysis of the roles and functions of English, a language the status of which is continually under discussion in Sweden, see, e.g., Hult (2017), and for a brief overview of the multilingual language situation, see Erickson et al. (2022: 157).

admitted for the autumn term 2018. The number of applications was much lower than for FRAM: nine out of sixteen eligible applicants were offered a place after a selection process similar to the one used for FRAM. The reasons for the much lower number of applications, experienced also by other research schools for teacher educators, are not known, but may be due partly to economic conditions for PhD students, which apply also to those already employed as university teachers as soon as they start their PhD studies and thus shift occupation.

Because of Covid-19 and the inevitable effects of the pandemic on data collection, a prolongation of the programme has been approved and SEMLA will officially end in 2024, although most theses have already been completed and approved (see 4.2).

3.3 The pedagogical model of FRAM and SEMLA – collaboration in practice

Following national standards for research education, the FRAM and SEMLA programmes were basically organized around two main activities, compulsory and optional PhD courses on the one hand and the writing of a thesis on the other. The activities started in parallel at the beginning of each programme, although the main focus during the first year was on the courses. Because the compulsory courses of the participating universities differed slightly, the students' course curricula were not identical. However, three courses were compulsory for each graduate school and were thus taken by all the students. Each of these courses comprised 7.5 higher education credits (ECs). In FRAM these were: 1. *Language education*, organized by Stockholm University in 2012; 2. *ICT, teaching and learning languages*, organized by Lund University in 2013; and 3. *Educational assessment focusing on language assessment*, organized by the University of Gothenburg in 2013. These courses were developed specifically considering the FRAM students' needs and the aim of the research programme.

In SEMLA the corresponding courses were the following: *Didactic dimensions of multilingualism*, 7.5 ECs, Stockholm university, 2019; *Mixed methods*, University of Umeå, 2019; *Educational assessment focusing on language assessment*, 7.5 credits, University of Gothenburg, 2020. In addition, an initial compulsory module of 3.5 credits in research ethics in language education research was taken by all SEMLA students at Stockholm University in 2018.

From the first semester, seminars were also organized at the different universities, where the students presented their work in progress. FRAM students and supervisors participated in three retreats and a study trip to Brussels. The latter included an international conference and institutional visits and gave the whole group the opportunity to meet and discuss the students' ongoing work. In parallel to these specially designed activities, the students followed the courses and seminars of the PhD programmes organized at their respective universities, and the defence of each thesis took place at the university where the student was registered. By the end of 2015, all 10 students, except for one who had been on parental leave, had defended their theses (the remaining student defended in 2016).

The plan for the SEMLA group was to arrange similar trips, meetings and seminars, and such activities took place during the first year and a half. However, due to the Covid-19 pandemic, a planned study trip to Tel Aviv and Haifa in 2020 had to be cancelled, and during 2020–2021 all meetings and seminars were held on Zoom.

Every student in both graduate schools was assigned a main supervisor at their university, but also at least one co-supervisor, often in another university and normally one of the participating universities. This fostered collaboration between the universities and often also across traditional disciplinary boundaries.

4 Outcomes

4.1 FRAM

The research conducted within FRAM has been presented by all the students in a collection of papers (Bardel et al. 2021) and references to all the licentiate theses are found in Bardel et al. (2017). Because of space limitations, a brief summary must suffice here.

A study of individual motivation to learn French by Rocher-Hahlin has several implications for teachers/future teachers and points at the importance of including learning activities that enhance pupils' Ideal L3 Self (Henry 2012) as early as possible in the curriculum. Two studies on the role of prior language learning (Gunnarsson, Smidfelt) indicate that pupils may benefit from drawing on their full linguistic repertoire when learning English or other foreign languages. Both authors point at the importance of considering this in the language classroom and call for teachers to pay attention to similarities and differences between languages and to encourage pupils to do so.

The studies conducted on ICT and language teaching and learning (Fredholm, Källermark-Haya) indicate that language teachers have an important role to play in the digital school environment and that pupils are too often left to their own devices when it comes to using the computer for learning purposes. Generally, young people are skilled in managing computers, but in order to achieve benefits in foreign language education, teachers' guidance on how to use the computer as a learning tool is crucial.

The research conducted on different aspects of assessment is of obvious relevance and importance in teacher pre- and in-service education. Pålsson Gröndahl's results call for clearer feedback, more time for pupils to process feedback, and for teaching to be more closely related to the feedback given. However, assessment has an important function in addition to feedback and formativity, namely to promote fairness and equity. In FRAM, two of the five theses within the assessment theme focus on aspects of large-scale, national assessment of oral language competence, hence the summative function, however not ignoring formative aspects (Borger, Frisch). Another dissertation (Håkansson Ramberg) analyses teachers' rating of written production of German, with particular reference to grammar and lexis, emphasizing the need for increased collaboration between teachers in rating, thereby enhancing aspects of consensus and fairness. Finally, one of the theses investigates assessment practices in the CLIL context (Reierstam). This has a high degree of relevance for teacher education, where the growing phenomenon of Content and Language Integrated Learning (CLIL) needs substantial attention. For more extensive summaries and references to the students' work, see Bardel et al. (2017) and Bardel et al. (2021).

The FRAM research school also organized various meetings and in-service activities for language teachers and teacher educators, for example a conference at Stockholm University with invited speakers, both from schools and from the NAE). It should also be mentioned that, after the completion of the research school, three of the FRAM students were employed by the NAE to work on language education projects. One of them was involved in the initiation and implementation of the so-called 'Language Leap' (Sw. *Språksprånget*),[8] an on-line tool to be used for in-service education among teachers of foreign languages.

4.2 SEMLA

As mentioned, the SEMLA programme focuses on language education in multilingual settings, targeting especially Swedish and English. To date (May 2023), seven of the students have finished their studies and received their PhD degrees. The first thesis to be defended was Ohlsson's study (2021) on Swedish academic writing with a special focus on vocabulary and the role of language of instruction in upper secondary school. CLIL is attracting a significant number of students and there is a debate on how English as language of instruction affects

---

[8] https://www.skolverket.se/skolutveckling/kurser-och-utbildningar/sprakspranget---kompetensutveckling-for–larare-i-moderna-sprak (accessed 1 May 2023).

students' Swedish language skills, especially their academic language. Ohlsson's analyses of productive written academic vocabulary do not indicate this kind of negative effect. Importantly, it seems that students benefit from instruction about academic writing and that revision work on their own texts might lead to an improvement of productive writing.

The second thesis to be discussed was Sturk (2022), who conducted a study exploring how writing is taught across the curriculum in Swedish compulsory school, with a mix of qualitative and quantitative methods and from the perspective of actual teaching practices and discussions about teaching. Two issues are mainly focused upon, namely what discourses of writing can be identified and how teachers use writing for pedagogical purposes across the curriculum. The results reveal that writing was rather infrequent across the curriculum, whereas writing as a tool for learning had a strong position.

The focus of Csöregh's thesis (2022) is assessment identity among student and novice teachers of English to 10–12-year-olds: what beliefs and assumptions characterize this identity and how it develops with increasing professional experience. A mixed-methods methodology was used; an initial questionnaire and recurring focus-group interviews were complemented by in-depth interviews. Based on the findings, a four-field model was constructed, positioning different assessment identities according to their approach and their relation to the accountability system.

In an ethnographically inspired study, Snoder (2023) investigated how five teachers with migrant backgrounds viewed their own multilingualism and how, and if, they found that their multilingualism was relevant for teaching in the early school years. Snoder concluded by calling for more research on multilingual language use in the early school years. Possible directions pointed out for future research were collaboration between different teacher categories and the teaching of multilingual language awareness.

Bylund (2023) explored young people's language use outside school in a study of students from school years 6 and 7 in some distinctly multilingual areas located in three Swedish cities. The focus of the thesis was on how patterns in daily language use and exposure interact with investment in language, language ideologies, and the formation of young people's identities. The findings signify the importance of bridging the gap between home and school contexts and for education to take a critical view on the role of language in educational equity.

Warnby (2023) analysed almost 1,000 Swedish upper secondary school students' receptive English academic word knowledge. Participants took vocabulary tests, questionnaires and a survey of out-of-school English activities. Results reveal that around half of the students leaving mandatory English courses in university preparatory programmes do not reach the minimum threshold score indicating mastery of academic lexis. This is discussed in terms of curriculum and equity in view of subsequent university studies.

The topic of Finndahl's (2023) study is young students' language choice in Swedish compulsory school, focusing on aspects of expectations and experiences of learning, teaching and assessment. Different methods are combined when following students at one school in French, German, and Spanish from their choice of language and during their first year of study. An important result is the impact of contextual factors both on students' choice and perceptions of language and language learning.

In addition, two theses are well under way: Clara Palm is studying Swedish for immigrants (SFI) in tertiary education, and Elisabeth Nilsson is focusing on the identification of language needs and assessment of language proficiency in pre-school.

As this brief summary shows, the SEMLA research school, like its predecessor FRAM, has generated several research projects on fundamental aspects of language education, diverse in content and methodology. In addition, its participants have formed networks that include teacher colleagues in different parts of Sweden, researchers in the national and international context, and schools where they have gathered data. Such networks are clearly beneficial to the further development of language education in an increasingly multilingual society.

5 Discussion

The work of the research schools FRAM and SEMLA is characterized by a wide array of topics as well as varying methodological approaches to the research questions posed. Furthermore, a consciously collaborative approach has been adopted between researchers involved in language teacher education in Sweden and abroad as well as between established researchers and teachers and teacher educators. Students of different ages and their teachers are also considered partners in this respect and have contributed in substantial ways.

As for national and international collaboration, FRAM had a network of reference which included staff from several Swedish universities and colleagues abroad, whereas SEMLA has an international advisory board. These scholars have been engaged in different tasks, from the evaluation of applications to giving talks, co-supervising, and discussing half-way or nearly final versions of the students' theses, given their expertise in areas of relevance for the research programme. This has obviously further added to the collaborative approach used and strengthened the intended reciprocity of the endeavour at large.

There has been regular collaboration with local schools, municipalities and/or regional centres for school development. The mutual benefit of this has been noticeable, in that all parties have gained useful experience and learnt from each other within areas not regularly focused upon in their own daily work. Some examples are given below.

A characteristic of FRAM was that the students taught part time in their schools during their studies, and this kept them in continuous contact with their professional contexts. Most of them gathered data for their empirical studies either in the school in which they were employed or in other schools. Consequently, colleagues and headteachers were continuously involved and informed about the research. The students as well as the steering committee have also been active in giving talks at different conferences and workshops in schools and teachers' associations, etc., and several of the FRAM students have published essays on their results outside the academic context after finishing their studies. It should be pointed out, moreover, that collaboration has also included the national policy level in a more indirect way, through the focus on the constructs of language education, expressed not least in national curricula and syllabuses. National authorities have also been actively involved via discussions and conferences and by appointing students and supervisors as experts in different school-related projects.

In the case of SEMLA, collaboration has been and is equally intense, although conducted in partly different forms. The students have been working full-time at their universities, though frequently collecting data in schools. Student teachers have been important participants in some of the studies.

As for content, many different aspects of language education have been focused on within the themes of the research schools – learning, teaching and assessment, and aspects of the multifaceted notion of multilingualism, referring to additive as well as simultaneous multilingualism (Cenoz and Genesee 1998), acquired in a variety of contexts. Focal points have been regulations and procedures as well as language development and purely linguistic aspects of learners' language and target languages, with a fairly even distribution between teachers' teaching and learners' learning. In this, the national regulatory documents, i.e., curricula and syllabuses, have played a more or less prominent role. Hence, using van den Akker's (2003) terminology, the intended curriculum has served as background to many of the studies, the implemented curriculum has been studied with the help of teachers' and students' practices and reflections, and the attained curriculum has been made visible not least in students' achievements and perceptions.

Finally, it needs to be recognized that a certain ambiguity of aims and duality of success can be identified, especially regarding research schools for teachers, like FRAM. Here, the intention was to enhance the level of scientific knowledge in schools, thereby also supporting and strengthening the amount of documented collegial work. However, national studies have shown that this was by no means always the case (Sveriges Riksdag 2016), since schools were not always prepared to make use of the added competence by offering their returning teachers new and stimulating tasks. Also, quite a number of students decided to stay in academia and continue their studies. This was clearly the case in FRAM, which led to a total of ten licentiate theses: only three students stopped at the licentiate level. Two of them returned to their work as schoolteachers, one took a permanent position at the NAE, and the remaining seven continued their academic careers. Six of these students completed PhD degrees and one is currently working on a PhD thesis. This is obviously positive from many points of view, though it does not contribute to the intended enhancement of the general level of scientific knowledge and documented experience in the regular school system.

6 Concluding reflections

As shown, research schools for professionals within the field of education may have many advantages, offering potential for all parties involved. Teachers are given the explicit opportunity to actively explore issues that are directly relevant for their profession and their professional development. Researchers are given insight into such issues and into teachers' experience and know-how. Participating students can contribute their perspectives in a way that raises awareness and enhances development for everybody concerned. Empirical studies which could not otherwise be carried out thus come into existence and results and implications are made visible.

Importantly, new professional and academic networks may arise in a multidirectional exchange of experience and ideas, and new knowledge can be achieved in collaborative development of the research field. Traditionally, academic research is assumed to be of positive value to schools, but the indispensable affordances of contributions 'from the field' – students, teachers and head teachers – to research and to the educational authorities responsible for the creation of national regulatory documents is less often acknowledged, except perhaps at the rhetorical level. We hope that the two research schools described in this chapter have illustrated this positive and mutual relationship. Their overarching thematics originated in academia and were enriched by the participating teachers' and teacher educators' specific research questions and points of view. Furthermore, the studies that have been conducted have prompted new queries that will inform and enrich the policy level and the decisions made there.

References

Bardel, Camilla, Gudrun Erickson, Jonas Granfeldt & Christina Rosén. 2017. Offering research education for in-service language teachers. *Language Teaching* 50(2). 290–293. https://doi:10.1017/S026144481600046X (accessed 5 November 2022).

Bardel, Camilla, Gudrun Erickson, Jonas Granfeldt & Christina Rosén (eds.). 2021. *Forskarskolan FRAM – lärare forskar i de främmande språkens didaktik* [The research school FRAM – teachers research the didactics of foreign languages]. Stockholm: Stockholm University Press. DOI: https://doi.org/10.16993/bbg (accessed 6 October 2022).

Bardel, Camilla, Gudrun Erickson & Rakel Österberg. 2019. Learning, teaching and assessment of second foreign languages in Swedish lower secondary school – dilemmas and prospects. *Apples. Journal of Applied Linguistic Studies* 13(1). 7–26. DOI: https://doi.org/10.17011/apples/urn.201903011687 (accessed 6 October 2022).

Biggs, John. 1996. Enhancing teaching through constructive alignment. *Higher Education* 32. 347–364. https://doi.org/10.1007/BF00138871 (accessed 6 October 2022).

Bonnet, Andreas & Peter Siemund (eds.). 2018. *Foreign language education in multilingual classrooms*. Amsterdam: John Benjamins.

Bylund, Jasmine. 2022. *Everyday language practices and the interplay of ideologies, investment and identities: Language use and dispositions among young adolescents in multilingual urban settings*. PhD thesis, University of Gothenburg.

Cenoz, Jasone & Fred Genesee. 1998. Psycholinguistic perspectives on multilingualism and multilingual education. In Jasone Cenoz & Fred Genesee (eds.), *Beyond bilingualism: Multilingualism and multilingual education*, 16–32. Bristol: Multilingual Matters.

Council of Europe 2001. *Common European Framework of Reference for Languages: Learning, teaching, assessment*. Cambridge: Cambridge University Press.

Council of Europe. 2020. *Common European Framework of Reference for Languages: Learning, teaching, assessment. Companion volume*. https://rm.coe.int/common-european-framework-of-reference-for-languages-learning-teaching/16809ea0d4 (accessed 28 October 2022).

Csöregh, Anna-Marie. 2022. *Fairest of them all? – Assessment identity development among Swedish student and novice teachers of EFL*. PhD thesis, Stockholm University.

Erickson, Gudrun, Linda Borger & Eva Olsson. 2022. National assessment of foreign languages in Sweden: A multifaceted and collaborative venture. *Language Testing* 39(3). 474–493. DOI: 10.1177/02655322221075067 (accessed 6 October 2022).

Erickson, Gudrun, Camilla Bardel, Rakel Österberg & Monica Rosén. 2022. Attitudes and ambiguities – teachers' views on second foreign language education in Swedish compulsory school. In Camilla Bardel, Christina Hedman, Katarina Rejman & Elisabeth Zetterholm (eds.), *Exploring language education: Global and local perspectives*, 157–201. Stockholm: Stockholm University Press. DOI: https://doi.org/10.16993/bbz.f (accessed 6 October 2022).

Finndahl, Ingela. 2023. *Young students' language choice in Swedish compulsory school: Expectations, learning and assessment*. PhD thesis, University of Gothenburg.

Henry, Alastair. 2012. *L3 motivation*. PhD thesis, University of Gothenburg.

Hult, Francis. 2017. More than a lingua franca: Functions of English in a globalized educational language policy. *Language, Culture and Curriculum* 30(3). 265–282. DOI: https://arkiv.lr.se/opinion--debatt/undersokningar/2022/2022-03-14-skolan-valet-och-de-svenska-valjarnas-prioriteringar (accessed 2 May 2023).

Lärarnas Riksförbund. 2022. *Skolan, valet och de svenska väljarnas prioriteringar* [School, general election, and Swedish voters' priorities]. https://arkiv.lr.se/opinion--debatt/undersokningar/ 2022/2022-03-14-skolan-valet-och-de-svenska-valjarnas-prioriteringar (accessed 2 May 2023).

Ohlsson, Elisabeth. 2021. *Den synliggjorda vokabulären och praktiken – gymnasielevers akademiska skrivande på svenska* [The visualized vocabulary and the practice. Upper secondary school students' academic writing in Swedish]. PhD thesis, University of Gothenburg.

Schleppegrell, Mary & Frances Christie. 2018. Linguistic features of writing development: A functional perspective. In Charles Bazerman, Arthur Applebee, Virginia Berninger et al. (eds.), *The lifespan development of writing*, 111–150. Urbana, IL: National Council of Teachers of English (NCTE). https://wac.colostate.edu/docs/books/lifespan-writing/development.pdf (accessed 6 October 2022).

SFS 2007:753. *Förordning om utbildning på forskarnivå för lärare* [Ordinance on postgraduate education for teachers]. Svensk Författningssamling. https://www.lagboken.se/Lagboken/start/ sfs/sfs/2007/700-799/d_169755-sfs-2007_753-forordning-om-utbildning-pa-forskarniva-for-larare (accessed 28 October 2022).

Skolinspektionen. 2019. *Vetenskaplig grund och beprövad erfarenhet. Förutsättningar och arbetsformer i grundskolan* [Scientific basis and documented experience. Prerequisites and work models in compulsory school]. Tematisk kvalitetsgranskning 2019. Dnr 400-2017:1022. https://www.skolins pektionen.se/sok/?q=beprövad+erfarenhet&_t_dtq=true (accessed 6 October 2022).

Skollag 2010:800 [Education Act]. https://www.riksdagen.se/sv/dokument-lagar/dokument/svensk-forfattningssamling/skollag-2010800_sfs-2010-800 (accessed 6 October 2022).

Skolverket. 2012. *Promemoria om vetenskaplig grund och beprövad erfarenhet* [Memorandum on scientific knowledge and documented experience]. Dnr 2012:1700.

Skolverket. 2020. *Att ställa frågor och söka svar – samarbete för vetenskaplig grund och beprövad erfarenhet* [Asking questions and seeking answers – collaboration for scientific basis and documented experience]. https://www.skolverket.se/publikationsserier/forskning-for-skolan/ 2020/att-stalla-fragor-och-soka-svar (accessed 6 October 2022). ISBN: 978-91-7559-351-7

Snoder, Sara. 2022. *'Det är inte så att vi exklusivt pratar svenska': Flerspråkighetens möjliga utrymmen i låg- och mellanstadieklassrum. En studie av flerspråkiga grundskollärares perspektiv* ['It's not the case that we speak Swedish exclusively': Possibilities for multilingual spaces in primary classrooms: A study of the perspective of multilingual teachers]. PhD thesis, Stockholm University.

SOU 1999:63. (Regeringskansliet, 1999). *Att lära och leda – En lärarutbildning för samverkan och utveckling* [Learning and leading – teacher education for collaboration and development]. https://www.regeringen.se/rattsliga-dokument/statens-offentliga-utredningar/1999/05/sou-199963/ (accessed 28 October 2022).

Sturk, Erika. 2022. *Writing across the curriculum in compulsory school in Sweden*. PhD thesis, Umeå University.

Sveriges Riksdag. 2016. *Forskarskolor för lärare och förskollärare – en uppföljning av fyra statliga satsningar* [Research schools for teachers and pre-school teachers – a follow up of four national projects]. Rapport från Riksdagen 2016/17:RFR4.https://www.riksdagen.se/sv/dokument-lagar/ dokument/rapport-fran-riksdagen/forskarskolor-for-larare-och-forskollarare-en_H40WRFR4 (accessed 6 October 2022).

Utbildningsdepartementet. 2021. *Ökad kvalitet i lärarutbildningen och fler lärare i skolan* [Increased quality in teacher education and more teachers in schools]. Promemoria. U2021/00301.

Regeringskansliet. https://www.regeringen.se/rattsliga-dokument/departementsserien-och-promemorior/2021/01/okad-kvalitet-i-lararutbildningen-och-fler-larare-i-skolan/ (accessed 2 May 2023).

van den Akker, Jan. 2003. Curriculum perspectives: An introduction. In Jan van den Akker, Wilmand Kuiper & Uwe Hameyer (eds.), *Curriculum landscapes and trends*, 1–10. Dordrecht: Kluwer Academic Publishers. DOI:10.1007/978-94-017-1205-7_1 (accessed 6 October 2022).

Warnby, Marcus. 2023. *English academic vocabulary knowledge among Swedish upper secondary school students*. PhD thesis, University of Gothenburg.

Afterword

Ema Ushioda
13 An ethical perspective on collaborative research

1 Introduction

My task here is to offer a concluding commentary on this diverse collection of studies, and to draw out some key insights for teaching and research in language education. Inevitably, my reading of the collection is influenced by my own experiences and shaped by the interests and perspectives I bring. These interests and perspectives will, in turn, shape the focus of my commentary and the themes and insights I wish to highlight.

I write from my position as a university academic working in language teacher education for a long time, with specific research interests in motivation in language learning. Over the past few years, I have grown increasingly concerned about the imbalance between the academic versus social purposes and values of the research we do on language learning motivation, and about whose interests are served and who ultimately benefits. In summary, my concerns are that our research tends to be driven by the academic purposes of developing and validating more powerful and generalizable theoretical accounts of motivation, and much less often by the social purposes of addressing the various challenges to motivation that language teachers and students face in their local classroom realities. These critical concerns have led me to propose a more socially responsive ethical agenda that prioritizes the actual needs and interests of teachers and learners, rather than the academic interests of the researcher (Ushioda 2020). Such an agenda calls for close mutual collaboration among all concerned, and for participatory forms of research involving teachers and learners as active agents rather than as the subjects or objects of inquiry. Clearly, the core themes of this edited collection resonate strongly with this proposed agenda for my own area of research within language education, and hence it is largely from an ethical perspective on collaborative research and reciprocity that I find myself writing this afterword.

2 Reciprocity as an ethical principle of collaborative research

This collection of studies focuses our attention on the concept of reciprocity in collaborative research in language education. While its subtitle might suggest an emphasis on practical benefits and challenges, I see the book as fundamentally concerned with reciprocity as an ethical principle of collaborative research, in the sense of referencing the complementary values and purposes underpinning a socially responsive collaborative research endeavour. I will expand further on what I mean by reciprocity as an ethical principle as I develop this discussion. In my view, this collection of studies offers a powerful and wide-ranging commentary on the underlying values and purposes of research in language education, and on the relational complexities among the individuals, communities, and institutions involved. In illustrating collaborative forms of inquiry that yield reciprocal benefits for all parties, the book points to the shortcomings of much language education research where the benefits for teachers and learners are often less direct and even questionable. Such 'benefits' are typically distilled into generalized and sometimes rather bland implications for pedagogy that are briefly summarized at the end of research articles.

As Larsen-Freeman (2015) has suggested, if language education research is to have direct benefits for teachers and learners and have a positive impact on their lives, it makes sense to take their actual interests, questions, and priorities as the starting point. The studies in this collection show that this does not mean simply engaging in tokenistic consultation so that teachers' (and learners') perspectives are acknowledged and their voices reported. For example, as Anna Elgemark and her colleagues explain (Chapter 3), collaborative research in their context entails focusing on specific recurring challenges that secondary school teachers of English in Sweden face in their practice and designing the research to support them in addressing these challenges. In this respect, they characterize the research as 'need-generated' and 'solution-focused', based on the principle that the knowledge collaboratively produced should be useable by the participating teachers to resolve their pedagogical problems. Similarly, Katherine Mueller and her colleagues (Chapter 2) give an account of teacher–researcher collaboration designed to address a specific practice-based issue in a German bilingual programme in Canada, which concerned the challenge of promoting learners' oral production skills. This kind of socially responsive approach to educational research is rather different from the versions of classroom research that Allwright (2005) has criticized as 'parasitic' activities, where researchers impose on the busy classroom lives of teachers and learners to obtain empirical data for their own academic purposes and benefit. Even where a research team has an academic agenda to collect standardized data for systematic analysis, the ethical principle of reciprocity in collaborative research means that researchers' needs should not dictate what happens in the project. Instead, as emphasized by Gabriele Pallotti and his colleagues (Chapter 8), the priority should always be the project's focus on addressing the teachers' needs, which in their study meant providing training and support for collaborative action research to enhance learners' writing skills.

Importantly, nevertheless, the principle of reciprocity in collaborative research means that it is not just the teachers (and learners) who gain but also the researchers. The benefits for researchers include direct access to ecologically rich classroom data and to teachers' professional networks and communities, with valuable opportunities for gaining insight into how pedagogical theory connects with classroom realities and practices, and with the lived experiences of teachers and learners. As David Little and Déirdre Kirwan emphasize (Chapter 6), such interdependence of pedagogical theory, classroom practice and empirical exploration should be core to all educational research. In other words, the ethical principle of reciprocity in collaborative research is not just a matter of ensuring equal distribution of benefits. Fundamentally, it is a matter of ensuring complete coherence and interdependence between the academic and the social values of the research. This contrasts with much research on language learning and teaching where, as Ortega (2005) has critically argued, academic goals and values tend to take precedence over social relevance and values. Of course, this hierarchical positioning reflects wider underlying imbalances in the traditional relationship between research and practice, or between researchers and teachers, in the field of language education. As illustrated in several of the studies in this collection, such inherent imbalances can create relational complexities in collaborative research in language education and may also give rise to potential ethical concerns in the relationships among different parties. In the next two sections I will discuss some of these relational complexities and ethical concerns, drawing on valuable insights from this collection.

3 Relational complexities in collaborative research

In the introduction to their study, Jessica Berggren and her colleagues (Chapter 1) problematize teacher–researcher partnerships where teachers are positioned as consumers of the knowledge that researchers produce. While such positioning could be construed as emphasizing the learning benefits to be gained by teachers, it also clearly presupposes a hierarchy of power and knowledge in such partnerships that accords a lesser status to (and a deficit view of) teachers. The underlying assumption that teachers should learn from academic research reflects wider critical debate around language teachers' general lack of engagement with research, and around the need for academic research findings to be made more practically and conceptually accessible to the professional teaching community (e.g., Borg 2010; Marsden and Kasprowicz 2017; Medgyes 2017; Sato and Loewen, 2019).

Within this critical debate, of course, there have been significant voices calling for 'more teaching-informed research to disrupt the current unidirectional flow of knowledge between teachers and researchers' (Rose 2019: 896) and encouraging us to rethink the 'teaching–research nexus' (McKinley 2019) in language education. Reciprocity in this sense of the bidirectional flow of knowledge between research and teaching, or between researchers and teachers, clearly underpins the collaborative relationships in the studies in this collection. The bidirectional flow of knowledge is reflected, for example, in David Little and Déirdre Kirwan's emphasis on the mutual relationship between research and practice in their collaboration (Chapter 6), and it is inherent in the 'third space' interactions between research and practice highlighted by Anna Elgemark and her colleagues (Chapter 3) in their project. More explicitly perhaps, Camilla Bardel and Gudrun Erickson (Chapter 12) essentially echo Rose's (2019) call to disrupt the unidirectional flow of knowledge from research to practice when they signal the important contribution that insights 'from the field' (i.e., from teachers, headteachers, and students) can make to the academic research community as well as to national educational policy.

A further major aspect of the critical debate around the 'teaching–research nexus' in language education is the involvement of teachers themselves in undertaking and producing their own research, instead of being merely consumers of other people's research. As Consoli and Dikilitaş (2021) highlight in their introduction to a special issue of *Educational Action Research*, the language teaching field has seen an increasing emphasis on promoting practitioner research and on encouraging teachers to engage in systematic inquiry to enhance their own classroom practice. This is reflected in a growing volume of professional development texts for language teachers providing guidance on how to do practitioner research in its different forms (e.g., Burns 2010; Hanks 2017; Smith and Rebolledo 2018), as well as a growing volume of edited collections focusing on language teacher research (e.g., Borg and Sanchez 2015; Dikilitaş and Hanks 2018) and even the publication of research monographs based on practitioner inquiry (e.g., Pinner 2019; Sampson 2016). At the same time, it is commonly acknowledged that language teachers' engagement in practitioner inquiry is often in the context of teacher education programmes, doctoral studies, or professional and institutional environments where teachers are supported or perhaps encouraged to undertake practitioner research (for critical discussion, see Burns 2005; see also Banegas and Consoli 2021).

In this regard, the studies in this volume similarly underline the valuable importance of appropriate institutional structures and collaborative partnerships to mediate and support teacher engagement in research inquiry. This aspect comes to the fore especially in the chapters in Part 3 addressing collaborative research in teachers' professional development, where teacher engagement in research is seen to mediate professional learning. In Chapter 8 focusing on 'interprofessional collaborative action research', for example, Gabriele Pallotti and his colleagues discuss how teachers in their project were trained to engage in action research by being supported to undertake systematic analysis of their learners' written texts, plan appropriate pedagogical actions, and evaluate the outcomes. Similarly, in Chapter 9 focusing on pre-service language teacher education in Israel, Ofra Inbar-Lourie and Orly Haim explore how student-teachers developed their professional knowledge through conducting collaborative participatory research with the support of one of the researchers, who was also the course instructor at the teacher education college. The chapter highlights the importance of the institutional framework and cross-institutional networks (between the teacher education college and the mentoring schools where teachers undertook their practicum) in supporting teachers' research engagement and professional learning. In Part 4 of this collection where the focus broadens to the national policy level, analysis of not only the institutional but also the wider educational policy framework for supporting teacher engagement in research is a major focus in Chapter 12. Here Camilla Bardel and Gudrun Erickson discuss how secondary school teachers and language teacher educators in Sweden have been enabled to pursue empirical research through their enrolment in graduate programmes that are collaboratively organized across various universities and funded by the national government.

Aside from illustrating how collaborative partnerships can give teachers agency to become producers and not just consumers of research, the studies in this collection consistently emphasize the importance of reducing power asymmetries in collaborative relationships as far as possible. For example, a non-hierarchical approach to their collaborative partnership is nicely captured in how Jessica Berggren and her colleagues (Chapter 1) describe teachers and researchers as working 'side by side' to produce knowledge together in their project. Similarly, Annamaria Pinter (Chapter 5) highlights the importance of explicitly promoting 'horizontal expertise' in her research collaboration with teachers and children in India, whereby everyone's knowledge and expertise shared equal status in the workshops that she and her academic colleague facilitated. As she comments, teachers appreciated the respectful non-hierarchical environment of the workshops and felt empowered to contribute actively. In the rather different context of collaboration between researchers and educational policymakers in Israel, Batia Laufer (Chapter 10) similarly emphasizes the complementary rather than competing or hierarchical nature of the perspectives and expertise brought by both parties to the shared enterprise of developing a lexical syllabus. In Chapter 7, Tanya McCarthy likewise highlights the important principle that all participants in collaborative research bring different knowledge structures, skills and experiences that enable the shared creation of new understandings. However, she further observes that in the Japanese institutional context where her work is located, how this principle plays out in certain partnerships can be affected by the traditional hierarchical structures operating in educational and professional settings.

4 Ethical concerns in collaborative research

In this respect, while emphasizing the importance of creating a culture of equality and mutual respect and of minimizing power asymmetries in collaborative research, the studies in this collection also illuminate some ethical challenges in this relational work. Two chapters give extensive attention to examining ethical perspectives in relation to how non-researcher participants engage in the collaboration under focus. In Chapter 4, Marie Källkvist and her colleagues examine researcher–student collaboration in the context of longitudinal ethnographic research in a Swedish multilingual school. Specifically, they focus on students' processes of giving consent to participate in the research and analyse how students' decision-making is mediated by the quality of their teacher's rapport with them, and by various associated classroom discourses around the nature and value of the research and the form of their participation in the research. The chapter provides an illuminating commentary on an essential aspect of procedural ethics (obtaining informed consent) that usually receives cursory reporting only in accounts of classroom research, where the relational complexities and power dynamics shaping students' decisions to participate in a research study often remain unexamined and unchallenged. After all, as Comstock (2012: 172) has pointedly commented, if participants agree to take part in a research study 'simply because they think an authoritative figure wants them to do it', does this really constitute consent?

The ethical challenges posed by the power structures in collaborative research partnerships are similarly given critical attention by Karita Mård-Miettinen and Anna Pittkänen-Huhta (Chapter 11) in their collaborative case study of new language policy implementation in a Finnish primary school. Analysing interview data, they examine complexities in how teachers and researchers (who are also teacher educators) relate to each other in these interactions, and they highlight challenges in the process of building mutual trust in the research collaboration despite the shared interests between parties. Specifically, their analysis reveals insecurities and defensiveness in how the teachers position themselves in relation to the research collaboration as well as in relation to the new language policy under focus. The analysis also reveals uncertainties and anxieties in how the researcher-interviewers try to manage and respond to teachers' feelings during their interactions with them. This reflexive analytical focus on the relational processes rather than the research outcomes of the collaboration demonstrates the researchers' awareness of and sensitivity to ethical tensions in their interactions with the teachers. In this respect, it illustrates their engagement with what Guillemin and Gillam (2004) call the 'ethics in practice' of research fieldwork processes, in terms of how we manage our relationships with participants and stakeholders in real time and deal with ethically important moments as they arise in our day-to-day research practices. As Guillemin and Gillam explain, this 'ethics in practice' dimension of research fieldwork often concerns relational complexities and tensions that are neither anticipated nor addressed in the more routinized procedural ethics dimension of institutional ethics committee applications.

Of course, the institutional perspective nevertheless remains important in this regard, since the relational and ethical complexities of collaborative research must be navigated not only on an interpersonal level but also on an institutional and structural level, as different organizational bodies and institutional processes come into interaction with one another. For example, Katherine Mueller and her colleagues (Chapter 2) explain how their research required ethical approval by both university and school boards, and they note how the researcher members of the project team had to stay mindful of their status as 'outsiders' from the perspective of the school board, despite teachers' natural propensity for sharing and working collaboratively. In summary, the wider institutional and environmental structures within which collaborative research is embedded clearly have an important bearing on how the collaboration is negotiated and managed, and on how effectively and successfully the ethical principle of reciprocity can be sustained.

5 Concluding thoughts

I began this afterword by stating that my task was to offer a concluding commentary on this collection and to draw out some key insights for teaching and research in language education. In this latter regard, the editors, contributors, and other readers will undoubtedly have observed that I have deliberately not separated out insights for teaching from insights for research in my commentary. In my view, such a separation would have rather undermined the fundamental principle of reciprocity characterizing the teaching–research nexus of these collaborative studies. While teachers, researchers, and others involved in such projects may each gain particular benefits and insights from their collaboration, the diverse studies in this collection consistently show that such benefits and insights should always be complementary, shared, and interconnected. In this sense, reciprocity in collaborative research in language education does not simply mean a transactional exchange of mutual benefits and concessions. As this thought-provoking collection of studies has richly illustrated, reciprocity in this context is the ethical principle of ensuring complete coherence and interdependence between the academic and the social values and purposes of the research, and of sensitively managing relational processes and power structures to sustain this coherence and interdependence to the collective benefit of everyone involved. These are valuable and important insights for all of us who engage in collaborative research relationships in the language education field.

References

Allwright, Dick. 2005. Developing principles for practitioner research: The case of exploratory practice. *Modern Language Journal* 89(3). 353–366.
Banegas, Darío Luis & Sal Consoli. 2021. Initial language teacher education: The effects of a module on teacher research. *Cambridge Journal of Education* 51(4). 491–507.
Borg, Simon. 2010. Language teacher research engagement. *Language Teaching* 43(4). 391–429.
Borg, Simon & Hugo Santiago Sanchez (eds.). 2015. *International perspectives on teacher research*. London: Palgrave Macmillan.
Burns, Anne. 2005. Action research: an evolving paradigm? *Language Teaching*, 38(2). 57–74.
Burns, Anne. 2010. *Doing action research in English language teaching: A guide for practitioners*. New York: Routledge.
Comstock, Gary. 2012. *Research ethics: A philosophical guide to the responsible conduct of research*. Cambridge: Cambridge University Press.
Consoli, Sal & Kenan Dikilitaş. 2021. Research engagement in language education. *Educational Action Research* 29(3). 347–357.
Dikilitaş, Kenan & Judith Hanks (eds.). 2018. *Developing language teachers with exploratory practice: Innovations and explorations in language education*. Cham: Palgrave Macmillan.
Guillemin, Marylis & Lynn Gillam. 2004. Ethics, reflexivity, and 'ethically important moments' in research. *Qualitative Inquiry* 10(2). 261–280.
Hanks, Judith. 2017. *Exploratory practice in language teaching: Puzzling about principles and practices*. London: Palgrave Macmillan.
Larsen-Freeman, Diane. 2015. Research into practice: Grammar teaching and learning. *Language Teaching* 28(2). 263–280.

Marsden, Emma & Rowena Kasprowicz. 2017. Foreign language educators' exposure to research: Reported experiences, exposure via citations, and a proposal for action. *Modern Language Journal* 101(4). 613–642.

McKinley, Jim. 2019. Evolving the TESOL teaching–research nexus. *TESOL Quarterly* 53(3). 875–884.

Medgyes, Péter. 2017. The (ir)relevance of academic research for the language teacher. *ELT Journal* 71(4). 491–498.

Ortega, Lourdes. 2005. For what and for whom is our research? The ethical as transformative lens in instructed SLA. *Modern Language Journal* 89(3). 427–443.

Pinner, Richard S. 2019. *Authenticity and teacher-student motivational synergy: A narrative of language teaching*. London: Routledge.

Rose, Heath. 2019. Dismantling the ivory tower in TESOL: A renewed call for teaching-informed research. *TESOL Quarterly* 53(3). 895–905.

Sampson, Richard J. 2016. *Complexity in classroom foreign language learning motivation: A practitioner perspective from Japan*. Bristol: Multilingual Matters.

Sato, Masatoshi & Shawn Loewen. 2019. Do teachers care about research? The research–pedagogy dialogue. *ELT Journal* 73(1). 1–10.

Smith, Richard & Paula Rebolledo. 2018. *A handbook for exploratory action research*. London: British Council.

Ushioda, Ema. 2020. *Language learning motivation: An ethical agenda for research*. Oxford: Oxford University Press.

Contributors

Camilla Bardel is a professor of Modern languages and Language education at Stockholm University. Her main research interests are multilingualism, second and third language development, cross-linguistic influence, language learning and teaching, and language policy. She currently coordinates the PhD program SEMLA for language teacher educators.

Jessica Berggren is a senior lecturer in a secondary school and researcher at the Department of Language Education, Stockholm University. Her research interests involve second language writing, oral interaction, task design, and assessment. She is the leader of the network for English and other foreign languages at Stockholm Teaching & Learning Studies.

Claudia Borghetti is Research Fellow in Educational Linguistics at the University of Bologna. She researches on (academic) writing, intercultural language learning, student mobility, and plurilingualism. She participates in numerous national and international research groups, and coordinated the European project IEREST (*Intercultural Education Resources for Erasmus Students and their Teachers*) as project manager.

Roswita Dressler PhD is an associate professor at the Werklund School of Education, University of Calgary. She studies in-service and pre-service teacher understandings of second language teaching and learning as well as linguistic identity and study abroad. She is a former teacher of German and French as a Second Language.

Anja Dressler Araujo, BA (German), BEd is an elementary teacher in the German Bilingual Program at Bowcroft School in Calgary, Alberta, Canada. Her research experience includes second language fluency, refugee education, incorporating Indigenous literatures, and the impact of family supports on the academic success of immigrant students.

Anna Elgemark is senior lecturer in English at University West (Sweden), and a qualified secondary teacher of English and social sciences. Her research interests include language awareness, language teacher awareness, and teacher identity development.

Gudrun Erickson is Senior Professor of Education in Language and Assessment at the University of Gothenburg. Her principal research interests lie within the field of language policy and assessment. She has long experience of teaching and teacher education, as well as national and international projects on language learning, teaching and assessment.

Stefania Ferrari is currently a researcher in second language teaching methodology at Eastern Piedmont University in Italy. Her main research interests are second language acquisition in migratory contexts, second language pragmatics, and task-based language teaching. She collaborates with different local authorities and schools in Northern Italy for the development and implementation of projects dedicated to the inclusion of migrant students. She is part of the professional network Glottonaute.

Henrik Gyllstad, PhD is an associate professor in English Language and Linguistics at the Centre for Languages and Literature, Lund University, Sweden. His research interests include language testing and assessment, second language acquisition, and bilingualism and multilingualism. Predominantly, his focus is on vocabulary, phraseology and lexical processing.

Malin Haglind is a teacher in a secondary school in Sweden. She teaches English and Spanish and has participated in the collaborative research project *From monologues to dialogues* for four years. She has published in *Lingua*, a journal for language teachers.

Orly Haim is a course instructor at Beit Berl College where she also serves as the chair of the Council of the Faculty of Education. Orly also teaches in the TEFL program at Tel Aviv University. Her research interests include bi/multilingualism, additional language acquisition, language policy, and language teacher cognition.

Alastair Henry is Professor of Language Education at Lund University and University West (Sweden), and a qualified secondary teacher of English and social sciences. His research focuses on second language motivation, multilingualism, teacher identity development, and language teacher motivational practice.

Amanda Hoskins participated in the collaborative research project *From monologues to dialogues* for three years, while she was working as an English and Spanish teacher in a Swedish upper secondary school. She is currently a PhD candidate at Linköping University; in her work she analyses task-based interactions with a conversation-analytic lens.

Ofra Inbar-Lourie lectures in the multilingual education department in the School of Education at Tel Aviv University. Her current research interests include teacher education with a focus on language teachers, language policy, language assessment and especially the acquisition of language assessment literacy, and the language of instruction in higher education contexts.

Petra Jansson is principal teacher in English and Swedish at Lagmansgymnasiet in Vara, Sweden, where she coordinates practice development in these subjects. An article showcasing her practice has appeared in the journal *Grundskoletidningen*.

Marie Källkvist, PhD is Professor of English, specializing in English Language Education, at Linnæus University, Sweden, and an associate professor at Lund University, Sweden. Her research is in the areas of language education and language policy and planning, both in schools and higher education.

Déirdre Kirwan was principal of Scoil Bhríde (Cailíní), Blanchardstown, Dublin from 1987 to 2015. She was awarded the European Language Label for her work in plurilingual education in 2008 and received her PhD from Trinity College Dublin in 2009. With David Little she co-authored *Engaging with linguistic diversity: A study of educational inclusion in an Irish primary school* (Bloomsbury, 2019).

Silvia Kunitz is an associate professor at Linköping University. She conducts conversation-analytic research focusing on how students and teachers do learning/teaching/testing as socially situated activities in and through embodied talk-in-interaction. Currently she also works at Stockholm Teaching & Learning Studies in the network for English and other foreign languages.

Batia Laufer is Professor Emerita of Applied Linguistics at the University of Haifa, Israel. She has lectured, supervised research and published widely on different areas of vocabulary acquisition in additional languages, such as effective teaching, reading, testing, cross-linguistic influence, ease and difficulty in learning, dictionary use, lexical attrition.

David Little is a Fellow Emeritus of Trinity College Dublin. His principal research interests are the theory and practice of learner autonomy in second language education, the management of linguistic diversity in schools and classrooms, and the use of the *Common European Framework of Reference for Languages* to support the design of curricula, teaching/learning programmes and assessment.

Anna Löfquist is a lead teacher in a primary school. She teaches English and music and has participated in the collaborative research project *From monologues to dialogues* for four years. She has published in *Lingua*, a journal for language teachers.

Tanya McCarthy received a PhD in Linguistics from Macquarie University and has been advising students on English learning for two decades. Her research interest is learner development, particularly language advising, out-of-class learning and professional development. She is currently researching the role of dialogue in L2 classroom, research, and industry contexts.

Karita Mård-Miettinen is professor in applied linguistics at the University of Jyväskylä, Finland. Her research focuses especially on practices and policies in early language learning and teaching in bilingual education and additional language teaching settings. She applies ethnographic, collaborative and visual methods and adopts content and discourse analytic approaches.

Frank Moeller, BA (German), BEd is an elementary teacher and Learning Leader in the German Bilingual Program at Bowcroft School in Calgary, Alberta, Canada. His research interest is second language education. He entered teaching after his army service and apprenticeship as a chef in Germany.

Katherine Mueller, PhD is an assistant professor (teaching), in the Werklund School of Education at the University of Calgary. She specializes in teaching pre-service teachers of French. She is a former teacher of French as a Second Language and is involved with school-based research involving the implementation of the strategies of the Neurolinguistic Approach.

Gabriele Pallotti is Professor of Language Teaching Methodology at the University of Modena and Reggio Emilia. His research focusses on interlanguage development, linguistic complexity, second language interaction, methodology, and epistemology in applied linguistics. He coordinates the project *Observing Interlanguage* and is associate editor of the EuroSLA Studies Series.

Annamaria Pinter is a reader at the Department of Applied Linguistics, University of Warwick, UK. Her research interests include all aspects of second/foreign language education for children, task-based second language learning, engaging children actively in research, and language teacher education.

Anne Pitkänen-Huhta is Professor of English at the University of Jyväskylä, Finland. Her research focuses broadly on issues related to practices of additional language learning and teaching, including multiliteracies and multilingualism in language education, early language learning, and language teacher education. She employs ethnographic, discourse analytic and visual methods.

Hanna Robertson is a teacher in an upper secondary school in Sweden. She teaches Swedish and English and has participated in the collaborative research project *From monologues to dialogues* for one and a half years.

Tanya Ronellenfitsch, BA, BEd is an elementary teacher at Bowcroft School in the German Bilingual Program in Calgary, Alberta, Canada. She also serves as President of the Alberta Association of Teachers of German to help support the professional development of other German teachers in the province.

Erica Sandlund, PhD is professor of English linguistics at Karlstad University, Sweden.
Her research centres on social interaction in institutional settings, including language testing, language teaching, language teachers' professional development, performance appraisal interviews, and broadcast interaction. With a conversation analytic approach, special interests include reported speech, code-switching, assessment, and apologies and their receipt.

Pia Sundqvist, PhD is professor of English language education at the University of Oslo, Norway. Her research interests are in the field of applied linguistics and include informal language learning, in particular the relation between Extramural English and gaming, English language teaching, and the assessment of second language oral proficiency.

Ema Ushioda is a professor in applied linguistics at the University of Warwick, with research interests in motivation and autonomy in language education. Recent books include *Teaching and researching motivation* (3rd edn.), co-authored with Zoltán Dörnyei (Routledge, 2021), and *Language learning motivation: An ethical agenda for research* (Oxford University Press, 2020).

Greta Zanoni is a research fellow at the University of Bologna. She researches on teaching and learning Italian as a foreign/second language, interlanguage pragmatics, and multilingualism. She has participated in national and international projects (*LIRA*, *ATIAH*) and she is involved in the Horizon2020 project *NEW ABC* (Networking the Educational World: Across Boundaries for Community-building).

Index

action research 12, 34, 49, 71, 75–76, 119–122, 201
– and collaboration 38
– and teacher training 123–124
– and process writing 125–126
– teachers' perspectives on 127–129
affordance 43, 45, 135, 145, 191
– linguistic 44, 45, 46, 47, 50–51, 52–53
– motivational 44, 45, 46, 47, 51–52
agency 182
– of learners 92
– of teachers 36, 124, 135, 145, 201
agentic child 72–74, 75
Akkoç, Hatice 134, 146
Alexander, Robin 90, 96, 110
Allwright, Dick 198, 204
Almasi, Janice 33, 37, 39
Alter, Jamie 135, 146
Altrichter, Herbert 120, 121, 130
Amdur, Lisa 145, 147, 151
Andrade, Maureen Snow 123, 130
Andrée, Maria 12, 24, 25, 26, 42, 43, 55
Andrews, Stephen 46, 55
Areljung, Sofie 23, 26
Armstrong, Matthew 104, 112, 117, 118
Arndt, Valerie 123, 132
Assadi, Nabil 135, 146
Atkinson, Paul 66, 70
autonomy, language learner 86, 90, 93, 95, 114, 123

Balaman, Ufuk 18, 27
Banegas, Darío Luis 201, 204
Bansal, Seema 103, 117
Bardel, Camilla 180, 183, 186, 187, 192, 200, 201
Barnes, Douglas 89, 90, 96
Barnes, Tina 106, 117
Barratt, Robert 74, 82
Barratt-Hacking 74, 82
Becker, Carl 113, 117
Beglar, David 153, 163
Benson, Phil 103, 117
Berggren, Jessica 13, 16, 24, 25, 26, 27, 199, 201

Bernstein, Katie A. 60, 70
Bigelow, Martha 60, 70
Biggs, John 182, 192
Bilash, Olenka 31, 40
bilingual programs (Canada) 30–31
British Council 71
British National Corpus 155, 162
Bonnet, Andreas 182, 192
Borg, Simon 120, 121, 127, 130, 140, 146, 200, 204
Borger, Linda 181, 182, 187, 192
Borghetti, Claudia 125, 126, 130, 132
Bouchard, Kate A. 3, 7, 59, 60, 68, 69, 70
Bradbury, Hilary 120, 121, 132
Bråten, Stein 90, 96
Braun, Virginia 169, 177
Brayko, Kate 77, 83
Brown, James Dean 159, 162
Brown, John 102, 117
Brumfit, Christopher 152, 162
Bruner, Jerome 89, 96
Buğra, Cemile 32, 37, 39
Bulterman-Bos, Jacquelien A. 12, 26
Burn, Katharine 135, 146
Burns, Anne 12, 17, 26, 80, 82, 120, 121, 122, 130, 131, 140, 142, 147, 200, 201, 204
Burzoni, Giulia 126, 131
Bylund, Jasmine 188, 192
Byrne, Bronagh 74, 82

Cammarata, Laurent 31, 39
capital
– educational 94
– intellectual and social 95–96
– linguistic 166
Carlgren, Ingrid 12, 13, 24, 25, 26, 42, 55
Ćatibušić, Bronagh Finnegan 92, 97
Cenoz, Jasone 190, 192
Childhood Studies 72–74, 77
Christie, Frances 182, 193
Clapham, Caroline 153, 163
Clarke, Matthew 81, 83
Clarke, Victoria 169, 177
Cloonan, Anne 32, 36, 37, 39
Cobb, Thomas 155, 162

COCA (Corpus of Contemporary American English) 155, 156, 162
Cochran-Smith, Marilyn 12, 26
Coggshall, Jane G. 135, 146
cognitive constructivism 102–103
collaboration
– cycles of 154, 157, 158
collaborative labour 60
– benefits
  – to researchers 65–66
  – to students 66–68
collaborative research
– benefits of 26, 35–36, 80–81, 116–117, 161
– challenges 25, 33, 35–36, 37, 60, 61, 80–81
– defining principles 103–104
– relational complexity of 198, 199–202
– tensions 81, 169–176, 199
Collins, Alan 102, 117
Collins, Julia 81, 82
Common European Framework of Reference for Languages 90, 92, 152
community of practice 134, 142–143
Comstock, Gary 202, 204
Consoli, Sal 200, 201, 204
Conversation Analysis 17–21
Copland, Fiona 74, 82
Corbin, Juliet 138, 147
Coulter, Janet 112, 117
Council of Europe 86, 90, 92, 96, 152, 162, 182, 184, 192
Covid-19 34, 35, 36, 48–49, 115, 168, 185, 186
Coxhead, Averil 156, 162
Csöregh, Anna-Marie 188, 192
Cummins, Jim 37, 38, 39
curriculum 90, 152, 190
– English as a Foreign Language (Israel) 152
– National Curriculum guidelines (Finland) 166–167
– Primary School Curriculum (Ireland) 86, 88, 89, 93, 96
– *see-also* lexical syllabus (Israel)

Dagenais, Diane 30, 33, 37, 39
Dam, Leni 86, 90, 97
Dang, Thi Ngoc Yen 153, 162
Davies, Alan 152, 162
De Fina, Anna 61, 70

Deci, Edward L. 90, 96, 97
Dewey, John 77, 90, 96, 103, 117
Dikilitaş, Kenan 33, 40, 200, 204
Dörnyei, Zoltán 68, 70
Doughty, Catherine 31, 39
Dressler, Roswita 29, 30, 31, 32, 33, 34, 35, 39, 40
Dubetz, Nancy E. 121, 131
Duguid, Paul 102, 117
Dunsmore, Kailonnie 123, 131

Eder, Donna 60, 66, 70
educational research
– fundamental concepts in 1, 182
EDUFI (Finnish National Agency for Education) 166, 167, 170, 175, 177
Edwards, Emily 140, 142, 147
Elder, Catherine 152, 162
Elgemark, Anna 198, 200
Eliasson, Stig 156, 162
Ellis, Elizabeth M. 142, 147
Ellis, Rod 14, 16, 22, 26
Ellström, Per-Erik 114, 118
Enever, Janet 74, 82
Englert, Carol Sue 123, 131
English Curriculum (Israel) 151, 159, 160, 162
Erickson, Gudrun 182, 183, 184, 192, 200, 201
Eriksson, Inger 12, 24, 25, 26, 42, 43, 55
Erman, Britt 156, 162
ethics – *see* research ethics
European Commission 166, 177
Evans, Carol 25, 27
Evans, Norman W. 123, 130
EVP (English Vocabulary Profile Online – British English) 155, 156, 162

Farrell, Thomas S. C. 121, 132
Ferrari, Stefania 126, 130, 131, 132
Fielding, Michael 81, 82
Fingerson, Laura 60, 66, 70
Flaste, Richard 90, 96
Freeman, Donald 121, 131, 133, 142, 147
Furey, Patricia 113, 118

Gallimore, Ronald 12, 26
Garton, Sue 74, 82
Genesee, Fred 190, 192

Germain, Claude 2, 7, 31, 39, 40
Gholkar, Radhika 121, 130
Gibbons, Anne 106, 117
Gibbons, Michael 47, 55
Gibson, James J. 45, 55
Gillam, Lynn 203, 204
Gilmore, Alex 44, 45, 49, 55
Given, Lisa 113, 118
Goldberg, Tsafrir 142, 145, 147
Graham, Ian 113, 118
Graham, Steve 124, 131
Granger, Sylviane 156, 163
Grimm, Sven 161, 162
Guida, Rochelle 34, 39
Guillemin, Marylis 203, 204
Gyllstad, Henrik 70

Hafernick, Johnnie 111, 118
Hahl, Kaisa 165, 167, 176, 177
Haim, Orly 142, 145, 147, 201
Hammersley-Fletcher, Linda 81, 82, 83
Hammersley, Laura 1, 7
Hammersley, Martyn 66, 70
Hamza, Karim 12, 22, 26
Hanks, Judith 200, 204
Hargreaves, David H. 95–96
Hart, Roger A. 75, 82
Hasselgreen, Angela 156, 162
Hawkins, Margaret 32, 37, 39
Henry, Alastair 43, 44, 45, 46, 55, 186, 192
heritage language 62–63, 65, 66, 67, 69
Hess, Michael E. 81, 82
Hiebert, James 12, 26
Hiver, Paul 140, 147
Holm, Claus 54, 56
home language 87
– inclusion in classroom discourse 91, 93
– literacy 94
– maintenance 91, 92
horizontal expertise 77, 201
Hult, Francis 184, 192
Hultman, Glenn 26
Hurmerinta, Elisa 166, 178
Hutchison, Kirsten 32, 36, 37, 39

Integrate Ireland Language and Training 92, 96
Inbar-Lourie, Ofra 134, 145, 147, 201

Inha, Karoliina 165, 167, 177
Inhelder, Bärbel 102, 118
Intensive German Weeks (Canada) 34
interlanguage approach 120, 123, 125

James, Allison 73, 82
Jenlink, Karen E. 77, 82
Jenlink, Patrick M. 77, 82
Jiménez-Silva, Margarita 134, 147
Johnson, David H. 134, 147
Johnson, Karen E. 4, 7, 134, 138, 147

Kähärä, Topias 165, 167, 177
Kahn-Horwitz, Janina 157, 162
Kahneman, Daniel 115, 118
Källkvist, Marie 60, 70, 202
Kasprowicz, Rowena 200, 205
Kasuya, Michiko 110, 118
Katz, J. Sylvan 103, 118
Kehily, Mary Jane 72, 82
Kellett, Mary 73, 74, 82
Kesby, Mike 120, 121, 131
Kim, Tae-Young 140, 147
Kim, Youngmi 140, 147
Kindon, Sara 120, 121, 131
Kirwan, Déirdre 88, 90, 93, 94, 95, 97, 199, 200
Kriewaldt, Jeana 135, 147
Krokfors, Leena 166, 178
Kuiken, Folkert 126, 131
Kunitz, Silvia 12, 14, 18, 23, 27

language awareness 45, 89, 94
– multilingual 188
– of teachers 46
language education policy
– Canada 29, 30–31
– Finland 165–167
– Sweden 180–181
Lärarnas Riksförbund 181, 193
Larsen-Freeman, Diane 198, 204
Larsson, Christer 42, 55
Lassonde, Cynthia 33, 37, 39
Laufer, Batia 155, 156, 162, 163, 202
Lave, Jean 134, 147
Lazenby Simpson, Barbara 92, 97
Leach, Tony 81, 82

learning to teach 134–136, 144–146
Leden, Lotta 23, 26
Legenhausen, Lienhard 86, 90, 97
Legler, Lynn 32, 37, 39
lexical syllabus (Israel) 152, 158–159
– implementation 159–160
– knowledge 157–158
– lemma 154–155
– multi-word unit 156
– vocabulary size 152–154
– word counting unit 154–156
– word family 154–155
Lieberman, Ann 159, 163
Lightfoot, Amy 121, 130
Lindgren, Eva 74, 82
Linell, Per 90, 97
Little, David 86, 87, 88, 90, 92, 94, 95, 97, 103, 118, 199, 200
Loewen, Shawn 1, 7, 200, 205
Lomax, Helen 74, 82
Lourenço, Monica 74, 83
Lowery, Charles L. 81, 82
Lundy, Laura 74, 82
Luukka, Minna-Riitta 170, 177
Lyster, Roy 29, 30, 31, 39, 40
Lytle, Susan L. 12, 26

MacDonald, Cathy 120, 131
Mackey, Alison 74, 83
Magnusson, Petra 42, 55
Malmström, Martin 42, 55
Mann, Steve 121, 122, 131
Mård-Miettinen, Karita 202
Mariage, Troy V. 123, 131
Marsden, Emma 66, 70, 200, 205
Marsh, Colin, J. 159, 163
Martin, Ben 103, 118
Martinez, Ron 156, 163
Masson, Mimi 31, 40
Mathew, Rama 78, 80, 82, 83
McCarthy, Tanya 103, 104, 112, 117, 118, 202
McEvoy, Lesley 74, 82
McIntyre, Alice 120, 131
McKay, Sandra Lee 120, 121, 131
McKinley, Jim 200, 205
McNiff, Jean 34, 40

McTaggart, Robin 120, 131
Medgyes, Péter 200, 205
Mena, Juanjo 143, 147
mentoring 133–134, 141–143, 146
Messerschmitt, Dorothy 111, 118
Mezei, Gabriella 140, 147
Mills, Geoffrey E. 34, 40, 120, 131
Mitchell, Rosamond 66, 70
Moje, Elizabeth Birr 47, 56
Moore, Danièle 30, 33, 37, 39
Moss, Peter 81, 82
motivation 43, 44
Mourão, Sandie 74, 83
Mueller, Katherine 29, 32, 33, 35, 39, 40, 198, 203
multilingual
– class/school 60, 119, 121, 122, 125, 126, 182, 184
– repertoire 64, 69
multilingualism 182, 190
– as a pedagogical and societal challenge 184
– as a resource 67
Murad, Tareq 135, 146
Mutton, Trevor 135, 146
Myles, Florence 66, 70

Nation, Paul 153, 156, 163
national graduate schools (Sweden) 179–180, 201
– FRAM 183–184, 190
  – outcomes 186–187, 190–191
  – research topics 190
– pedagogical model of FRAM and SEMLA 185–186
– SEMLA 184–185
  – outcomes 187–189, 191
  – research topics 190
needs 60, 68–69, 198
– learners' 45, 65, 66, 102, 107, 108, 114, 116, 119–120, 122, 123, 124, 128, 129, 160, 185, 189
– researchers' 47, 62, 65, 105, 116, 199
– teachers' 12, 45, 122, 127–128, 197, 199
Nesselhauf, Nadja 156, 163
Netten, Joan 31, 40
Neurolinguistic Approach 31, 34, 35–36, 37, 38
Nichols, Beverly 159, 163

Nielsen, Diane Corcoran 133, 148
Nihlfors, Elisabet 42, 56
Nikolov, Marianne 74, 83
Noguchi, Junko 103, 118
Nuclear Word Family 160
Nunan, David 120, 131

Observing Interlanguage/Osservare l'Interlingua 119–120, 122
– future prospects 129–130
– teachers' perspectives 127–129
O'Connor, Arlene 31, 33, 44
Oliver, Rhonda 74, 83
Olson, Kate 134, 147
Olsson, Eva 44, 56, 181, 182, 192
Opfer, V. Darleen 5, 7, 133, 134, 135, 137, 138, 139, 141, 144, 148
Orland-Barak, Lily 142, 145, 147
Ortega, Lourdes 199, 205
Österberg, Rakel 183, 192

Paatsch, Louise 32, 36, 37, 39
Pain, Rachel 120, 121, 131
Pallotti, Gabriele 120, 122, 123, 125, 126, 131, 132, 199, 201
Palm, Clara 189
Papert, Seymour 102, 118
Paquot, Magali 156, 163
Pashby, Ian 106, 117
Payne, Katherina A. 77, 83
Pedder, David 133, 134, 135, 137, 138, 139, 141, 144, 148
Peltoniemi, Annika 166, 177
Persson, Sven 25, 27
Peters, Elke 156, 163
Pettitt, Nicole 64, 70
Philp, Jennifer 74, 83
Piaget, Jean 102, 118
Pietarila, Maija 165, 167, 176, 177
Pinner, Richard S. 200, 205
Pinter, Annamaria 78, 80, 82, 83, 201
Pitkänen-Huhta, Anne 202
plurilingual and intercultural education 86, 87–89
Prabhu, N. S. 23, 27
practicum (Clinical Practice model) 133–134, 135–136, 201

professional development
– and action research 12, 25
– of graduates 101–102, 103, 105, 107, 113, 117
– of teachers 25, 30, 42, 72, 79, 134–135, 200–201
– partnership 133, 137
Prøitz, Tine S. 47, 56
Prout, Alan 73, 82
Pyykkö, Riitta 165, 166, 167, 177

Rasmussen, Jens 54, 56
Ravenhorst-Kalovski, Geke 151, 153, 163
Reason, Peter 120, 121, 132
Rebolledo, Paula 200, 205
reciprocity 25, 54, 77, 95–96, 110, 123, 145, 189, 200, 204
– as ethical principle 198, 199, 203
– benefits 66, 68–70, 93, 111, 116, 161, 199
– defined 60, 85
– in classroom discourse 88
Reinhardt, Jonathon 46, 56
research
– and practice
  – gap between 12, 42
  – interdependence of 89–90, 95–96, 181, 199
– design 14, 15, 33–34, 47–48, 75–77, 125, 137–138
– dissemination 23–24, 42, 129–130
research data
– blogs 137, 139–142, 143–144
– classroom recordings 93
– examples of learners' work 86
– interviews 62, 86, 137, 168–169, 170–176
– lesson plans 86, 137
– teaching materials 137
research ethics
– challenges 199, 202–203
– dilemmas 80–81
– informed consent 60–61
research exchange 102, 104–106
research partnerships 106–111, 160–161
– learner/learner 111–113
– schools and universities (Sweden) 13, 42, 47
– teacher (instructor)/learner 113–114
– teacher (instructor)/teacher (instructor) 114–115
research purpose 197, 199

Richards, Jack C. 121, 132, 152, 163
Rinaldi, Carlina 73, 83
Robinson, Carol 74, 83
Rose, Heath 1, 7, 200, 205
Rosi, Fabiana 125, 132
Ryan, Richard M. 90, 97
Rycroft-Malone, J. 113, 118

Sabatier, Cécile 30, 33, 37, 39
SACI 105, 118
Salaberry, M. Rafael 18, 27
Saldaña, Johnny 65, 70
Sampson, Richard J. 200, 205
Sanchez, Hugo Santiago 200, 204
Sandmel, Karin 123, 131
Sato, Masatoshi 1, 7, 200, 205
Scarino, Angela 121, 132
Schleppegrell, Mary 182, 193
Schmitt, Diane 153, 163
Schmitt, Norbert 153, 156, 163
Schostak, John 81, 83
Segalowitz, Norman 45, 56
Selinker, Larry 123, 132
Sensevy, Gérard 12, 15, 24, 27
Sharkey, Judy 31, 33, 40
Shier, Harry 74, 83
Shin, Dongkwang 156, 163
Shkedi, Asher 138, 148
Sibbald, Shannon 113, 118
Sidnell, Jack 2, 7, 17, 27
Siemund, Peter 182, 192
Sivenbring, Jennie 14, 27
Sjöberg, Lena 42, 56
Sjöberg, Sannina 166, 167, 177
Skinnari, Kristiina 166, 167, 177
Skogmyr Marian, Klara 18, 27
Skolinspektionen (Sweden) 179, 181, 193
Skollag 2010:800 [Education Act] 179, 193
Skolverket 181, 193
Smith, Cameron W. 31, 40
Smith, Richard 200, 205
Smith, Will 49–52
Snoder, Sara 188, 193
social constructionism 102–103
Spada, Nina 60, 70
Spyrou, Spyros 74, 83
Stewart, Timothy 33, 40

Stigler, James W. 12, 26
Stivers, Tania 17, 27
Storch, Neomy 123, 132
Strauss, Anselm 138, 147
Stringer, Ernest T. 34
Sturk, Erika 188, 193
Sundqvist, Pia 43, 44, 45, 55, 56
Svalberg, Agneta M.-L. 45, 46, 56

Taylor, Carol A. 74, 83
teacher learning 78–80
– ecological levels 134, 138–139
    – pre-service teacher 139–142
    – professional activities 143–144
    – school 142–143
teaching focus
– authentic texts 43
– oral interaction 11, 13–15, 17–19
– oral proficiency 31, 32
– process writing 125–126
– task design 15–17, 22–23
Tedick, Diane 29, 30, 31, 40
Tetroe, Jacqueline 113, 118
Thompson, Amy S. 135, 137, 140, 148
Thornbury, Scott 46, 56
Thorne, Steven. L. 46, 56
Thorsen, Cecilia 43, 44, 45, 46, 55
Timmons, Kristy 34, 40
Tomlinson, Brian 44, 56
Toth, Paul D. 53, 56
Trainor, Audrey 3, 7, 59, 60, 68, 69, 70
Trent, John 135, 145, 148
Trevarthen, Colwyn 90, 97
Turnidge, Dagmar 135, 147

UNCRC (United Nations Convention on the Rights of the Child) 73
Ushioda, Ema 44, 45, 56, 197, 205

van den Akker, Jan 1, 7, 182, 194
van Lier, Leo 135, 145, 148
Vandrick, Stephanie 111, 118
Varghese, Manka 133, 148
Vedder, Ineke 126, 131
Vetenskapsrådet 15, 27
Vitikka, Erja 166, 178
Vygotsky, Lev 102, 103, 118

Walkerdine, Valerie 73, 83
Waring, Michael 25, 27
Warren, Beatrice Cecilia 156, 162
Warriner, Doris S. 60, 70
Webb, Stuart 153, 162
Wenger, Etienne 134, 147
West, Michael 157, 163
WFF (Word Family Framework) 155, 156, 163
White, Ronald V. 123, 132
Wiblom, Jonna 23, 26
Willegems, Vicky 136, 148

Williams, Jessica 31, 39
Wine, Osnat 106, 118
Woods, Devon 137, 140, 148
Wu, Joe 31, 40
Wyatt, Mark 32, 33, 37, 39, 40

Yazan, Bedrettin 134, 148
Young Knowles, Sarah 65, 70

Zeichner, Ken 77, 83
Zigo, Diane 59, 60, 64, 69, 70

www.ingramcontent.com/pod-product-compliance
Lightning Source LLC
Chambersburg PA
CBHW050524170426
43201CB00013B/2079